# The Government
# Against the Economy

# THE GOVERNMENT AGAINST THE ECONOMY

The story of the U. S. government's on-going destruction of the American economic system through price controls

## George Reisman, Ph.D.

## Foreword by William E. Simon

TJS Books, Laguna Hills, California

George Reisman, Ph.D., is Pepperdine University Professor Emeritus of Economics and the author of *Capitalism: A Treatise on Economics* (Ottawa, Illinois: Jameson Books, 1996; Kindle Edition, 2012). See his Amazon.com author's page. His website is www.capitalism.net. His blog is www.georgereismansblog.blogspot.com. Follow him on Twitter @GGReisman and on YouTube at http://bit.ly/2pNZmwz.

Published by TJS BOOKS, PO Box 2934, Laguna Hills, CA 92654.

All inquiries should be addressed to TJS Books, PO Box 2934, Laguna Hills, CA 92654-2934 or to TJS.Books@capitalism.net. Phone: (877) 843-3573. Fax: (949) 831-1783.

ISBN: 978-1-931089-64-7

Library of Congress Catalogue Card Number 79-83689

Manufactured in the United States of America

To Edith

# CONTENTS

# Contents

## Contents

# FOREWORD

President Carter's program of "voluntary" price and wage "guidelines," announced last Fall, highlights the necessity of this book. We are on the brink of price controls, if we have not already gone headlong over it, and very few people, indeed, understand what is at stake and what the consequences are likely to be if controls should exist for any substantial period of time.

Professor Reisman, an academic economist, is one of the handful of people who does thoroughly understand these issues. His book is an extremely clear, step-by-step explanation of what free-market prices accomplish and what price controls destroy.

First of all, Professor Reisman briefly acquaints us with the cause of the problem of rising prices, which controls are supposed to solve. He argues, in agreement with Milton Friedman and most of the leading economists of the last two centuries, that when prices rise across the board, year after year, the explanation is not any deficiency in production or the alleged machinations of sellers, but the inflationist monetary policies of the government—i.e., the government's hand-over-fist increase in the quantity of money, which necessarily reduces the value of the monetary unit. (As I explained in my own book, *A Time For Truth*, the money supply is inflated to finance irresponsible, vote-buying fiscal policies that stem from the something-for-nothing, egalitarian philosophy that nowadays goes under the name "liberalism.")

Professor Reisman shows that given the nature of the *cause* of rising prices, the imposition of price controls to deal with the problem is as illogical a solution as trying to hold down expanding pressure in a boiler by manipulating the needle in the boiler's pressure gauge—and is just as dangerous. Price controls, he argues, do not solve the problem of inflation at all. They merely *combine* with it to produce a much worse problem. Instead of the problem being inflation alone, it becomes inflation *plus* the destruction of the price system.

Professor Reisman gives an excellent explanation of what free-market prices actually accomplish. He develops a cohesive set of economic principles, each of which explains a major aspect of how the free market's price system works and what it achieves. After laying this foundation he turns to a systematic analysis of price controls and where they must lead.

Every principle set forth in this book is fully illustrated by means of true-to-life examples and is in turn used to explain recent economic history. The reader of this book may very well finish it with a radically different understanding of such events as the oil and natural gas crises, chronic power failures, and the decline of rental housing in places like New York City. He may also come away with a different opinion about the alleged prosperity caused by World War II, which gave us our most extensive experience with price controls thus far.

The basic conclusion of this book is that what we must ultimately expect from price controls is mounting chaos, declining production, and radical discontent—culminating in an economic *and* political system closely resembling that of Soviet Russia and Nazi Germany in its essential features.

I earnestly hope that this book will succeed in reaching a large audience—which will read it and understand the consequences of price controls—and that we will change our path in time.

WILLIAM E. SIMON

New York
January 1979

# PREFACE

As this book goes to press, a new oil crisis appears to be in the making, replete with waiting lines at gas stations and renewed talk of "outrageous profits" and sinister "conspiracies" on the part of oil companies. The reader of this book will be extremely well informed on how to interpret such phenomena, either now or in the future.

Also, the drift toward a totally controlled economic system continues, which brings closer the specter that the later chapters of this book will also have immediate relevance to events in the United States in the years ahead.

It is true that President Carter has proposed the gradual decontrol of oil prices. At first thought, this might be taken to indicate an important step toward freeing the economic system. However, within days of the announcement of that proposal, the President's chief "inflation fighter," Mr. Kahn, publicly raised the possibility of mandatory price and wage controls being imposed throughout the economic system if the present "voluntary guidelines" do not "work."

Furthermore, the proposed decontrol of oil prices would not be a significant step toward a freer economy, because the President simultaneously proposed a special, additional tax on the oil companies that would have the effect of confiscating most of the profits that would otherwise accrue to them as the result of decontrol. The result of this would be that the oil companies would be deprived of the incentives and the capital that high profits would provide. Thus they would not be able to expand American oil production, and, therefore, oil would continue to grow scarcer and its price continue to rise—with the further result that sooner or later powerful pressure groups would almost certainly bring about the reimposition of controls on oil prices.

Whatever the resolution of our immediate crises, it is virtually certain that inflation and, therefore, price controls are going to be the leading politico-economic issues of the coming decade. I hope that my book will be found of value by readers who want a serious understanding of these vital subjects.

In writing this book I have freely borrowed and applied the ideas of many great economists. I would like to acknowledge them all by name, not only in order to objectify my indebtedness to them, but in the hope that the readers of this book who may wish to study economics further will turn to their works.

First and foremost, I am indebted to the late Ludwig von Mises, my teacher and mentor, whose contributions to the subject areas of this book were especially profound. Von Mises was the leading economic defender of capitalism and the leading critic of socialism and price controls.

I am indebted to Professor F. A. Hayek, the Nobel Laureate and one of von Mises' first students, for important elaborations of the master's ideas. I am also indebted to Doctor Henry Hazlitt, whose writings expounding the theories of von Mises and the classical economists have always been both an inspiration and a standard for my own work.

The older economists I have borrowed from are Adam Smith, David Ricardo, James Mill, J. R. McCulloch, John Stuart Mill, Frederic Bastiat, Carl Menger, and Eugen von Böhm-Bawerk.

I recommend the works of all of the above authors as being indispensable to the analysis of contemporary economic problems.

I would also like to acknowledge my indebtedness to the philosopher-novelist Ayn Rand, and recommend her works. Miss Rand's philosophy of Objectivism has had a very major influence on my approach to capitalism and economic theory.

I am grateful to Professor James Buchanan and Mr. George Koether for suggestions concerning my manuscript, and to the following individuals for their favorable comments about it, which helped to secure its publication: Professor Buchanan, Professor Milton Friedman, Professor F. A. Hayek, Doctor Henry Hazlitt, Mr. Leonard Read, and Mr. William Simon.

I am especially grateful to Mr. Simon for having, in addition, graciously written the Foreword to this book so that it might be called to the attention of the widest possible audience.

I would like to thank my very good friend Mr. Michael Marcus for his kind encouragement when it appeared that my book might go unpublished.

Finally, my greatest debt is to my partner in life, my beloved wife, to whom this book is dedicated. Without her beside me, I would not have been able to write it.

GEORGE REISMAN

Laguna Hills, California
April, 1979

# Introduction

This book is about the destructive effects of price controls. It explains why price controls are destructive in principle and shows how they have actually been destructive in practice, within our own recent experience. It shows, for example, how price controls were responsible for the oil shortage of 1973-74, with all of its accompanying chaos; the natural gas crisis of the winter of 1977; and the New York City blackout of the following summer. It shows how price controls (reenforced by so-called environmental legislation) are continuing to undermine vital energy-producing industries, and how rent controls have already totally destroyed large segments of the housing supply in places like New York City. Finally, it shows why price controls are sooner or later likely to be extended to all industries and that, if this happens, it will be tantamount to the socialization of the economic system and will be followed by economic chaos and a totalitarian dictatorship. In support of this last contention, it is shown that the economic chaos and totalitarianism of Soviet Russia, which have only recently been brought to the attention of the present generation,[1] are logically necessary consequences of socialism's destruction of the free market's price system.

This book is by no means merely a critique of price controls, however. It is also a positive exposition of the virtues of a free market. The critique of price controls is carried out only after an adequate foundation has been laid in explaining the relevant principles of operation of a free market. Furthermore, it is explained in detail just how the existence of a free market would have enabled us to avoid the hardships we have experienced in connection with price controls—even, indeed, especially, those associated with the Arab oil embargo and the Arab-led oil cartel.

1

Price Controls No Remedy for Inflation

Price controls are advocated as a method of controlling inflation. People assume that inflation means rising prices and that it exists only when and to the extent that businessmen raise their prices. It appears to follow, on this view, that inflation would not exist if price increases were simply prohibited by price controls.

Actually, this view of inflation is utterly naive. Rising prices are merely a leading symptom of inflation, not the phenomenon itself. Inflation can exist, and, indeed, accelerate, even though this particular symptom is prevented from appearing. Inflation itself is not rising prices, but an unduly large increase in the quantity of money, caused, almost invariably, by the government. In fact, a good definition of inflation would be, simply: an increase in the quantity of money caused by the government. A virtually equivalent definition would be: an increase in the quantity of money in excess of the rate at which a gold or silver money would increase. These two definitions are virtually equivalent, because without government interference in money over the course of our history, the supply of money today would consist mainly or even entirely of precious metals and fully backed claims to precious metals. The increase in the supply of such a money would almost always be quite small and at all times would be severely limited by the high costs of mining additional quantities of the precious metals. Rising prices as a chronic social problem are a consequence of governments overthrowing the use of gold and silver as money and putting in their place unbacked paper currencies and checking deposits whose quantity can be increased without limit and virtually without cost.

The Quantity Theory of Money

Because it is necessary to approach the subject of price controls with clear ideas about why prices are rising in their absence, it should be definitely understood that the quantity theory of money—i.e., in this context, an expanding quantity of money—is the only valid explanation of this phenomenon.

The truth of the quantity theory of money follows from the most elementary and basic principle in the theory of prices, which is that prices are determined by demand and supply and vary directly with demand and inversely with supply. By *demand* is to be understood the willingness combined with the ability to spend money. By *supply* is to be understood the existence of goods combined with the willingness to sell them. Demand manifests itself in the spending of money; supply, in the quantity of goods sold.

When people complain of "inflation," what they have in mind is not an isolated rise in some prices here and there, offset by a fall in prices elsewhere, but a rise in prices in general, i.e., a rise in the "consumer price level." The consumer price level is a weighted average of all consumer prices.

It follows from the law of supply and demand that the consumer price level can rise only if the aggregate demand (the total spending) for consumers' goods rises, or the aggregate supply (the total quantity sold) of consumers' goods falls. Indeed, the consumer price level can be conceived of as an arithmetical quotient, with demand (spending) as the numerator and supply (quantity of goods sold) as the denominator, for the average of the actual prices at which things are sold *is*, literally, nothing more than the total spending to buy them divided by the total quantity of them sold. In effect, in any given year, some definite mass—however measured—of houses, cars, soap, matches, and everything else in between, exchanges against some definite overall expenditure of money to buy them, and the result, the arithmetical quotient, *is* the general consumer price level.

Rising prices in the United States are obviously not the result of falling supply, since supply has been growing in practically every year. The same is true of the countries of Western Europe, Japan, and even many of the Latin American countries. There can be no question, therefore, but that the rise in prices in these countries can be the result only of an increase in aggregate demand. Moreover, in the few cases in which supply appears to have fallen, such as Chile and Uruguay, the rise in prices has been enormously out of proportion to any possible decrease in supply in those countries. In those countries above all, demand has grown.[2]

An increase in aggregate demand is the result of an increase in the quantity of money in the economic system. When new and additional money enters the economic system, whether it is newly mined gold in a country using gold as money, or newly created paper currency or checkbook money, as in the present-day United States, that money will be spent, and those who receive it in the sale of their goods and services will respend it. The additional money will be spent and respent in every year of its existence, thereby raising aggregate demand and spending in the economic system to a correspondingly higher level. Indeed, the more rapidly new and additional money enters the economic system, the more rapidly the previously existing quantity of money tends to be spent, because people progressively lose the desire to hold balances of such money.[3] (For example, who wants to hold Argentine pesos? Who wants to hold U.S. dollars as much today as ten or twenty years ago?) Aggregate demand and spending thus begin to rise more than in proportion to the increase in the quantity of money. The rise in aggregate demand is what bids up the prices of all goods and services in limited supply, and is what enables price increases initiated by sellers, whether businessmen or labor unions, to take place as a repeated phenomenon. In the absence of the rise in aggregate demand, price increases initiated by sellers would reduce the amount of goods and services that could be sold. This loss of sales volume, and the mounting unemployment that goes with it, would soon put an end to such price increases.

Once the truth of the quantity theory of money is recognized, the government's responsibility for rising prices follows immediately. Under the conditions of the last sixty years or more, the government has had virtually total control over the quantity of money. It has deliberately brought about its rapid increase. Since the inauguration of the New Deal in 1933, the quantity of money in the United States has been increased approximately nineteenfold, from little more than $19 billion to more than $360 billion. Since 1955, the rate of increase has shown a pronounced tendency to accelerate, despite the absence of any major war. Today, rates of increase are considered "normal" and even "modest" that only a decade ago would have been considered huge.[4]


Inflation Plus Price Controls

The imposition of price controls to deal with inflation is as illogical as would be an attempt to deal with expanding pressure in a boiler by means of manipulating the needle in the boiler's pressure gauge. It is no less self-destructive, as well. This book will show that prices are equivalent to an instrument panel on the basis of which everyone plans his economic activities and which enables the plans of each individual to be harmoniously adjusted to the plans of all other individuals participating in the economic system. When price controls are imposed, the gauges on this instrument panel are frozen. Not only do the gauges no longer record the fact of inflation, which still continues and probably accelerates because the government need no longer fear rising prices, but the gauges also no longer reflect any other aspects of the state of supply and demand, which people must be able to take into account if their actions are to be coordinated with one another. Thus, economic activity becomes discoordinated and chaos ensues. It follows, and every page of this book will confirm it, that a government which imposes price controls is in process of destroying the economic system of its own country.

# Free-Market Principles and Applications
## I

1. The Tendency Toward a Uniform
Rate of Profit on Capital Invested

Price controls are advocated out of a lack of knowledge of what free-market prices accomplish. The best way to begin to understand the function of such prices is by understanding a very simple and fundamental principle.

This is that *there is a tendency in a free market toward the establishment of a uniform rate of profit on capital invested in all the different branches of industry*. In other words, there is a tendency for capital invested to yield the same percentage rate of profit whether it is invested in the steel industry, the oil industry, the shoe business, or wherever.

The reason is that investors naturally prefer to earn a higher rate of profit rather than a lower one. As a result, wherever the rate of profit is higher, they tend to invest additional capital. And where it is lower, they tend to withdraw capital they have previously invested. The influx of additional capital in an initially more profitable industry, however, tends to reduce the rate of profit in that industry. Its effect is to increase the industry's production and thus to drive down the selling prices of its products. As the selling prices of its products are driven down, closer to its costs of production, the rate of profit earned by the industry necessarily falls. Conversely, the withdrawal of capital from an initially less profitable industry tends to raise the rate of profit in that industry, because less capital means less production, higher selling prices on the reduced supply, and thus a higher rate of profit on the capital that remains.

5

To illustrate this process, let us assume that initially the computer industry is unusually profitable, while the motion-picture industry is earning a very low rate of profit or incurring actual losses. In such conditions people will obviously want to invest in the computer industry and to reduce their investments in the motion-picture industry. As investment in the computer industry is stepped up, the output of computers will be expanded. In order to find buyers for the larger supply of computers, their price will have to be reduced. Thus, the price of computers will fall and, as a result, the rate of profit earned in producing them will fall. On the other hand, as capital is withdrawn from the motion-picture industry, the output of that industry will be cut, and the reduced supply it offers will be able to be sold at higher prices, thereby raising the rate of profit on the investments that remain in the industry.

In just this way, initially higher rates of profit are brought down and initially lower rates of profit are raised up. The logical stopping point is a uniform rate of profit in all the various industries.

This principle of the tendency of the rate of profit toward uniformity is what explains the amazing order and harmony that exists in production in a free market. It was largely the operation of this principle that Adam Smith had in mind when he employed the unfortunate metaphor that a free economy works as though it were guided by an invisible hand.

In the United States production is carried on by several million independent business enterprises, each of which is concerned with nothing but its own profit. Knowing this, and knowing nothing about economics, one might easily be led to think of such conditions as an "anarchy of production," which is how Karl Marx described them. One might easily be led to expect that because production was in the hands of a mass of independent, self-interested producers, the market would randomly be flooded with some items, while people perished from a lack of others, as a result of the discoordination of the producers. This, of course, is the image conjured up by those who advocate government "planning." It is the view of many advocates of price controls.

The uniformity-of-profit principle explains how the activities of all the separate business enterprises are harmoniously coordinated, so that capital is not invested excessively in the production of some items while leaving the production of other items unprovided for. The operation of the uniformity-of-profit principle is what keeps the production of all the different items directly or indirectly necessary to our survival in proper balance. It counteracts and prevents mistakes leading to the relative overproduction of some things and the relative underproduction of others.

To understand this point, assume that businessmen make a mistake. They invest too much capital in producing refrigerators and not enough capital in producing television sets, say. Because of the uniformity-of-profit principle, the mistake is necessarily self-correcting and self-limiting. The reason is that the effect of the overinvestment in refrigerator production is to depress profits in the refrigerator industry, because the excessive quantity of refrigerators that can be produced can be sold only at prices that are low in relation to costs. By the same token, the effect of the underinvestment in television set production is to raise profits in the television set industry, because the deficient quantity of television sets that can be produced can be sold at prices that are high in relation to costs. The very consequence of the mistake, therefore, is to create incentives for its correction: The low profits—or losses, if the overinvestment is serious enough—of the refrigerator industry act as an incentive to the withdrawal of capital from it, while the high profits of the television set industry act as an incentive to the investment of additional capital in it.

Moreover, the consequence of the mistake is not only to create incentives for its correction, but, simultaneously, to provide the means for its correction: The high profits of the television set industry are not only an incentive to investment in it, but are themselves a *source* of investment, because those high profits can themselves be plowed back into the industry. By the same token, to the extent that the refrigerator industry suffers losses or earns a rate of profit that is too low to cover the dividends its owners need to live on, its capital directly and immediately shrinks, and it is thereby made unable to continue producing on the same scale.

In this way, the mistakes made in the relative production of the various goods in a free market are self-correcting.

With good reason, the operation of profit and loss in guiding the increase and decrease in investment and production has been compared to an automatic governor on a machine or to a thermostat on a boiler. As investment and production go too far in one direction, and not far enough in another direction, the very mistake itself sets in motion counteracting forces of correction. Moreover, the greater the mistake that is made, the more powerful are the corrective forces. For the greater the overinvestment and overproduction, the greater the losses; and the greater the underinvestment and underproduction, the greater the profits. Thus the greater the incentives and the means (or loss of means) to bring about the correction. In this way, the mistakes made in a free market are not only self-correcting, but self-limiting, as well: the bigger the mistake, the harder it is to make it.

Further, in a free market, most of the mistakes that might be made in determining the relative size of the various industries and the relative production of the various goods are not made in the first place. This is because the prospect of profit or loss causes businessmen to weigh investment decisions very carefully in advance and thus to avoid mistakes as far as possible from the very beginning. In seeking to avoid losses, businessmen necessarily aim at avoiding overinvestment and overproduction. In seeking to make the highest possible profits, they necessarily aim at providing the market with those goods in whose production they do not expect other businessmen to invest enough. This last fact, incidentally, makes each businessman eager to invest sufficiently in his own industry, lest the opportunities he does not seize be seized by others instead.

In addition, the free market performs a constant process of selection with respect to the ownership of capital. Capital gravitates, as it were, to those businessmen who know best how to employ it and is taken away from those who do not know how to employ it. For those who invest in providing goods that are relatively more in demand make high profits and are thereby able to expand their capitals and, consequently, their influence over future production; while those who invest in producing goods that are relatively less in demand earn low profits or suffer losses, and are correspondingly deprived of capital and of influence over future production. At any given time, therefore, capital in a free market is mainly in the hands of those who are best qualified to use it, as demonstrated by their past performance in investing. For this reason, too, most of the mistakes that might be made in determining the relative production of the various goods are avoided in the first place in a free market.

The uniformity-of-profit principle not only explains how a free market prevents and counteracts such mistakes, but also how the consumers in a free market have the power of positive initiative to change the course of production. All the consumers need do to cause production to shift is to change the pattern of their spending. If the consumers decide to buy more of product A and less of product B, the production of A automatically becomes more profitable and that of B less profitable. Capital then flows to A and away from B. The production of A is thus expanded, and that of B contracted, until, once again, both A and B afford neither more nor less than the general or average rate of profit.

Of course, businessmen do not sit back and passively wait for the consumers to shift their demand. On the contrary, businessmen seek to anticipate changes in consumer demand and to adjust production accordingly. In addition, of course, they seek constantly to introduce whatever new or improved products they believe will attract consumer demand once the consumers learn of the product. Businessmen will produce anything for which they believe the consumers will pay profitable prices, and they will cease to produce anything for which the consumers are unwilling to pay profitable prices. In this sense, business is totally at the disposal of the consumers—the consumer is king, as the saying goes. It should not be difficult to see that the real advocates of the consumers—their virtual agents—are businessmen seeking profit, not the leaders of groups trying to restrict the freedom of businessmen to earn profits. Such groups, called, ironically, the "consumer movement," seek to force businessmen to produce things the consumers do not want to buy, like automobile seatbelts, and to prohibit them from producing things the consumers do want to buy, like breakfast cereals that are enjoyable to eat.

The uniformity-of-profit principle explains how the profit motive acts to make production steadily increase in a free market. It explains how the profit motive becomes an agent of continuous progress.

In order to earn a rate of profit that is above average, it is necessary for businessmen to anticipate changes in consumer demand ahead of their rivals, to introduce new and/or improved products ahead of their rivals, or to cut the costs of production ahead of their rivals. I say, "ahead of their rivals," because as soon as any innovation becomes general, then, in accordance with the uniformity-of-profit principle, no special profit can be made from it. For example, the first firms that produced shoes by machinery rather than by hand, or that put zippers in clothing, or found a way to sell a cigar for ten cents, or whichever, were able to make above-average rates of profit by doing so. But once such things became general, no special profit could any longer be made from them. They became the ordinary standard of the industry and were taken for granted. Sooner or later, virtually every innovation does become general. This implies that for any firm to continue to earn an above-average rate of profit, it must *repeatedly* outdistance its rivals: it must work as an agent of continuous progress.

Perhaps one of the most dramatic examples of this is provided by the career of the first Henry Ford. When the Ford Motor Company began, in the early part of this century, the automobile was a rich man's toy. Extremely primitive models by our standards were selling for about $10,000—in the very valuable money of the time. Henry Ford began to find ways to improve the quality of automobiles and at the same time cut the costs of their production. But it was not possible for Ford to make a single improvement or a single cost reduction and stop there, because it was not long before those innovations were generally adopted in the industry and, indeed, superseded. Had Ford stood pat, it would not have been long before his once profitable business was destroyed by the competition. In order for Ford to go on making a high rate of profit, he had to continuously introduce improvements and reduce costs ahead of his rivals.

The same is true in principle in a free market of any individual or firm that earns an above-average rate of profit over an extended period of time. What was good enough once to make a high profit, ceases to be good enough as soon as enough others are able to do the same thing. In order to go on earning an above-average profit, one must continue to stay ahead of the competition. By the same token, any business that stands pat is necessarily finished in a free economy, no matter how great its past successes. For the technological advances of any given time are further and further surpassed as time goes on. Think how absurd it would be in virtually any industry to try to make money today by producing with the most advanced, most profitable technology of 1900, 1920, or even 1950, and not bothering to adapt to the changes that have taken place since then.

It is necessary to explain in more detail how the competitive quest for an above-average rate of profit expands the total of production.

It is probably self-evident that the introduction of new and/or improved products constitutes an increase in production or is a source of an increase in production. One has only to think of such cases as the automobile replacing the horse and buggy or the automobile with the self-starter replacing the hand-cranked automobile, or such cases as the tractor bringing about a vast increase in the production of agricultural products, or the electric motor bringing about a vast increase in the production of all kinds of manufactured goods. It may be less obvious, however, how the day-by-day attention of businessmen to costs, and their constant efforts to reduce the costs of production, are no less a source of the increase in production. Still less obvious is the role in increasing production that is played by correct anticipations of changes in consumer demand. Therefore, let us briefly consider the contribution of these factors to increasing production.

Reducing the costs of production means, for the most part, that one finds a way to produce the same amount of a good with less labor. This acts to increase production because it makes labor available to produce more of this good or more of other goods, somewhere else in the economic system. The saving of labor is clearest in the case in which the businessman achieves the cost reduction by employing labor-saving machinery. But even if the cost reduction is achieved by finding a way to use less of some material or a less costly material, labor will also be saved. If less of a material is required, less labor is required to produce the smaller quantity of the material. If a less costly material is required, it is probable that labor will be saved, since it is probable that the less costly material is less costly because less labor is required to produce it. To this extent, then, saving costs means saving labor and, therefore, making the means available for increasing production.

Even if a saving in the quantity of labor is not involved in a cost reduction, the ability to produce something with a less costly material or with less costly labor, for that matter—say, unskilled labor in place of skilled labor—still brings about a net increase in total production. What happens in these cases is that the more costly material or labor is released to expand the production of something else which is comparatively important, while the less costly material or labor that replaces it is withdrawn from the production of something else which is comparatively unimportant.

The principle here is perhaps best illustrated by the case of employing nurses and other aides for many of the tasks that would otherwise have to be performed by doctors. What is gained is the added work that can only be performed by doctors, and which otherwise would have been impossible for lack of availability of doctors' time. What is lost is only the work that the nurses or whoever might have performed as secretaries, bookkeepers, or whatever. Every substitution of less costly labor for more costly labor is comparable to this case in its effect. The same applies to the substitution of less costly for more costly materials. In this way, a net economic gain, equivalent to an increase in production, takes place, because the production of something more important is increased at the expense of the production of something less important. As far as labor goes, the ability to substitute unskilled for skilled labor and achieve equal results can also be viewed as the equivalent of increasing the intelligence and ability of workers, which in the very nature of the case must increase production.[1]

The correct anticipation of changes in consumer demand is also a necessary part of the process of increasing production. To understand this point, it must be realized that increases in production are one of the most important causes of wide-ranging changes in the pattern of consumer spending. For example, the steady improvements in agriculture and the consequent drop in the proportion of people's income that has had to be tied up in buying food has made possible a continuously growing demand for the whole range of industrial goods. Similarly, the introduction and development of the automobile brought about far-reaching shifts in demand: it made possible the development of the suburbs and a whole host of new businesses from gas stations to motels; expanded the demand for other businesses, such as ski resorts; reduced the demand for passenger railroads and horses; and virtually destroyed the businesses of buggymaking and blacksmithing. Every improvement in production exercises a similar, if less dramatic, effect on the demand for other goods.

In order for these shifts in demand to be accompanied by corresponding shifts in production, it is necessary for wide-ranging changes in the investment of capital to occur. Thus, to continue with the examples of agriculture and the automobile, capital had to be diverted from agriculture to industry, from cities to suburbs, from railroads, horsebreeding, buggymaking, and blacksmithing, to automaking, gas stations, motels, and ski resorts. To the extent that the appropriate shifts of capital did not occur, or occurred with undue delay, the benefit from the improvement in production was lost. For example, to the extent that capital was not shifted out of farming rapidly enough—as a result of government farm subsidies or the inertia of many farmers—the effect of the improvements in agriculture was limited to a relatively unwanted increase in agricultural production and correspondingly less of an increase in much more desired industrial production. Similarly, to the extent that capital would not have been shifted rapidly enough out of buggymaking and horsebreeding, the benefits from the automobile would have been held down: capital would have been wasted in buggymaking and horsebreeding which could have been employed with infinitely greater benefit in any of the new or expanding industries brought about by the automobile. In all such cases, to fail to make the appropriate shifts of capital is to lose some or all of the benefit of the improvement in production. For this reason the correct anticipation of changes in consumer demand is an integral part of the process of increasing production.

To summarize the discussion of the free market thus far: The desire of businessmen to earn profits and avoid losses, and to earn higher profits in preference to lower profits, brings about a tendency toward a uniform rate of profit on capital invested in all the different branches of industry. The operation of this tendency counteracts, delimits, and largely prevents mistakes from being made in the relative production of the various goods. Because of it, consumers have the power of positive initiative to shift the course of production simply by changing the pattern of their spending; because of it, businessmen are made to act virtually as the consumers' agents. The operation of the tendency toward a uniform rate of profit requires that high profits be made by continuously introducing productive innovations in advance of competitors. These innovations are the base of a continuous increase in production, whether they take the form of new and improved products, reduced costs of production, or correct anticipations of changes in consumer demand.

On the basis of the foregoing, we must conclude that the free market, operating through the profit motive, has been responsible for the tremendous success of the American economic system. It has ensured the maximum possible effort to introduce innovations and to extend their application as rapidly as possible, with the result that in comparatively short periods of time revolutionary improvements have become commonplace. Because of this and because of the rapid adaptation it assures to all changes in economic conditions, it has rendered every crisis, from natural disasters, to wars, to absurd acts of government, a merely temporary setback in a steady climb to greater prosperity.

## Profits and the Repeal of Price Controls

What we have learned about the free market can be applied to a number of cases in which the free market does not presently exist in our country. A brief consideration of these cases will both illustrate the principle of the tendency of the rate of profit toward uniformity and provide a demonstration of the value to be gained by extending the free market.

Consider the case of government farm subsidies. Let us imagine that the government stopped buying up farm products to be stored or given away, and at the same time reduced taxes by the amount of money it saved in abolishing the farm program.

The effect would be a drop in the demand for farm products. But since the taxpayers would now have the money previously used to pay the subsidies, there would be a rise in the demand for a host of other products—products which the taxpayers judged would satisfy the most important of their needs or wants which previously had had to go unsatisfied, such as an extra room on a house, a newer or better car, extra education, and so on, depending on the needs and desires of the various individuals concerned. The immediate effect of this shift of demand would be to depress prices and profits in farming and to raise them in these various other industries. The further consequence would be a withdrawal of capital and labor from farming and their transfer to the production of these other goods.

The movement of capital and labor out of farming would take place until the rate of profit in farming was raised back up to the general level, and the rate of profit earned on the various goods in additional demand by the taxpayers was brought down to the general level. Until this result was achieved, incentives would exist for a further movement of capital and labor out of farming and into these other fields. When the process was finally completed, therefore, the rate of profit earned in farming would be on a par with the rate of profit earned everywhere else. In accordance with the uniformity-of-profit principle, it would simply not be possible for the rate of profit in farming to be permanently depressed.

It follows from this analysis that in the long run those who remained in agriculture would tend to earn, on average, the same level of income they had earned before the repeal of the subsidies. Even the incomes of ex-farmers would, on average, come to be on a level comparable to what they had been initially. This would be the case as soon as the former farmers acquired industrial skills on a level comparable to those they had possessed in agriculture and so could take appropriate advantage of the new employment opportunities created by the expansion in the demand for industrial goods. The one permanent difference that would now exist and which would be of benefit to everyone, farmers and ex-farmers included, would be that the taxation of everyone's income would be smaller and everyone would be enabled to buy more of the goods he himself desired. Instead of everyone being forced to spend a part of his income, through the government, for the purchase of farm products to be uselessly stored or given away, he would be able to spend that part of his income for industrial goods of value and importance to his life. And those goods would be produced by the capital and labor previously employed in producing the farm products.

I chose the example of farm subsidies to illustrate how the free market reacts when the profitability of an industry is initially rendered low. Farm subsidies, however, represent a form of price controls different from the kind we are concerned with in this book. Farm subsidies are a way the government achieves artificially high prices. They are an illustration of legal minimum prices, i.e., prices below which the government prevents the producers from selling. They are comparable in their effects to minimum-wage legislation. The kind of price controls that we want to focus on, of course, are controls designed to keep prices artificially low—that is, legal maximum prices or ceiling prices, as they are often called, i.e., prices above which one is not allowed to sell.

So let us take as a second major illustration the consequences that would follow if rent controls were repealed.

To simplify this discussion, let us assume that the entire supply of rental housing in a given locality has been under controls. In this case, the first effect of the repeal of controls would simply be a jump in all rents. As a result of the jump, however, rental housing would again become profitable—in fact, as a result of previously inadequate building due to rent controls, extremely profitable. However, it is impossible that the rental housing industry should be permanently more profitable than other industries. The high rate of profit would be the incentive, and would itself provide much of the means, for expanded investment in the rental housing industry. There would be a building boom in rental housing. As a result, the supply of rental housing would be stepped up and the rents and the profitability of rental housing would begin to fall and would go on falling until the rate of profit in rental housing was no higher than the rate of profit in industry generally. The long-run effect of the repeal of rent controls, therefore, would simply be an increase in the supply of rental housing. Rents themselves in the long run would be no higher than corresponded to the costs of constructing and operating apartment houses, with profits only enough to make the industry competitive.

Exactly the same effects would follow the repeal of price controls on crude oil, natural gas, or any other good. There would be a temporary surge in price and profit, followed by expanded production and a reduction in price and profit to the point where the price corresponded to the good's production cost and allowed only enough profit to make the good's production competitive.

Of course, it should not be forgotten that once a price control is repealed, the dynamic effects of the uniformity-of-profit principle take over. As we have seen, if someone wants to make an above-average rate of profit on a free market, he must strive to reduce his costs of production and improve the quality of his products, and repeatedly succeed in doing this ahead of his rivals. This means that in the absence of controls, costs and prices tend steadily to *fall*—if not in terms of a depreciating paper money, then nevertheless in terms of the time people must spend to earn the money to buy goods. Once controls are repealed and a free market established, the free competitive quest for high profits causes prices to fall further and further below the point at which they were controlled, while the quality of goods rises higher and higher.

It should be obvious that the repeal of rent controls would act to end New York City's housing shortage and make possible an enormous improvement in the quantity and quality of housing for the average person in New York City. It should be equally obvious that the repeal of price controls on crude oil and on natural gas would act to expand energy supplies and make possible a return to America's traditional abundance and growth of energy supplies.

In sum, it should already be clear, even at this stage of our knowledge, that the problems we are experiencing in all these areas are the result of controls and would be solved by the establishment of economic freedom.


Why There Are No Limits to Progress in a Free Economy

The picture I have painted of a free economy is one of continuous progress and improvement. And so it has been in the United States over the last two hundred years, during most of which time we had a substantially free economy. As the free economy has come to be steadily undermined and the transition to a form of socialism drawn even closer, however, the foundations of economic progress have been eroded. For reasons that should become progressively clearer from now on, a controlled or socialist economy cannot have economic progress. I believe that the advocates of socialism know this, or at least that they sense it, and that, as a result, they have launched a widespread campaign to try to deny the very possibility of continuous economic progress. The nature of their attempt is summed up in the phrase "The Limits to Growth." The motivation of the supporters of that phrase, I believe, is to be able to blame the end of economic progress not on the end of capitalism, but on the fundamental nature of the world.

Therefore, let us consider the basic facts that underlie the possibility of continuous economic progress.

As far as man himself is concerned, the basic fact is that knowledge can be transmitted from generation to generation and that each generation has the ability to add to the total of what it has received. The only limit to this process would be the attainment of omniscience.

Let us consider the physical world in which man lives. Is there a limit to the supply of natural resources on earth?[2]

Yes, there is. But the limit is utterly irrelevant to human action. For practical purposes it is infinite, because the limit is the entire mass of the earth. The entire earth, from the uppermost limits of its atmosphere to its very center, four thousand miles down, consists exclusively of natural resources, of *solidly packed natural resources*. For what is the earth made out of? It is made exclusively out of chemical elements found in different combinations and in different proportions in different places. For example, the earth's core is composed mainly of iron and nickel—millions of cubic miles of iron and nickel. Aluminum is found practically everywhere. Even the soil of the Sahara desert is comprised of nothing but various compounds of silicon, carbon, oxygen, hydrogen, aluminum, iron, and so on, all of them having who knows what potential uses that science may someday unlock. Nor is there a single element that does not exist in the earth in millions of times larger quantities than has ever been mined.

Now this limit of natural resources has existed from the very first day that man appeared on earth, and in all the millennia since, it has not diminished by so much as a single atom. This is because chemical elements are never destroyed. They simply reappear in different combinations, in different proportions, in different places. Apart from what has been lost in a few rockets, the quantity of every chemical element in the world today is the same as it was before the Industrial Revolution. The only difference is that instead of lying dormant, out of man's control, the chemical elements have been moved about, as never before, in such a way as to improve human life. For instance, some part of the world's iron has been moved from the interior of the earth, where it was useless, to now constitute buildings, bridges, automobiles, and a million and one other things of benefit to human life. Some part of the world's carbon, oxygen, and hydrogen has been separated from certain compounds and recombined in others, in the process releasing energy to heat and light homes, power automobiles and railroad trains, and in countless other ways serve human life. Nor is the world running out of energy by virtue of the energy released in these ways. For heat from the sun every year provides a constantly renewed supply that is millions of times greater than the energy consumed by man. It follows from these facts that all that has occurred as a result of the Industrial Revolution is that man has *improved his environment*.

It should be realized that by its very nature, production means an improvement in the environment. All that production of any kind fundamentally consists of is the rearrangement of the same chemical elements that nature gives us, but in ways that make them stand in a more useful relationship to man. Consider further examples. To live, man needs to be able to move his person and his goods from place to place. If an untamed forest stands in his way, such movement is difficult or impossible. It represents an improvement in the environment, therefore, when man moves the chemical elements that constitute some of the trees of the forest somewhere else, and lays down chemical elements brought from somewhere else to constitute a road. It is an improvement in the environment when man builds bridges, digs canals, opens mines, clears land, constructs houses, or does anything else that represents an improvement in the external, material conditions of his life. All economic activity has as its sole purpose the improvement of the environment: it aims exclusively at the improvement of the external, material conditions of human life.

In trying to restrict man's freedom to improve his living conditions, the misnamed "environmental movement" seeks to force man to live in a less favorable environment.

Now because the world is composed entirely of natural resources and possesses a virtually irreducible and practically infinite supply of energy, the problem of natural resources is simply one of being able to obtain *access* to them, of being able *to obtain command over the resources*, that is, of being in a position to direct them to the service of human well-being. This is strictly a problem of science, technology, and the productivity of labor. Its solution depends merely on learning how to break down and then put together various chemical compounds in ways that are useful to man, and having the equipment available to do it without requiring an inordinate amount of labor. Human intelligence certainly has the potential for discovering all the knowledge that is required, and in a free, rational society, the incentive of profit virtually guarantees that this knowledge will both be discovered and provided with the necessary equipment to be put to use.

The record of the last centuries, certainly, demonstrates that such a society has no problem of a scarcity of accessible natural resources. While the total volume of chemical elements in the world has remained the same, the volume of *useful* elements and compounds *at the disposal of man* has been enormously *increased*. Today, for example, because of improved knowledge and equipment, it is probable that man can more easily extract minerals from a depth of a thousand feet than he could a century ago from a depth of fifty feet. In the same way, he has learned how to use elements and compounds he previously did not know how to use—such as aluminum and petroleum, which have only been in use for approximately a century, and, more recently, uranium. There is no reason why, under the continued existence of a free and rational society, the supply of accessible natural resources should not go on growing as rapidly as in the past or even more rapidly. Further advances in mining technology, for example, that would make it possible to mine economically at a depth of, say, ten thousand feet, instead of the present limited depths, would so increase the portion of the earth's mass accessible to man, that all previous supplies of accessible minerals would appear insignificant by comparison. And even at ten thousand feet, man would still, quite literally, just be scratching the surface, because the radius of the earth extends to a depth of four thousand *miles*. In the same way, dramatic advances are possible in the field of energy, such as may occur through the use of atomic energy, hydrogen fusion, solar power, tidal power, or thermal power from the earth's core, or still other processes as yet unknown.

Because the earth is literally nothing but an immense solid ball of useful elements and because man's intelligence and initiative in the last two centuries were relatively free to operate and had the incentive to operate, it should not be surprising that the supply of accessible minerals today vastly exceeds the supply that man is economically capable of exploiting. In virtually every case, there are vast *known* deposits of minerals which are not worked, because it is not necessary to work them. Indeed, if they were worked, there would be a relative overproduction of minerals and a relative underproduction of other goods—i.e., a waste of capital and labor. In virtually every case, it is necessary to choose *which* deposits to exploit—namely, those which by virtue of their location, amount of digging required, the degree of concentration and purity of the ore, and so forth, can be exploited at the lowest costs. Today, enormous mineral deposits lie untouched which could be exploited with far less labor per unit of output than was true of the very best deposits exploited perhaps as recently as a generation or two ago—thanks to advances in the state of mining technology and in the quantity and quality of mining equipment available.

As just one example, and a very important one, consider the fact that there are petroleum deposits in shale rock and tar sands in our own Rocky Mountain states and in Canada of a size far exceeding the petroleum deposits of the Arab countries. Until now, these deposits have not been exploited, because it has been cheaper to obtain petroleum from liquid deposits. Even though oil obtained in these ways would be more expensive than oil obtained in its liquid state, still, it is undoubtedly cheaper—in terms of the labor required to produce it—to obtain oil in these ways today than it was to obtain liquid petroleum a century ago and probably even a generation or two ago. There is no reason why further advances in mining technology and in the availability of mining equipment would not enable oil obtained in these ways in the future to be less expensive than oil obtained in its liquid state today. Similarly, there are vast untapped known coal fields in the United States containing enough coal to supply present rates of consumption for many centuries.

In some important respects, these coal fields must be considered not merely a substitute, but the full equivalent of petroleum deposits. For it is possible to produce some of the identical products from coal as from oil—for example, gasoline. This too has not been done commercially until now, because it has been cheaper to produce gasoline from petroleum. But there is no reason why, with the further progress of technology and the availability of equipment, gasoline produced from coal in the future should not be cheaper than gasoline produced from oil today, just as gasoline produced from coal today would undoubtedly be cheaper than was gasoline produced from oil in the past. If it were necessary, a free American economy could respond to a loss of foreign supplies by turning to such other sources of oil and gasoline as these, and, in not very much time, both through reducing their costs of production and by developing other, newer sources of fuel, would enjoy lower costs and more abundant supplies of energy than ever before. In a free American economy, it would not matter in the long run if the Arabian peninsula and its oil simply did not exist. As a free economy, we would not need Arab oil. Neither our survival nor our long-run progressive prosperity would depend on it.

The growing threat to the supply of natural resources that people are beginning to complain about is not the result of anything physical—no more than it was the result of anything physical in the days when these terrible words of despair were written:

"You must know that the world has grown old, and does not remain in its former vigour. It bears witness to its own decline. The rainfall and the sun's warmth are both diminishing; the metals are nearly exhausted; the husbandman is failing in the fields, the sailor on the seas, the soldier in the camp, honesty in the market, justice in the courts, concord in friendships, skill in the arts, discipline in morals. This is the sentence passed upon the world, that everything which has a beginning should perish, that things which have reached maturity should grow old, the strong weak, the great small, and that after weakness and shrinkage should come dissolution."[3]

That passage is not a quotation from some contemporary ecologist or conservationist. It was written in the *third century*—ages before the first chunk of coal, drop of oil, ounce of aluminum, or any significant quantity of any mineral whatever had been taken from the earth. Then as now, the problem was not physical, but philosophical and political. Then as now, men were turning away from reason and toward mysticism. Then as now, they were growing less free and falling ever more under the rule of physical force. That is why they believed, and that is why people in our culture are beginning to believe, that man is helpless before physical nature. There is no helplessness in fact. To men who use reason and are free to act, nature gives more and more. To those who turn away from reason or are not free, it gives less and less. Nothing more is involved.

There are no significant scarcities of accessible raw materials as yet. But the enemies of reason and capitalism sense the consequences of the social system that they hope to impose, and they project it on to the present. Thus they admonish us to save every little tin can and every scrap of paper. Their world, if it ever comes, will have to live like that. But we, who are capable of producing in abundance—we do not have to regard bits of garbage as priceless treasures. To us, used tin cans, paper wrappings, and the like, which cost us hardly any labor to produce or to replace, are generally not worth the trouble of saving or reusing. In fact, it is usually wasteful for us to do so: it wastes our labor and our time, which are the only things in life we should be concerned about not wasting. For if we can produce new tin cans easily, by scooping iron ore out of the earth in ten or twenty-ton loads, it is simply ludicrous to take the trouble to gather up each little tin can and carry it off to some recycling center, because in doing so we spend far more labor than we save.

Nor is it "wasteful" or uneconomic in any way that we use so many tin cans or so many paper wrappings. If we consider how little labor it costs us—in terms of the free time it takes us to earn the money we spend for it—to have things brought to us clean and fresh and new, in new containers and new packaging, and what the alternatives are for the spending of that money or the use of that time, it becomes clear that the expenditure is well made. For consider the alternatives: We could have our food and other goods wrapped in old newspapers and put in jars, bags, or boxes that we would have to carry along with us whenever we went shopping, or which we would have to make a special trip to go and fetch whenever we came on something unexpectedly that we wanted to buy. We could then use the money we saved in that way to buy a handful of other goods. Conceivably, we could use the money we saved to work a few minutes less at our jobs each day, and earn correspondingly less. But these alternatives would simply be bizarre, because neither a handful of extra goods nor working a few minutes less at our jobs each day would compensate us for the loss of cleanliness, convenience, aesthetic satisfaction, and also time saved in shopping that is provided by modern packaging.

Let the ecologists adopt the poverty-stricken life-style of Eastern Europe if they choose. Let them go about like old Russian grandmothers in Moscow, with an ever-present shopping bag and herring jar, if that is what they like. Let them pick through garbage pails while pretending that they live in a spaceship—"spaceship Earth," they call it—rather than in the richest country of the planet earth. But there is absolutely no sane reason why anyone should or needs to live this way, and certainly not in modern America. Above all, let them keep their peculiar values to themselves and not seek to impose them on the rest of us by the enactment of laws.

### 2. The Tendency Toward a Uniform Price for the Same Good Throughout the World

A second principle of economics, similar and closely related to the uniformity-of-profit principle, is that *in a free market there is a tendency toward the establishment of a uniform price for the same good throughout the world.*

The basis of this principle is the fact that any inequality in the price of the same good between two markets creates an opportunity for profit. In order to profit, all one need do is buy in the cheaper market and sell in the dearer market. The very fact of doing this, however, acts to reduce the inequality in price. For the additional buying raises the price in the cheaper market and the additional selling lowers it in the more expensive market. The process tends to continue until the inequality in price between the two markets is totally eliminated and a uniformity of price achieved.

The reason that uniform prices among different geographical markets are not actually established is mainly the existence of transportation costs. The existence of these costs means that before a price discrepancy between two markets becomes profitable to exploit, it must exceed these transportation costs. These costs, however, then set the limits which geographical price discrepancies do not tend to exceed. Or, to put it positively, the price of the same good tends to be uniform throughout the world except for transportation costs between markets.

The significance of this principle is very great. Its operation explains, for example, why local crop failures in a free market do not result even in significant scarcities, let alone famines. The effect of a local crop failure is to begin raising the price of grain in the local market. Once the local price of grain exceeds prices in outside markets by more than transportation costs, it becomes profitable to buy in those outside markets and sell locally. The effect is that the reduction in the local supply is almost entirely made good by drawing on the production of the rest of the world. Consequently, instead of a disastrous reduction in the local supply and an enormous rise in the local price, there is a modest reduction in the world supply and a modest rise in the world price of grain.

A good analogy to what happens is provided by the physical principle that water seeks its level. Imagine that you have just filled an ice tray—the kind in which water is able to flow around and underneath the plastic or metal insert that marks off the separate compartments for the ice cubes. If you now remove water from one compartment of the tray, you will not reduce the water level in that compartment by the amount of water you take from it. You will reduce the water level in that compartment and in the whole tray very slightly, because the loss from the one compartment will be spread over the whole tray.

In just the same way, if half the wheat crop of France were lost, the supply of wheat in France would not fall by half. On the contrary, the supply in France and in the whole world might fall by 2 or 3 percent—or however much of a decline the French loss represented in the world supply.

Water seeks its level by virtue of the force of pressure. It moves from places of higher pressure to places of lower pressure. Commodity supplies seek their level by virtue of the attraction of profits. They move from places of lower prices to places of higher prices, in the process equalizing prices as the movement of water equalizes pressure.

It should be realized that the principle of the tendency toward a geographical uniformity of prices is not only descriptively analogous to a law of physics, but, as far as the ability of governments to act is concerned, has the same *existential status* as a law of physics. (And so, incidentally, do all the principles of economics.) That means it is impossible even for the world's most powerful governments to annul its operation. Governments can frustrate its operation, but even in the cases in which they do so, they cannot annul its operation. The existence of the principle is confirmed by the very attempts to frustrate it, because to frustrate it, definite means must be adopted, which are necessary only because the principle exists, and is working. For example, governments may adopt tariffs, or they may prohibit imports or exports altogether, and in that way stop the equalization of prices. But why must they resort precisely to such measures, and not other measures? The answer is because the principle does exist and is at work even in a controlled economy. Controls of a specific kind are needed to counter it. There is no difference here between economics and the example of water seeking its level. We can make ice trays in which each compartment is totally insulated from the others. That does not contradict the principle that water seeks its level. It confirms it, because the insulation is required only

because water does seek its level, and for some reason one wishes to stop
it from doing so. It is the same way with all economic laws and government
attempts to frustrate them.

Why the Arab Oil Embargo Would Not Have Been a Threat to a Free
Economy

The principle that in a free market there tends to be a uniform price for
the same good throughout the world has important application to the Arab
oil embargo of 1973-74. The principle shows that if the United States had
had a free market in oil when the Arabs imposed their embargo, our oil
supplies could not have been seriously jeopardized.

Let us think back to the time of the embargo, and imagine that everything
else is the same except that the United States has a free market in oil.

The Arabs now launch their embargo. The immediate effect is that a large
part of the oil supplies of the northeastern United States—the major importing region and the one dependent on the Arabs—is cut off.

In a free market, no sooner would this have happened, than the price of
oil and oil products in the Northeast would have begun to rise. Once prices
in the Northeast came to exceed those in the rest of the country by more
than the costs of transportation, supplies would have moved from the rest
of the country to the Northeast. The effect would have been largely to
replenish supplies in the Northeast and to reduce supplies somewhat in the
rest of the country. The reduction in imports from the Arabs, in other
words, would have been spread over the whole country instead of being
concentrated in the Northeast, where it threatened to cripple the economy
of the region. In this way, its impact would have been minimized. Prices
in the Northeast would have been held down by the inflow of the new
supplies, and those in the rest of the country raised up by the shipments
to the Northeast.

In fact, the higher level of oil prices in the Northeast and in the country
as a whole would have acted as a magnet to supplies of oil from outside the
country. The same motives that would have impelled a southern or mid-
western oil producer to send additional supplies to New York or Boston
would also have impelled a Venezuelan producer to do so. In fact, additional
imports could have come from the most remote places. As the rise in prices
in the Northeast pulled up prices in the rest of the country, it could very
well have become profitable to start shipping additional supplies to the West
Coast from oil-producing areas like Indonesia, thereby freeing more of domestic production for supplying the Northeast.

Indeed, the United States could have gone on—indirectly—importing
Arab oil! This would have occurred simply as a result of expanding the
import of refined petroleum products made from Arab oil in places not

subject to the Arab embargo. For example, if the Arabs continued to supply Spanish refineries, say, and the price of refined products had risen in the United States, those refineries would have diverted more of their output to the United States.

It thus becomes apparent that within a fairly short time an embargo by the Arabs against oil shipments to the United States would have had very little effect on the supply of oil in the United States. To the extent that the United States had been importing Arab oil, it would, for the most part, merely have changed importers, and, for much of the rest, it would even have continued to import Arab oil, but by a circuitous route.

The reason the Arab embargo did threaten us was the existence of our price controls. When oil supplies to the Northeast were cut off by the embargo, price controls prohibited the people in the Northeast from bidding up oil prices. The people in the Northeast were therefore made powerless to bring about the shipment of additional supplies from the rest of the country. In the same way, price controls prohibited the people of the United States as a whole from bidding up prices, with the result that it was not possible to bring about stepped-up imports from non-Arab sources. The effect of our controls was to cause the reduction in imports from the Arabs to be experienced with full force at its initial point of impact and to make it impossible to obtain replacement imports. Our price controls paralyzed us——they made it impossible for us to take the actions needed to deal with the situation.

Indeed, because of our price controls, we were not only prevented from finding replacement imports for the loss of Arab imports, but were forced to lose imports from non-Arab sources as well! This happened because other countries in the world, such as West Germany, became better markets in which to sell oil than the United States. As a result, our non-Arab foreign suppliers were led to sell more of their oil to those countries and less to us. Because of our price controls, we tied our hands in the international competition for oil, and made it possible for countries far poorer than ourselves to outbid us for oil we had normally consumed.

There is more to say about why a free American economy would have had nothing to fear from an Arab embargo.

In late 1973 and early 1974, the Arabs were apparently threatening to cut off oil supplies to the world. There was near panic over whether they would do so. There seemed to be no solution except either to give in to their demands, whatever they might be, or go to war with them.

If we had had a free economy, the only lasting effect of any embargo the Arabs might have launched against the rest of the world would have been to strengthen our oil industry at the expense of their oil industry.

To understand this point, let us assume that the American economy had been free of all price controls in 1973 and that the Arabs had launched their embargo with the serious intention of cutting off their supply of oil to the world. Let us assume that the worst fears people had at the time came true, and that the Arabs simply stopped selling oil to anyone, in an effort to blackmail the world into doing their bidding.

The effect, of course, would have been a skyrocketing of the price of oil.

But observe. The Arabs wouldn't have gotten the benefit of the higher price, because *they* wouldn't have been selling any oil.

The benefit of the higher price of oil would have gone to the non-Arab producers, mainly to the producers in the United States.

The American oil companies in that case really would have made fabulous profits. They might have been making profits at a rate fast enough to double their capitals in a single year, or less. They would have made the kind of money the Arabs have made.

In the face of the Arabs' withdrawal from the market, a tendency would have set in to reestablish the United States as an oil exporter, because Western Europe and Japan would have had to turn to us. However much prices skyrocketed here, they would have skyrocketed still more there. Instead of our high prices pulling oil in, we would have begun to ship oil out, in response to their still higher prices. Billions of dollars would have begun to flow from Western Europe and Japan to the United States, not to Iran or Saudi Arabia.

With vast profits starting to pour in from the rest of the world and, of course, from the American consumer too, huge sums would have become available for every kind of oil and energy project in the United States. It would not have taken long, with such profits, for the domestic oil industry to have been entirely rejuvenated and established on an enormously larger scale than ever before, and who knows what other new sources of energy along with it.

Now consider the Arabs. While the American oil producers would have been making money hand over fist, the Arabs would have been starving for lack of income. In this context, it would have been virtually certain that the Arab alliance would soon have broken up. The less fanatical Arab countries would soon have resumed the sale of oil in order to cash in on the profits. Probably, in very short order, all of them would have begun selling again. So, in fact, the supply of oil in the world would almost certainly not have been drastically reduced for very long, despite whatever intentions the Arabs may originally have had. And, therefore, the United States would not, in fact, have had to switch for very long, if at all, from the role of an oil importer to the sudden role of an oil exporter. But to whatever extent the Arabs had delayed in resuming the sale of oil, the effect of their action would have been to impoverish themselves while enormously enriching the oil industry in every other country, especially the United States.

In the years that followed, the American oil industry would have been bigger and richer. American oil production and the production of other forms of energy in the United States would have been expanded because of the additional profits that American firms had earned. Very possibly, a year or two after the embargo, the price of oil would have fallen below its level in the period before the embargo, because of expanded American production. The oil industry at that point might have run at losses for a while. The American firms would have been able to cover their losses out of the profits the Arabs had handed them. The Arabs would not have been able to cover their losses as easily. Consequently, the effect of the whole process would have been a larger American oil industry and, quite possibly, a smaller Arab oil industry.

This is what economic freedom would have accomplished.

The question might be raised of just how high prices could have gone during the Arab embargo if we had not had price controls. It is impossible to answer such a question with any accuracy. Perhaps for a brief period we might have had dollar-a-gallon gasoline or even more expensive gasoline. While they lasted, such prices would certainly have represented a hardship for many people, the author of this book included. But later we would have had far lower oil prices than we do have. Furthermore, as we will see in later chapters, even while a high price lasts, the real problem is not the high price, but the scarce supply. No one's hardship is alleviated by a low price for goods he cannot buy, which is always the effect of price controls. If we in fact have a scarcity, and consumption must be restricted, then, as we will see, the high price is necessary and positively beneficial, because it leads people to restrict their consumption in the ways that are least damaging to themselves.

The policy of price controls on oil during the embargo, therefore, cannot even be said to have sacrificed our long-run economic well-being to our short-run economic well-being. It sacrificed both our long-run and our short-run economic well-being.

### 3. The Tendency Toward Uniform Prices Over Time: The Function of Commodity Speculation

*In a free market there is a tendency toward the equalization of the price of a good in the present with the expected price of that good in the future.* For example, there is a tendency for the price of wheat or crude oil or whichever, today, to be equal to the expected price of wheat or crude oil or whichever next month, six months from now, or next year. This principle applies to any good that is capable of being held in storage.

The basis of this principle is the familiar fact that any discrepancy in price creates an opportunity for profit, the exploitation of which reduces the discrepancy. If, for example, wheat is expected to be more expensive six months from now than it is today, then speculators begin to buy wheat at today's comparatively low price for the purpose of storing it and later selling it at the comparatively high price that is expected to exist in the future. The effect of their action is to raise the price of wheat in the present, and, by enlarging the supply available in the future, reduce the price of wheat in the future. As a result, the present and expected future prices are brought closer together.

The present and expected future prices will never actually be equalized, for two important reasons. First, there are costs of storing any commodity. In addition, since every business must yield the going rate of profit, if it is to continue in existence, it is necessary to earn as good a rate of profit in storing commodities as in any other line of business. Consequently, the actual relationship between present and future prices is that they tend to differ by no more than the costs of storage plus an allowance for the going rate of profit on the capital that must be invested in the storage.

The practical significance of this principle can be seen in the following example. Assume that the wheat harvest is one-twelfth below the size of the average annual harvest. It is therefore necessary to stretch what would normally be an eleven months' supply of wheat over twelve months. If the price of wheat did not rise at harvest time, the consumption of wheat and wheat products would go on at the usual rate, requiring a more severe restriction of consumption later on. Imagine that the price did not rise until after ten months had gone by, during which consumption had occurred at the usual rate. In that case, two months would be left to go until the next harvest, and it would be necessary to stretch the remaining supplies, equal to only one month's usual consumption, over that period. By the rise in price being delayed this long, one month's supplies would have to be made to do the work of two, instead of eleven months' supplies doing the work of twelve. The rate of consumption would have to be cut in half instead of merely by one-twelfth. It is the same in principle for all shorter periods during which the rate of consumption is excessive. Always, an excessive rate of consumption in the earlier months must be balanced by a more severely reduced rate of consumption in the later months.

The existence of speculation on future prices prevents such calamities and minimizes all such imbalances in the rate of consumption. Speculators anticipate the future prices of commodities and buy or sell the commodity in question for the purpose of profiting from every discrepancy between the present price and the prices they expect to exist in the future. In our example, the activity of the commodity speculators would serve to bring about the minimum necessary restriction in the rate of wheat consumption. For if they see that in the absence of their activity prices will reach famine levels in the future, or levels reflecting a severe scarcity, or even any level whatever that exceeds the present price by more than the costs of storage and the going rate of profit, they begin to buy the commodity in question for the purpose of profiting from the future high price. Their additional buying raises the price of the commodity in the present and thus restricts the rate of its consumption. Later, as the future unfolds, the goods in the hands of the speculators constitute a larger supply and serve to reduce prices in comparison with what they would otherwise have been. The activity of the speculators therefore serves to transfer supplies from a period in which they are less urgently needed, as indicated by their lower price, to a period in which they are more urgently needed, as indicated by their higher price. In this way, it brings about the optimum rate of consumption of limited supplies.

Speculative activity, of course, is not limited to anticipating just future scarcities. Rather, it seeks in general to balance consumption and production over time by accumulating stocks of commodities and regulating their rate of consumption. If it is anticipated, for example, that a future harvest will be larger than originally forecast, and thus that the price of wheat in the future will be lower than originally expected, the activity of the speculators will bring about a lower price immediately. In anticipation of the lower future price, some of the speculators will begin to sell their holdings of the commodity now, in order to find a more profitable employment for their capitals. As a result of their sales, the price begins to fall right away. As a consequence of the lower price, the rate of consumption in the present is expanded. In this case, the effect of speculative activity is to permit present consumption to expand in the knowledge that larger future production than originally expected necessitates the holding of smaller present stocks.

Much speculative activity occurs on organized commodity exchanges. However, only a relatively small number of basic commodities are traded on the exchanges—principally various agricultural commodities and nonferrous metals. For the rest, speculation is largely limited to those who are engaged in the actual production or use of the commodity.

It should be realized that every businessman is a commodity speculator when he decides what size inventory to hold and whether it is a good time to increase or decrease the size of his inventory. For he is basing his decision on a comparison of present prices and the prices he expects to exist in the future. In the same way, every consumer engages in commodity speculation when he decides to buy more or less than his normal requirements on the basis of a comparison of present prices with the prices he anticipates in the future.

The speculative activities of businessmen and consumers serve to equalize present and future prices in additional ways than the one we have considered. For example, if, in anticipation of higher prices, businessmen simply hold back on selling their inventories, they are decreasing the supply available in the present and increasing the supply available in the future, which, of course, acts to narrow the discrepancy in price. By the same token, if consumers step up their purchases in the present, in anticipation of higher prices in the future, then, to that extent, their demand for the item in the future will be less because it will already have been provided for. In this case, a larger present demand and smaller future demand act to reduce the discrepancy in price.

Like almost every economic activity that goes beyond manual labor, commodity speculation is frequently denounced. Because speculation transmits the higher prices expected to exist in the future to the present, it is denounced as the cause of the higher prices. What is overlooked in this accusation is that the supplies accumulated as a result of speculation must ultimately be used, and at that time they necessarily act to reduce prices—because either they are put on the market and sold, thereby increasing the supply of the commodity, or, by sparing their owners the need to purchase, they reduce the demand for the commodity. Moreover, if the speculators are mistaken—if they raise the present price and there is no independent cause of a higher price in the future—*they* pay the penalty of their mistake: they have bought at high prices and must sell at low prices, or they have stocked up at high prices when they might later have bought at low prices.

Rebuttal of the Charge that Large Stocks of Oil Proved the Oil Shortage Was "Manufactured" by the Oil Companies

Our knowledge of speculation can be applied to the charge that the oil shortage of late 1973 and early 1974 was "manufactured" by the oil companies, an accusation which was repeated again and again in the press and on television at the time.

The proof offered that the oil companies were artificially creating the oil shortage was the allegation that their storage depots were full of oil. I remember one television news story, filmed at an oil company tank farm, in which the reporter pointed to the tanks, said he had personally seen that they were full, and, therefore, that there could be no real shortage of oil, but just an "artificial" one created by the oil companies.

The reporter, his editor, station, and network evidently forgot, or did not know, the major news item of the time, which was the prospect that in the coming months the United States would be deprived of a significant part of its customary imports of oil, while having to meet the possibility of a long, severe winter. The tanks and storage depots most certainly *should* have been full, *in anticipation* of that terrible prospect. Any fullness of the tanks and depots was not, as the news media claimed, a proof of the abundance of oil, but of its *prospective scarcity*. (The reader should imagine what it would mean if the day ever came when he thought it necessary to fill every spare inch of his kitchen with food. His large stockpile would not be a proof of the abundance of food, but of the prospective scarcity of food.)

Apparently, the media were simply unaware of the need to hold supplies of oil for future sale. For it appears that they would have been satisfied with the genuineness of the shortage only if their reporters had visited the tank farms and found them empty. By that time, however, it would have been too late: millions would have died.

The unfortunate fact was, however, that the oil company storage depots and tank farms were *not* full. The media erroneously inferred from their observation of a large quantity of oil at some tank farms that there must be a large supply of oil in the country. Their logic was the same in principle as that of someone travelling to India and seeing a few warehouses full of food, and then concluding that there is a large quantity of food in India. In reality, because of price controls, the stocks of crude oil, gasoline, and residual fuel oil in the United States in the period from October 31, 1973, to April 1, 1974—the time of the oil crisis—were all substantially less in most months than their respective averages had been for that period of the year over the preceding *five years*; distillate fuel (home heating oil) was the only major oil product whose stock had been increased. Overall, that is, if one simply adds up the number of barrels of crude oil and of the various kinds of oil products, stocks were significantly lower in all but two months, when they were very slightly higher. Table 1, based on data compiled by the Commodity Research Bureau, shows the facts.[4] (It should be realized, incidentally, that the table tends to understate somewhat the deficiency of stocks, because the figures for the average of the previous five years are all pulled down by their inclusion of data for 1972-73, which was itself a year of very low stocks, as a result of price controls.)

Table 1
*Stocks of Oil and Oil Products in the*
*United States During the Oil Crisis*
(all figures in millions of barrels)

*a. Stocks of Crude Oil in the U. S. at Beginning of the Month*

|  | *Nov.* | *Dec.* | *Jan.* | *Feb.* | *Mar.* | *Apr.* |
|---|---|---|---|---|---|---|
| 1973-74 | 246.3 | 250.0 | 242.5 | 233.0 | 240.7 | 244.7 |
| Average of Previous Five Years | 263.1 | 264.9 | 264.0 | 261.0 | 258.0 | 261.8 |

*b. Stocks of Finished Gasoline on Hand in the U. S. at End of Month*

|  | *Oct.* | *Nov.* | *Dec.* | *Jan.* | *Feb.* | *Mar.* |
|---|---|---|---|---|---|---|
| 1973-74 | 218.2 | 211.4 | 213.4 | 221.3 | 223.0 | 223.6 |
| Average of Previous Five Years | 201.5 | 207.6 | 216.8 | 230.8 | 237.3 | 234.6 |

*c. Stocks of Residual Fuel Oil in the U. S. at Beginning of Year* (data available only for January 1 and July 1)

Jan. 1, 1974                    53.5

Average of
Previous                        58.5
Five Years

*d. Stocks of Distillate Fuel in the U. S., First of the Month*

|  | Nov. | Dec. | Jan. | Feb. | Mar. | Apr. |
|---|---|---|---|---|---|---|
| 1973-74 | 203.0 | 200.2 | 196.5 | 181.2 | 149.2 | 128.9 |
| Average of Previous Five Years | 211.0 | 204.1 | 177.0 | 142.2 | 116.5 | 105.3 |

*e. Total Stocks of Oil and Oil Products in the U. S.* (end of month gasoline data added to beginning of month data for crude oil and distillate; residual oil shown separately for January)

|  | Nov. | Dec. | Jan. | Feb. | Mar. | Apr. |
|---|---|---|---|---|---|---|
| 1973-74 | 667.5 | 661.6 | 652.4 | 635.5 | 612.9 | 597.2 |
|  |  |  | 53.5 |  |  |  |
| Average of Previous Five Years | 675.6 | 676.6 | 657.8 | 634.0 | 611.8 | 601.7 |
|  |  |  | 58.5 |  |  |  |

The fact that stocks of oil in storage were actually below average in 1973-74 should not be surprising. Such a result is to be expected from price controls. It is implied in our example of the deficient wheat harvest in which the price does not rise. It is only necessary to realize that price controls not only induce buyers to buy up commodities too rapidly for supplies to last, but also induce sellers to sell them too rapidly. Sellers are led to sell too rapidly because it is more profitable to sell goods at the fixed, controlled price in the present rather than in the future. By selling in the present, a seller saves storage costs and can earn profit or interest by investing the sales proceeds. If he is going to have to sell at the controlled price, it pays him to sell as soon as possible and simply put the money in the bank if he has to.[5]

The only reason that stocks of distillate oil were built up in the crisis period was that the government ordered it. Distillate stocks had declined sharply in early 1973, with the result that shortages began to appear even then. The government feared vastly worse shortages in the winter of 1974: it feared the prospect of people freezing to death.

It should be understood that if we had not had price controls, any build-up in stocks of oil that would have occurred, would not have caused a shortage, even though it reduced the supply of oil currently available. In the absence of price controls, the build-up would have raised the current price of oil. At higher prices, people would have economized on their use of oil products to whatever extent it was necessary to reduce current consumption. Of course, higher prices would also have pulled in supplies from other markets, making the necessary reduction in current consumption that much less. As will be shown in later chapters, anyone able and willing to pay the higher current prices would have been able to buy whatever oil products he wished. There would have been no shortage in the sense of people being able and willing to pay the asking price of oil but unable to obtain it. Thus, even if there had been a build-up of stocks of oil, as the media claimed, it could not have caused a shortage of oil in the absence of price controls.

In charging the oil industry with "manufacturing" the oil shortage by holding large stocks of oil, the media displayed ignorance in four respects. First, they were ignorant of the fact that, with the exception of distillate, stocks of oil were not actually large, but significantly below normal. Second, they were ignorant of what large stocks of oil would have signified had they existed (or, in the case of distillate, what the large stock did signify)—i.e., not proof of abundance, but of prospective *scarcity*. Third, they were apparently ignorant even of the fact that it is necessary to hold stocks of oil in the first place, for their attitude was, it seems, that so long as oil was on hand, there could be no problem of a lack of it. Fourth, they did not know that in the absence of price controls, no accumulation of a stock could cause a shortage in the current market.

In their treatment of the oil shortage, the media functioned on the level of men without the ability to think conceptually. They proceeded as though they were unable to make distinctions between quantities that are perceptually large, i.e., between a tank farm full of oil, and an adequate national supply. They proceeded as though they were unable to think beyond the range of the immediate moment, i.e., to realize the need to hold supplies for future sale. They proceeded as though they were incapable of understanding connections among concrete events, i.e., the connection between the prospect of the loss of imports and the need to build up stocks of oil. They proceeded, in short, as though they had never heard of, and were incapable of grasping, a single principle of economics. Only because they functioned at this incredibly low mental level, was it possible for the media to assert that the oil shortage was "manufactured" by the oil companies.

I will have much more to say about this accusation in later chapters. I will show that it is only correct to say that the oil shortage was "manufactured" and "artificial," if one realizes that it was manufactured by the government, through price controls, not by the oil companies and their perfectly natural desire to earn profits.

### 4. The Tendency Toward Uniform Wage Rates
### for Workers of the Same Degree of Ability

*In a free market there is a tendency toward an equalization of wage rates for workers of the same degree of ability.*

The basis of the tendency toward equality is the fact that men prefer to earn a higher income rather than a lower income, and therefore seek higher-paying jobs in preference to lower-paying jobs. The movement of labor into the higher-paying fields and out of the lower-paying fields reduces wage rates in the higher-paying fields and raises them in the lower-paying fields. The stopping point is an equality of wage rates.

This is not to say that forty or fifty-year-old workers suddenly give up their work of many years to change to a brand-new occupation in response to a 5 or 10 or even 20 percent difference in wages. No. In view of the costs and the various other problems such workers would have to incur in the learning of new skills, it would not pay them to switch occupations except in cases of really major differences in wages—brought about, for example, by their previous jobs being rendered obsolete through technological progress.

The movement of labor from occupation to occupation in response to less-than-gross differences in wage rates is accomplished in a different way. It is accomplished by virtue of the fact that each occupation continually loses members through death or retirement and must continually be resupplied with young workers. Changes in the flow of young workers into the various occupations produce the same effect as an actual movement of labor between occupations. Where the number of young workers entering an occupation exceeds the number of old workers dying or retiring, the supply of labor in that occupation rises. Where the number of young workers entering an occupation is less than the number of old workers leaving, the supply of labor in that occupation falls.

Now by the time young people are ready to begin preparing themselves for a career, there are very marked differences in their ability and willingness to learn. And, for this reason, the labor force necessarily assumes a hierarchical structure, with the tendency toward an equalization of wage rates being operative only within the respective levels of this structure, not throughout the structure as a whole.

Those with the greatest ability and willingness to learn are potentially capable of performing practically any job. For example, the young man who is capable of learning to be a surgeon is also certainly capable of learning to be a printer. In turn, the young man who is capable of learning to be a printer is also certainly capable of learning to work on an assembly line. Everyone, in other words—the potential surgeon, the potential printer, and the potential assembly line worker—is capable of learning the work of the assembly line worker. But only the potential surgeon and the potential printer are capable of learning the work of the printer. And only the potential surgeon alone is capable of learning the work of the surgeon.

In conformity with the principle contained in this example, let us think of the young people ready to prepare for a career as divided into three broad groups: those capable of entering the professions, those capable of learning to do skilled work, and those capable of learning no more than unskilled work.

Such a division of the potential labor force necessarily prevents any tendency toward a general equalization of wage rates. No matter how high the wage rates of the professions may climb in relation to those of skilled and unskilled labor, it is simply impossible for young people who lack the necessary capacity, to go into the professions instead of skilled or unskilled labor. Similarly, no matter how high the wages of skilled labor may climb in relation to those of unskilled labor, there is, again, no way for the young people who lack the necessary capacity, to enter the field of skilled labor instead of unskilled labor. On the other hand, the wages of skilled labor *are* limited in relation to those of professional-level labor. For as soon as the wages of skilled labor begin to exceed those of professionals, it is possible for young people capable of the professions to enter the field of skilled labor. In the same way, the wages of unskilled labor are limited in relation to those of skilled labor. For as soon as the wages of unskilled labor begin to exceed those of skilled labor, it is possible for young people capable of skilled labor to enter the field of unskilled labor.

It is because of this hierarchical division of the total pool of human talent—of the fact that ability can flow downward to lower channels, but not upward to higher channels, so to speak—that we observe in actual life that the wages of professionals markedly and permanently exceed those of skilled workers, while those of skilled workers, in turn, markedly and permanently exceed those of unskilled workers. And we observe that the wages of the highest-paid skilled workers cannot get very far ahead of the wages of the lowest-paid professionals, nor the wages of the highest-paid unskilled workers very far ahead of the wages of the lowest-paid skilled workers.

This explains inequalities in wages. Let us return to the question of why wage rates for any given level of ability tend to be equal.

Let us consider the wage rates of a number of skilled occupations, for example, the various building trades, such as carpenters, electricians, and plumbers, and other skilled occupations, such as printers, draftsmen, mechanics, and locomotive engineers. All of these occupations, and others of a similar nature, require the same basic level of intelligence and education on the part of the workers. As a result, they are all potentially capable of being performed by the same people. All of them, in effect, can be supplied with labor that is drawn from a pool of human talent on the same basic level. Because of men's preference for a higher income over a lower income, this pool of talent naturally runs more heavily into those occupations which offer higher wages and less heavily into those which offer lower wages. As a result, there is a tendency toward an increase in the supply of labor in the better-paying kinds of skilled work and a decrease in the supply of labor in the poorer-paying kinds of skilled work. Since the effect of the increases in the supply of labor in the initially higher-paying fields is to reduce wages in those fields, while the effect of the decreases in the supply of labor in the initially lower-paying fields is to raise wages in those fields, the discrepancy in wages among the different kinds of skilled labor is narrowed, and thus they tend toward equality.

In exactly the same way, there is a tendency toward a uniformity of wages among the various unskilled or low-skilled occupations, such as assembly line workers, machine tenders, truck and bus drivers, clerks, stevedores, and so on. There is a tendency toward a further uniformity of wage rates among the various professions, such as doctors, lawyers, scientists, engineers, professors, and so on. In these cases, too, the original pool of talent flows into the various channels on its level in accordance with the wages to be made; and, in flowing more or less heavily, lowers or raises those wages, thereby reducing the discrepancies among them and driving them toward equality.

There are, of course, important differences in wages of a permanent nature even within the three broad groups of workers that I have delineated. At each level, there is a tendency for some particular occupations to earn more than others—for example, for doctors to earn more than professors, and for stevedores to earn more than clerks. There are also important differences in earnings within each occupation, especially at the professional level. For example, there are always some doctors or lawyers who earn five or ten times as much as the average of their profession, and there are some printers or mechanics who earn significantly more than others.

These differences are due in part to the existence of further categories of division in human ability. There are those who have the ability and willingness to learn how to be a doctor or lawyer, and others who have the ability and willingness to learn how to be a great doctor or lawyer. In other cases, willingness and ability to learn is not the sole criterion of division. Other factors have to be added. For example, in many types of work, especially unskilled work, it is necessary to possess a significant degree of physical strength. Those who have it are in a narrower category than those who do not and, accordingly, tend to be higher paid. In other cases, workers are differentiated by the special development of other physical or psychological potentials—such as muscular coordination, an ear for music, special visual acuity, and so on. In the case of great athletes, opera singers, musicians, and actors—all the really star performers—the combination of special characteristics is such as to make the labor of these persons virtually unique. As a result, when they are in demand, their earnings do not have any fixed limit in relation to the earnings of others, because no one is able to increase the supply of what they are offering.

For the rest, the differences in wages within the various broad groups are the result of the fact that considerations other than money income are associated with each job. There are such considerations as how interesting or uninteresting is the work, how pleasant or unpleasant are the conditions of the work, how safe or dangerous is it, how regular is the employment, how long and how expensive is the special preparation required, and, perhaps, still other, similar considerations. Considerations of this kind explain, for example, why scientists tend to earn less, and tax lawyers more, than is commensurate with their respective levels of ability. In the one case, the work itself may be the highest pleasure in life to those who perform it; in the other, it is more likely to be experienced as painfully dull. As a result, those with the necessary ability to be scientists are willing to enter the field even to the point of accepting substantially lower wages in comparison with what they could earn elsewhere. By the same token, people would cease to enter such a field as tax law as soon as that field no longer offered significant monetary advantages over other fields they might enter. The principle that emerges is that any occupation which offers special nonmonetary advantages tends to offer correspondingly lower wages, while any occupation that imposes special disadvantages of any kind tends to offer correspondingly higher wages. These discounts and premiums in wages balance the special advantages and disadvantages of the various occupations.

In sum, in a free market there are at least three principles of wage determination at work simultaneously. One is a tendency toward a uniformity of wages for labor of the same degree of ability. A second is a tendency toward unequal wage rates for labor of different degrees of ability—primarily intellectual ability, but also other abilities as well. And a third is a tendency toward the inclusion of discounts and premiums in wages as an offsetting element to the special advantages or disadvantages of the occupations concerned. The combined operation of these three principles helps to explain the full range of the various wage rates we observe in actual life.

Now, as far as it operates, the principle of the uniformity of wage rates is similar in its consequences to the uniformity-of-profit principle. That is, it serves to keep the various occupations supplied with labor in the proper proportions. Too many people do not rush into carpentering and not enough go into printing, say, because the very effect of such a mistake is to reduce the wages of carpenters and raise those of printers. This acts to delimit and counteract the mistake. In addition, the operation of this principle gives to consumers the ultimate power to determine the relative size of the various occupations. If the consumers buy more printed matter and fewer products made of wood, then the effect of the change is to cause the demand for printers to rise and that for carpenters to fall. As a result, the wages of printers rise and more young men are induced to become printers, while the wages of carpenters fall and fewer young men become carpenters.

It should be realized, as this example of the printers shows, that in seeking to earn the highest wages, the individual worker is seeking to do the kind of work the consumers most want him to do. This is true of every individual who seeks to take the best-paying job he can find at any given level of ability or who seeks to raise his level of ability. For what enables any job to pay more is only the fact that the consumers want its products sufficiently. Let them decide to reduce their demand for its products, and the wages it pays will tend to fall, while if they raise their demand for its products, the wages it pays will tend to rise still higher.

In a free market, within the limit of his abilities, each man chooses that job which he believes offers him the best combination of money and non-monetary considerations. In so doing, he simultaneously acts for his own maximum well-being and for that of the consumers who buy the ultimate products his labor helps to produce.

### 5. Prices and Costs of Production

*In a free market the prices of products tend to be governed by their costs of production.*

This principle follows directly from the uniformity-of-profit principle, and we have already glimpsed it in discussing the long-run consequences of repealing price controls. The uniformity-of-profit principle implies that the prices of products tend to equal their costs of production plus only as much profit as is required to afford the going rate of profit on the capital invested. If prices exceed costs by more than this amount of profit, then there is a tendency toward expanded production and lower prices. If they fail to exceed costs by as much as this amount of profit, then there is a tendency toward reduced production and higher prices. The stopping point is, as I say, where prices equal costs of production plus the amount of profit required to yield the going rate of profit on the capital invested.

Now there are two ways that cost of production governs prices. One way is indirectly—through variations in the supply of the good, as above. The other way is directly—through the decisions of the sellers of the good in setting their prices.

Let us consider first the cases in which the role of cost is indirect—for example, all or most agricultural commodities. In any given year, the price of wheat, or potatoes, or cotton, or whichever, is determined simply by supply and demand. Over a period of years, however, the price of such a good tends to gravitate about its cost of production. This is because whenever the price begins to exceed cost by more than what is required to afford the average rate of profit to the industry, additional capital will be invested, supply will be expanded, and the price and profit will decline. If the price fails to provide the average rate of profit to the industry, capital will be withdrawn, supply will be reduced, and the price and profit will be restored. What ties price to cost in such a case is variations in supply.

However, there is a vast category of cases in which the connection between price and cost is far more direct. This is the case of most manufactured or processed goods. In these cases, the sellers typically maintain inventories of their goods and have plant capacity available to produce more. In such a situation, a rise in demand, provided it is not too large, is met out of inventories, and before the inventory is exhausted, production is stepped up from plant capacity held in reserve. Similarly, when a fall in demand occurs, inventory is temporarily allowed to build up, and production is cut back. Provided the changes in demand are not of major proportions, there is little or no change in price. It can be observed, for example, that the price of bread, automobiles, newspapers, restaurant meals, paper clips, and countless other goods does not change with every change in demand. A change in demand must be fairly substantial to raise or lower the price of these goods. In cases in which the demand changes are not too substantial, they are simply accompanied by corresponding changes in production, while the price of the product remains the same.

In cases of this kind, it is not correct to say that the price of the product is determined simply by supply and demand. On the contrary, the price of the product determines the quantity of the product the buyers buy, and the quantity that they buy determines the quantity the sellers produce and sell.

The prices themselves in these cases are set by sellers on the basis of a consideration of costs of production. It is not that each seller sets his price on the basis of his own costs. But some seller in an industry—usually, the most efficient large firm and one that is in a position to expand its production significantly from existing capacity—sets its price on the basis of a consideration of costs, and the other firms are forced to match its price. The other firms cannot exceed its price, because it has the additional production capacity required to supply many of their customers if they should try to sell at higher prices. Nor, as a rule, can the other firms undercut its price, because it is the lowest-cost, most efficient producer, and sets its price accordingly.

The cost of production on the basis of which such a firm sets its price is not primarily its own cost of production, but the costs of production of its less efficient competitors or, if it has no current competitors, the costs of production of potential competitors. It sets its price in such a way as to prevent its competitors from earning too high profits, because it does not want them to accumulate the capital that would enable them to become more efficient and to expand at its expense. Nor does it want to invite new firms into its field. It wants to avoid creating a situation in which it makes it possible for others to make inroads into its business, which, once started, might lead to its own downfall. It therefore tries to set its price in such a way as to prevent this, which means it tries to set prices not very far above their costs—as a maximum. At the same time, of course, it strives to reduce its own costs of production even further, so as to be able to expand its own profits and to be able comfortably to meet any price reductions inaugurated by competitors that in the meanwhile may have grown more efficient. It is only when the demand for the product becomes so strong that it is not possible to meet it at a price determined in this way, that the price rises to permit high profits to all in the field.

In the case of manufactured and processed goods, therefore, the direct determinant of price is cost of production.[6]

However, if we examine costs of production, we find that they are reducible to two things: to the physical quantities of the means or factors of production employed to produce a good and to the prices of those factors of production. For example, the cost of producing an automobile equals the quantity of each type of labor employed in turning out a car times the wage rates of that labor, plus the quantity of steel used times the price of that steel, and so on. Now the prices of these factors of production are themselves directly determined either by supply and demand or by cost of production. For example, the wage rates are determined by supply and demand, while the price of steel is determined by cost of production. Now the costs of producing steel and all the other elements of an automobile whose prices are determined by cost are themselves resolvable in the same way as the cost of producing an automobile. That is, they in turn are based on prices directly determined by supply and demand and prices directly determined by cost of production.

It should be observed that as we keep pushing the matter back and back, the cumulative role of prices directly determined by supply and demand becomes greater and greater. In the case of our automobile, the production cost of an automobile ultimately depends on the wages of auto workers, the wages of steel workers, the wages of iron miners, and so on, all of which are determined by supply and demand. And, along the way, the prices of some of the materials, such as the copper and zinc the auto companies may have to buy, the raw rubber the tire manufacturers buy, the scrap metal the steel producers need—these prices, too, are directly determined by supply and demand. Ultimately, therefore, as far as it rests on prices, cost of production itself is determined entirely by supply and demand.

Consequently, when prices are determined by cost of production, what they are ultimately determined by is still supply and demand, but supply and demand operating in a wide context—that is, by supply and demand operating in the context of the labor market and in certain broad commodity markets, not in the relatively narrow market of the individual product itself.[7]

The analysis of cost of production into elements which are themselves determined by supply and demand tells us that if we want an ultimate explanation of prices determined by costs, we must explain prices determined by supply and demand. This will be our task in the next chapter, as we complete our presentation of the free market's laws of price determination.

# Free-Market Principles and Applications II

1. The General Pricing of Goods and
Services in Limited Supply

The determination of price by supply and demand applies to all goods and services whose supply is a given fact and therefore limited for a longer or shorter period of time to come. As we have seen, it also applies indirectly (via determining the prices that constitute their costs of production) to products whose supply can be immediately varied in response to changes in demand.

It is necessary to consider a kind of catalog of goods and services in limited supply, in order to understand concretely the range of application possessed by the principle of supply and demand.

The most important item in this list is, of course, human labor, which is always limited by the number of people able to work. Furthermore, the labor of each person is limited by his need for rest and relaxation. And, as the general level of real wages—i.e., the quantity of goods a worker can buy with his money wages—goes up, the fewer are the hours that people are prepared to work. This occurs because to the degree that people can earn a higher standard of living from any given number of hours of labor, their need for the additional real income that extra hours could provide is less. In addition to this, of course, the supply of skilled labor is always still further limited, and that of professional-level labor even more so; and, at any given time, the supply of labor in each occupation and each location is very narrowly limited.

After labor services come materials whose supply is temporarily limited, such as agricultural commodities between harvests. Housing and buildings of all kinds are in a state of temporarily limited supply, because considerable time is always required before their supply can be increased through new construction. Any material, any product whatever, is capable of being in limited supply temporarily, if the demand for it outruns the ability to supply it from existing facilities at a price based on cost of production.

Land sites are in the category of goods in limited supply on a long-run basis, insofar as there is anything special or unique about them that makes them superior to other land, such as their superior location or superior fertility.

In a few cases, the products of such land sites are also in the category of goods in limited supply on a more or less permanent basis: for example, wines of a special flavor that can be produced only from grapes grown on a soil of a very limited extent, or caviar found in sturgeon beds located only in a few places.

Goods such as paintings and statues by old masters, first editions, rare coins, and so on, are in the category of goods in limited supply on an absolutely permanent basis, because their production is necessarily past.

Finally, all second-hand goods are in a state of limited supply.

The prices of all goods and services in limited supply are determined in an essentially similar way in a free market and have a similar significance. One basic determinant is *the quantity of money* in the economic system. As previously indicated, the quantity of money determines aggregate demand. It can do this, of course, only in determining at the same time the demand for the various individual goods and services. We will not go too far wrong if we assume that once the economic system becomes adjusted to a change in the quantity of money, the effect of the change is to change the demand for everything more or less to the same degree. For example, in the long run, if the quantity of money doubles, and everything else remains the same (including such things as the rate at which the money supply increases and is expected to go on increasing), the demand for each individual good and service in the economic system should also tend to double. With a doubled quantity of money, we should expect that eventually the demand for shoes, baseballs, zinc, skilled and unskilled labor, and all other goods and services should all just about double. This means that, in the long run at least, we can regard the quantity of money as acting more or less equally on the price of everything.[1]

The second major determinant of the prices of goods and services in limited supply is *the value judgments of the consumers with respect to the various goods and services on which they spend the quantity of money*. The value judgments of the consumers determine, in effect, how the aggregate demand that is made possible by any given quantity of money is distributed among the products of the various industries and among all the different goods and services in limited supply. The value judgments of the consumers determine, for example, how much is spent for shoes versus shirts, and indirectly, therefore, how much is spent for leather versus cloth, cowhides versus cotton, and grazing land versus cotton land; similarly for the labor services at each stage. In determining the relative spending for all the different consumers' goods, each with its own requirements for labor of specific types, the consumers determine how much is spent in the economy as a whole for each type of labor in relation to every other type of labor, both in terms of specific occupations and in terms of wide groups of occupations, such as skilled labor versus unskilled labor. Similarly for all other goods and services in limited supply, such as diamonds versus wheat, real estate in New York City versus Des Moines, Iowa, and so on. In this way, the value judgments of the consumers ultimately determine the prices of all goods and services in limited supply in relation to one another. It is the value judgments of the consumers that ultimately determine how much more professional-level labor must be paid relative to skilled labor, and how much more skilled labor must be paid relative to unskilled labor.

In sum, the quantity of money determines the absolute height of the prices of goods and services in limited supply, and the value judgments of the consumers determine their relative heights.

## 2. The Pricing and Distribution of Consumers' Goods in Limited Supply

For our purposes, the most important characteristic of the price of a good in limited supply is the fact that *in a free market it always tends to be set high enough to level down the quantity of the good demanded*—i.e., the quantity of it that buyers are seeking to buy—*to equality with the limited supply of it that exists.*

For the sake of simplicity, consider the case of a rare wine, for example. It may be that, potentially, millions of people would enjoy drinking this wine and would be prepared to buy tens of millions of bottles of it every year. But because of the limitation of the special soil on which the necessary grapes can be grown, no more than, say, ten thousand bottles of the wine can be produced in an average year. What happens in this case is that the price of the wine rises to such a point that the great majority of potential buyers are simply eliminated from the market. They look at the high price and say to themselves, "This wine is simply too expensive for me, however delicious it may taste." In fact, in the knowledge that this would be their decision, the very existence of such a wine would probably never even be called to the attention of the great majority of people. As for those who do buy the wine, the high price probably makes almost all of them restrict the amount of it that they consume. At fifty dollars a bottle, say, even millionaire wine lovers probably drink it much less often than they would at, say, ten dollars a bottle.

The case of apartment rentals is essentially the same. In a free market, rents go high enough to level down the quantity of rental space demanded to, or somewhat below, equality with the limited supply of it that exists. The only difference is that in an economy like that of the United States, no one need be excluded from the rental market entirely. Everyone is always able to afford to rent *some* space, even if it is only half of a room he must share with someone else.

Always, a free-market price acts to level the quantity demanded of any good or service in limited supply down to equality with the supply that exists.

This characteristic of a free-market price has a major implication. *It implies that shortages cannot exist in a free market, even in cases of the most severely limited supply.* That is because, however limited the supply may be, a free-market price always rises high enough to level down the quantity demanded to equality with the supply available. In a free market, limited supplies do not cause shortages, but high prices. At the high price, there is no shortage.

In order to further prove this point, let us take an extreme example—one that is very unfair to the free market, namely, the case of the gasoline shortage of 1973-74. In a variety of ways, many of which I have not yet mentioned, the government was responsible for vastly reduced supplies of gasoline, especially in the Northeast. Let us start with these artificially low supplies of gasoline and imagine that at that point the government had simply repealed its price controls on gasoline.

Think back to the sight of service stations faced with multi-block-long lines of cars waiting for gasoline. Let us imagine a service station that has 1,000 gallons of gasoline in its own tanks and is confronted with a line of cars whose drivers are seeking 2,000 gallons of gasoline for their tanks. This is a case of 1,000 gallons of gasoline available, 2,000 gallons demanded. Even in this case, a free market would have equalized the quantity demanded with the supply available. If the owner of the gas station had been free to set his own price, he would have set a price high enough to make those drivers reduce their demand by 1,000 gallons. Such a price undoubtedly existed. If the reader doubts this, he should imagine the gas station owner simply auctioning his gasoline off to the highest bidders. As the price at the auction rose, more and more bidders would have restricted the quantities they bid for, and some would have dropped out of the bidding altogether. At some point, the quantity of gasoline demanded would have been cut back to equality with the 1,000 gallons available. It makes no difference, of course, if instead of conducting an auction, the service station owner had simply set his price where such an auction would have set it. In either case, people who previously were prepared to buy 2,000 gallons of gasoline would have found that they could not afford more than 1,000 gallons and would have limited their purchases accordingly.

In fact, things would have gone further than this. A service station owner not restricted by price controls would have considered the demand not only of the cars presently in line, but of all the cars that might have shown up later in the day, or the next day, or any time before his next deliveries were to arrive. He would not have been willing to sell gasoline to someone presently in line if he expected that someone else would show up later willing to pay more. The price he set, in other words, would have corresponded to the price set in an auction market that extended over time and represented future bidders as well as present bidders.

The effect of the owner's pricing gasoline in this way would have been not only to further reduce the quantity demanded on the part of those presently in line, thereby reducing the waiting line further, *but actually to make gasoline available at all times at his service station.* Since all other service station owners would also have been pricing gasoline in the same way, motorists would soon have realized that gasoline was in fact available whenever they wished it and in whatever quantity they wished it—provided they were willing to pay the price. There would have been no shortage and motorists would have known that they did not have to fear a shortage; they would have ceased to be afraid to drive with less than a full tank of gasoline. This would have totally eliminated the lines. (It should be realized that this is largely a description of what actually happened. Shortages ended because the controls on oil prices were substantially relaxed, and totally eliminated as far as imported oil goes.)

Of course, in the case of a good like gasoline, a rise in price to the free-market level not only restricts the quantity demanded, and eliminates the need to hoard, but also pulls in supplies from other geographical areas. As we will see, it also causes oil refineries to step up the production of gasoline at the expense of other petroleum products, if necessary. And, in the long run, it increases the total production of oil products. In these ways, a free market not only balances the demand and supply of gasoline, but does so at the point of large and, indeed, continuously growing supplies.

However, the crucial point here is that even in the case of goods in strictly limited supply, there are no shortages, no waiting lines, in a free market. Whoever has the price is always able to buy as and when he wishes, and as much as he wishes.

There is a further very important point that follows from our discussion. This is the fact that in the context of limited supplies, it is not only to the self-interest of the sellers that prices rise when conditions make it necessary, but, no less, to the self-interest of the *buyers.* It is simply not true, as most people seem to believe, that the interests of buyers are always served by low prices. On the contrary, *it is to the self-interest of buyers of goods in limited supply that prices be high enough to exclude their competitors from the market.*

To grasp this point in the clearest possible way, imagine an art auction, with two bidders for the same painting. One of them is willing to go as high as $1,000; the other, as high as $2,000. The man whose limit is $2,000 would certainly like to pay as little as necessary. He would be glad to pay just $100, or less, if he could. But given the fact that someone else at the auction is prepared to bid up to $1,000, it would be very foolish for this man to insist on paying any preconceived figure below $1,000. If he arbitrarily insisted on bidding any amount below $1,000, the effect of his action would simply be to allow the painting to go to his rival. If he bid exactly $1,000, and refused to bid any more, he would make it a matter of accident to whom the painting went—if the other bidder bid the $1,000 first, it would probably go to that other bidder. In either case, by refusing to outbid the other bidder, he would prevent himself from getting the painting he wants and which he really values above the other bidder's maximum of $1,000. It is, therefore, to the self-interest of this man to bid above $1,000 for the painting.

There is absolutely no difference as far as this man is concerned if, instead of his having to appear personally at an auction and outbid his rivals, the art dealer who possesses the painting anticipates the strength of his bid, and simply sets a price on the painting in his gallery that is high enough to deter other potential buyers and thus to reserve it for him. From the standpoint of the rightly understood self-interests of this man, it is a positively good thing that the art dealer asks more than $1,000, because if he did not, someone else would buy the painting and it would be gone by the time our man got around to trying to buy it.

The only difference between the cases of the art auction and the art dealer and that of all other commodities in limited supply is simply one of size. Instead of it being a unique painting that is put up for auction or for sale and which is of interest to a relatively small number of bidders or potential buyers, it is more common to have millions of units of the same good offered in the market and sought after by large numbers of bidders or potential buyers. Just as in the case of the painting, in all these cases, too, the fact that a price is high enough to level down the quantity of the good demanded to equality with the limited supply of it that exists is very much to the interest of all those buyers who are willing and able to pay that price. That price is their means of eliminating the competition for the good from other bidders or potential buyers not willing to pay as much. It is their means of being able to secure the good for themselves. In our example of the wine, for instance, the price of fifty dollars a bottle—if that is the price necessary to level the quantity demanded down to equality with the supply available—is in the interest of everyone who values the wine at or above fifty dollars. If the price were any lower, the wine would be within reach of other potential buyers, who did not value it so highly, and it would, therefore, to that extent, not be available to those who did. In the same way, whatever price of a square foot of rental space, or any other good, is required to level the quantity demanded down to equality with the supply available, that price is to the interest of all those who value that space or that good at that price or any higher price. If the price were any lower, they would simply lose their ability to secure the good for themselves—the good would be bought up by those not able or willing to pay as much, and to that extent it would be unavailable to those who did value it sufficiently.

There are two possible misunderstandings of what I am saying that I want to anticipate and answer before going any further.

First, I want to stress that the ability to outbid others for the supply, or part of the supply, of a good is by no means the exclusive prerogative of the rich. The fact is that absolutely everyone exercises this prerogative to the extent that he earns an income or has any money to spend at all. Even the very poorest people outbid others, and the others whom they outbid can include people who are far wealthier than themselves. Of course, this is not true in a case such as our example of the rare wine, where the entire supply is obviously consumed by those who are quite well-to-do.

But it is true in a case such as rental space, or housing in general, where everyone succeeds in obtaining some part of the supply. In a case of this kind, a wealthier family will obtain a larger share of the supply than a poorer family, but what stops it from obtaining a still larger share is the fact that the poorer family outbids it for part of the supply. For example, a wealthier family may rent an eight-room apartment, while a poorer family rents only a four-room apartment. The reason that the wealthier family does not rent a nine-room apartment is the fact that the poorer family is able and willing to pay more for its fourth room than the wealthier family is able and willing to pay for a ninth room.

This competition, of course, does not take place at an actual auction, but the result is exactly the same as if it did. If, for example, apartments are renting at some given figure per room, such as seventy-five dollars a month, and the poorer family decides it can afford a four-room apartment, while the wealthier family decides it cannot afford a nine-room apartment, the implication is that the poorer family values a fourth room above seventy-five dollars, while the wealthier family values a ninth room below seventy-five dollars. In effect, the poorer family outbids the wealthier family for this extra room or, as economists often say, for this "marginal" room. If this poorer family wants to be sure of obtaining its four rooms, it is just as important to it that rents be high enough to level the quantity of space demanded down to equality with the supply available, as it is to the richer family.

If the price were any lower than the necessary equilibrium price, then while some poorer families might be able to afford a fifth room, wealthier families would just as often be able to afford a ninth room. And as often as poorer families succeeded in grabbing off a fifth room at the expense of a wealthier family's eighth room, a wealthier family would succeed in grabbing off a ninth room at the expense of a poorer family's fourth room. The same results apply to any good that is universally consumed: an artificially low price permits the "rich" to expand their consumption at the expense of the "poor" just as often as it permits the poor to expand their consumption at the expense of the rich.

Thus, the setting of prices at levels high enough to achieve equilibrium between the quantity demanded and the supply available is to the rational self-interest of everyone, irrespective of his income. Moreover, a harmony of interests exists in a free market even in those cases in which the price totally excludes some people from the market for particular goods. It exists on a remoter plane. For example, the price of Rembrandt paintings excludes the author of this book from the market for those paintings entirely and without question. Nevertheless, it is to my self-interest that if someone must be excluded, it be me, and not an industrial tycoon. For if his vastly greater contribution to production did not enable him to live at a better level than I do, I would be in serious trouble. To put this another way, if an industrial tycoon can have his art collection and other super-luxuries, then I can have all the food I want, a house, an automobile, and so on, and more and better all the time. If I were to be able to compete on equal terms with him for the super-luxuries, he would have no motive to conduct production in such a way that I am assured of all the necessities and lesser luxuries.

In order to avoid a second possible misunderstanding about the interest buyers have in prices being sufficiently high, I want to stress that I am *not* saying that people should simply welcome higher prices and be glad to pay them. Obviously, rising prices are currently imposing major hardships on large numbers of people, and they cannot simply look on stoically and be glad of their ability to pay those prices. However, there are two separate things here that must be very carefully distinguished, namely, the fact of the rise in prices and the cause of the rise in prices.

Our example of the art auction will serve to make this distinction clear. Assume that the losing bidder, whose maximum bid was previously $1,000, is now placed in a position in which he is able to bid as high as $1,500. In order to outbid him, our man will now have to bid above $1,500, whereas before he only had to bid above $1,000. Obviously, this is not a pleasant development for our man. But nevertheless it is still to his interest to bid a price that is sufficiently high to secure him the painting. Our man should, indeed, still value the opportunity to outbid his rival. His sorrow should be directed only at that which now makes it more difficult for him to do so.

In the same way, people today should, indeed, still value the opportunity to outbid their rivals and the fact that sellers set prices high enough to achieve this objective for them. Their anger should be directed only at that which makes it more and more difficult for them to accomplish this over-bidding. What they should be angry about is not the existence of a market economy and the way the market economy works, *but at the presence in the market of a vast gang of dishonest bidders and dishonest buyers*, a gang that does its bidding and buying with *newly created money*, a gang that bids and spends dollars created out of thin air in competition with their earned dollars. The source of these dollars created out of thin air is, of course, the government itself. And the dishonest gang consists of it and of everyone else who demands and receives such fiat money.

In other words, it is inflation and the pressure-group demands for inflation that the victims of rising prices should denounce, not the market economy or the opportunity it affords them for outbidding their rivals. It is the entry of newly created money into the economy that they should seek to stop, not the registry of that newly created money in the form of higher prices. Instead of, in effect, calling for the closing of the market, they should simply call for an end to the government's inflation of the money supply, and for the establishment of a *fully free* market.

On the basis of the way their prices are determined, the distribution of consumers' goods in limited supply—in the sense of who actually ends up with them—always tends to take place in a free market in accordance with two criteria: the relative wealth and income of the various potential buyers and the relative intensity of their need or desire for the good in question. The wealthier a buyer is, the more of any good he can afford to buy—obviously. But wealth is not the sole criterion of distribution. Where two buyers possess the same wealth, the one who needs or desires a good more intensely will be willing to devote a larger proportion of his wealth to its purchase, and he will therefore be able to outcompete an equally wealthy buyer who values the good less intensely. And, of course, in many cases a buyer who possesses a sufficiently strong desire will be able to outcompete a wealthier buyer. In our example of the wine, for instance, a wine connoisseur of relatively modest means might very well be willing to pay prices that a millionaire would not. Or, because of their relative preferences, some poorer families might outcompete some wealthier families not just for a marginal room, but for an equal-size apartment by devoting a sufficient proportion of their income to rent.

In a free market, therefore, consumers' goods in limited supply are distributed in accordance with purchasing power directed by needs and desires, or, equivalently, in accordance with needs and desires backed by purchasing power. Everyone consumes these goods in accordance with a combination of his means and his needs and desires.

### 3. The Pricing and Distribution of
### Factors of Production in Limited Supply

All that we have learned about the prices of consumers' goods in limited supply applies to the prices of factors of production in limited supply, i.e., to the prices of materials, labor, machinery, and anything else that is bought for business purposes and that is limited in supply.

The price of a factor of production in limited supply is also determined in such a way that the quantity of it demanded is levelled down to equality with the limited supply of it that exists, just like a consumers' good in limited supply. What pushes the price to the necessary height is, once again, a combination of the self-interests of the sellers and the buyers. The immediate buyers, directly concerned, are, of course, businessmen. Businessmen desire a factor of production not for the satisfaction of their own personal needs or wants, but in order to secure the means of producing goods for profit. Nevertheless, it is just as much against the interests of businessmen to try to pay too little for a factor of production as it is for a consumer to try to pay too little for something he buys. Like a consumer, a businessman must be willing to pay prices that are high enough to secure him the things he wants. This means that he must be willing to pay prices that outbid what other businessmen are able to offer for the same part of the supply. (It follows that the doctrine that self-interest drives employers to arbitrarily pay subsistence wages is as absurd as the belief that self-interest drives the bidder at an art auction to offer scrap-paper prices for a valuable painting. Employers who would arbitrarily decide to pay too low wages would simply enable other employers to hire away their labor. The employer who wants labor must be willing to pay wages that are high enough to make that labor too expensive for all its other potential employers.)

The only complication that is introduced by the price of a factor of production in limited supply is that it does double duty, so to speak. It not only levels down the quantity of the factor that is demanded to equality with the supply available, but, indirectly, the quantity of all the various products of the factor as well.

Let us consider first a simple case, such as cigarette tobacco, whose only product is cigarettes. The price of cigarette tobacco not only levels down the quantity of cigarette tobacco that is demanded, but, as a major part of the cost of producing cigarettes, it carries through to the price of cigarettes and also levels down the quantity of *cigarettes* demanded. The price of cigarette tobacco thus adjusts the demand for cigarettes to the supply of cigarette tobacco. Observe just how this happens. As the price of cigarette tobacco rises, the cost of producing cigarettes rises, which, in turn, raises their price. As the price of cigarettes rises, the quantity of cigarettes demanded falls. In fact, it is this fall in the quantity demanded of cigarettes, as their price rises, that necessitates a fall in the quantity demanded of cigarette tobacco, as its price rises. As the price of cigarette tobacco rises, businessmen purchase less of it because they know that they cannot sell as many cigarettes at the higher prices that are necessary to cover the resulting higher costs of production. In this way, therefore, the price of cigarette tobacco levels down the quantity demanded both of cigarettes as well as cigarette tobacco to equality with the supply of cigarette tobacco available.

Nothing is changed if we now consider the somewhat more complicated case of wheat or any other factor of production that has a variety of products, such as skilled labor. As the price of wheat rises, the cost of production and prices of all products made from wheat—such as bread, crackers, macaroni, whiskey, and wheat-fed cattle and chickens—also rise. The rise in the prices of wheat products reduces the quantity of the various wheat products demanded, and this reduces the quantity demanded of wheat. Again, as the price of wheat rises, businessmen cut back their purchases in anticipation of the fact that they will not be able to sell as many wheat products at the higher selling prices necessary to cover the higher cost of wheat. In this way, therefore, through its effect on the cost of production and the selling prices of all the various wheat products, the price of wheat equalizes not just the quantity of wheat demanded, but also the quantity demanded of all wheat products as a group, with the supply of wheat available.

There is a further important similarity between what is accomplished by the price of a factor of production in limited supply and the price of a consumers' good in limited supply. If we look at the whole range of products of such a factor as forming a single group, we can observe the same essential principle of distribution with respect to the factor that we previously observed with respect to a consumers' good in limited supply. Namely, the benefit of the factor, as conveyed by its various products, is distributed to the various individual consumers in accordance with their relative purchasing power and in accordance with their relative desire for products of that type. For example, the benefit of the supply of wheat is distributed to the ultimate consumers in accordance with a combination of their relative wealth and relative preferences for products made of wheat. Other things equal, richer buyers obtain the benefit of more of the supply of wheat than poorer buyers. Not that richer buyers eat more bread—they probably eat less of it—but they eat more meat, which employs far more wheat in its production pound for pound (in the feeding of cattle) than does bread. In the same way, a buyer with a relatively strong preference for wheat products, such as a buyer who especially likes steak and scotch, is able to obtain a larger share of the benefit of the wheat supply than a buyer of equal wealth who values these things less.

The benefit of the supply of crude oil, skilled and unskilled labor, and all other factors of production in limited supply is distributed to the ultimate consumers in just the same way.

Thus far, it is evident that the prices of factors of production in limited supply have the same characteristics and the same significance as the prices of consumers' goods in limited supply. The great difference between them pertains to the fact that there is an added dimension to the distribution of the factors of production. Not only is the benefit of a factor of production distributed to different persons, in accordance with their relative wealth and relative preferences, but the factor itself must be distributed to *different concrete uses in production.* Its benefit goes to the persons only by means of those specific uses. For example, consumers do not buy the benefit of wheat or skilled labor as such, but the various specific products of wheat or skilled labor. The supply of the factor must be distributed among its various specific products—in order to produce them.

This distribution of a factor of production among its various products is the result of a further process of mutual bidding and competition among the consumers. Only this time, it is not merely one consumer bidding against another consumer, *but the different needs, desires, or purposes of one and the same individual consumers bidding against each other, as well.* For instance, there is a competition for wheat between its use for baking bread, its use for making crackers, its use for making whiskey, feeding meat animals, and so on. There is a competition for crude oil between its use for making gasoline, its use for making heating oil, and so on. And there is a competition for the labor of each ability group between all of its various possible employments. Since the same individual consumers consume most or all of the various products of these factors of production, the competition is, as I say, ultimately largely one between the competing needs, desires, or purposes of the same individuals.

In order to grasp the nature and the importance of this competition, let us consider the question of why just so many bushels of wheat—to continue with that example—are devoted to each of its specific uses. Why aren't a million bushels, say, withdrawn from making crackers and added on to baking bread? The reason this does not occur is that the consumers of the quantity of crackers requiring the million bushels in question are perfectly willing and able to pay a price for the crackers that makes it profitable to cracker manufacturers to produce them at the current price of wheat. The consumers of the crackers, in other words, are willing to allow the producers of the crackers to pay the present price of wheat. But suppose that a million bushels of wheat were used to produce additional loaves of bread. In order to find customers for the additional bread, its price would have to be reduced. In fact, in a country like the United States, where even the very poorest people can already buy all the bread they desire to eat, the price would probably have to be cut so drastically as to induce people to feed the extra bread to pigeons. Conceivably, the extra bread might not be saleable at any price. In any case, it is clear that the bakers of bread would not be able to buy any additional wheat except at a lower price of wheat. And that means that the bread industry, in effect, bids less for the million bushels of wheat in question than the cracker industry. The cracker industry gets the wheat by outbidding the bread industry. And this happens because ultimately the consumers of crackers are outbidding the consumers of bread for the benefit of that wheat.

For the same reasons, the reverse situation does not occur either—that is, a million bushels of wheat are not withdrawn from the bread industry and added on to the cracker industry. For the consumers of the present quantity of bread are willing to pay prices for that quantity that allow the bread industry to be profitable at the present price of wheat. But the consumers of crackers would only be willing to buy a larger quantity of crackers at a lower price. In order for crackers to be profitable at a lower price, the price of wheat would have to be lower. As a result, the only way the cracker industry could buy an additional quantity of wheat would be at a lower price of wheat than the bread industry is willing to pay for it. Thus, the bread industry outbids the cracker industry for this particular quantity of wheat. Again, ultimately it is the consumers of the one product outbidding the consumers of the other product for the benefit of the quantity of wheat in question. And since it is the same people who consume both products, it is really one kind of need, desire, or purpose of the same individuals outcompeting another.

In exactly the same way, any other such transfer of wheat from one use to another is prevented by the fact that in its changed employment the quantity of wheat in question could only be employed profitably at a lower price than in its present employment. In other words, the present employments outbid the potential changed employments, and thus they get the wheat. And the reason they outbid them is because of the fact that the ultimate consumers are willing to allow more for the use of wheat in its present employments than in its changed employments.

In this way, the distribution of wheat to its various uses is determined by a process of competition among those uses, which in turn reflects a process of competition among the needs, desires, and purposes of one and the same individual consumers.

We can substitute any factor of production for wheat, and the results will be the same. If we ask why a million man-hours of unskilled labor are not withdrawn from one industry and added on to another, the answer again is that the consumers are willing to pay product prices in its present employments that enable businessmen to employ that labor profitably at its going wage rate; if the labor were shifted, however, the consumers would only buy the resulting products at prices that would require lower wage rates for their production to be profitable. These products, therefore, are unable to compete for the necessary labor. They are unable because of the choices and value judgments of the consumers, which enable the existing employments to outbid them.

A principle which emerges from our discussion is that *in a free market a factor of production in limited supply always tends to be distributed to its most important employments, as determined by the value judgments of the consumers themselves.* In our example of the distribution of wheat, it was more important for the million bushels to be employed in producing crackers that people wanted—as demonstrated by their willingness to pay for them—than additional bread that people did not want or wanted less. It was more important for a million bushels to be retained in producing bread that was desired than to be added on to producing crackers that were less strongly desired—as manifested, this time, in the willingness of consumers to allow more for wheat used to produce bread than for wheat used to produce additional crackers.

It is this way in every case. A factor of production in limited supply is employed in those uses that can afford to pay the highest prices for it. And that is determined by the willingness of the consumers to pay prices for the resulting final products. Every factor of production in limited supply is distributed to those employments where the consumers are willing to allow the most for it in the prices of the goods they buy. That is, it is distributed to those employments which the consumers regard as the most important to their own well-being.

It must be stressed that the concept "the most important employments of a factor of production" is *a variable range* that expands or contracts with the supply of the factor of production available. What it means is the most important employments *for which the supply of the factor suffices*. For example, if the supply of the factor is extremely limited, the most important employments for which the supply suffices might be as important as life itself. If the supply is very great, the most important employments can extend downward to include many luxury uses. The case of wheat again provides a good example. In a country like India, or medieval France, devoting wheat to its most important employments means, essentially, producing as much bread as possible to ward off starvation. In a country like the present-day United States, devoting wheat to its most important employments ranges downward through totally satisfying the desire for products such as bread and pasta, heavily satisfying the desire for such things as cakes and cookies made from wheat, substantially satisfying the desire for alcoholic beverages made from wheat, and partly satisfying the desire for wheat-fed meat.

A second major principle follows from this discussion. Namely, the price of every factor of production in limited supply, and thus the prices of all of its various products, is determined by the importance attached to the *least important of the employments for which its supply suffices*; that is, by the importance attached to its "marginal employments." In our example of wheat, for instance, the price of wheat in the present-day United States is determined by the importance attached to the use of wheat in feeding meat animals—its marginal employment in the context of our economy. This results from the fact that the price of wheat has to be low enough to permit its use to be profitable in *all* of its employments. If it is to be used in feeding meat animals, its price has to be low enough to make that use profitable at prices consumers are willing to pay for wheat-fed meat. However, there is only one uniform price of wheat in the same market at the same time. As a result, the bread industry pays no more for wheat than the cattle-raising industry. And because the price of bread is determined by its cost of production, the price of bread in the United States is actually determined not by its own importance, which may be as great as the stilling of hunger, but by the relatively low importance attaching to the use of wheat in producing meat.

Or, to take another example, the price of surgical instruments, on which countless lives may depend, is not determined by the importance of the needs they serve directly. It is not even determined by the importance attached to the marginal employments of iron and steel, but by the importance attached to the marginal employments of the ability groups of the labor that produces iron, steel, and surgical instruments. For the price of the surgical instruments is determined by their cost of production. And the wage rates which constitute that cost are low enough to make the employment of the different ability groups of labor profitable in their marginal employments. To put it another way, the price even of surgical instruments is no higher in relation to the wages of the ability groups of labor employed to produce them than the marginal products of such labor, which may be a quantity of razor blades or even magazines or chocolate bars or who knows what.

To summarize our discussion of factors of production in limited supply, we have seen that all the principles apply that we developed in relation to consumers' goods in limited supply, plus two others. First, that factors are distributed to their most important employments through a process of the different needs, desires, and purposes of the same individual consumers bidding against one another. And second, that the prices of the factors are determined with respect to the *least important* among the employments for which their supply suffices. Determination of price by cost, we have seen, therefore, ultimately means determination with respect to the consumers' value judgments concerning the *marginal products* of factors of production.[2]

It is necessary to return briefly to our earlier discussion of the pricing of consumers' goods in limited supply, and point out what may by now be obvious, namely, that their prices, too, are determined with respect to their marginal importance to consumers. For example, the price of rental space must be low enough to find customers for all of the space, which means, in most cases, to find customers for extra bedrooms, garages, larger size rooms, and so forth. And since space of the same quality has the same rent in the same market, the whole supply rents at a price conformable to the importance of the marginal quantity. Similarly, the price of the rare wine we discussed must probably be low enough to permit some people to buy second or third bottles, and so on; and, therefore, it too must conform to the importance attached to a marginal quantity. Thus, we can reformulate our principle of price determination, and say that the prices of goods and services in limited supply are determined not simply by the value judgments of consumers, but by their value judgments with respect to *marginal* quantities of those goods or services.

## 4. The Free Market's Efficiency in
## Responding to Economic Change

On the basis of the way their prices are determined, every change in the demand or supply of a factor of production in a free market tends to be dealt with in the most rational and efficient manner possible—that is, in a way that maximizes gains and minimizes losses.

To understand why this is so, imagine that the demand for one product in the economic system rises, while the demand for another product falls. For the sake of simplicity, assume for the moment that the two products are produced with the same factors of production. Washing machines and refrigerators are a good illustration of such products, because both of them require just about the same overall proportions of skilled and unskilled labor in their production, use largely the same materials, and can probably be produced in the very same factories without great difficulty. If the demand for one of these products increases while the demand for the other decreases, there will probably be little or no change at all in the demand for factors of production that cannot be matched by an immediate corresponding shift in their supply. Essentially, all that occurs in this case is that more of the same kinds of factors are employed in one capacity, less in another. The production of the one item is expanded in accordance with a change in consumer demand, and the production of the other item is contracted. In this case, there is obviously no tendency toward a change in the prices of the factors of production.

But now let us consider a more complicated case, which will bring out an important new principle of the free market. Assume that a change in fashion occurs which dictates that the average person own one extra wristwatch, and which, at the same time, encourages him to own one less suit or dress. I choose this example because the labor used to produce clothes cannot be transferred to the production of watches, due to the enormous skill differences involved. Here, therefore, we have a case of changes in the demand for factors of production that cannot be matched by offsetting shifts in their supply. Let us see what happens in such a case in a free market.

The wage rate of watchmakers and the cost of production and price of watches, of course, will rise; while the wage rate of garment workers and the cost of production and price of clothing will fall. However, the effects will not be confined to these initial areas of impact. A rise in the wages of watchmakers will begin to attract other workers into the field, say, some workers who would have gone into instrument making, optics, jewelry making, and so forth—that is, whatever fields employ labor of a kind that can be used to make watches. A fall in the wage rates of garment workers, on the other hand, will begin to push some of these workers out of that field and into other fields. As a result, a tendency develops toward widening and diffusing the initial impact of the change in demand.

As workers leave fields such as instrument making and optics to go into watchmaking, the wage rates and thus the production costs and product prices in these fields will begin to rise. Thus, the rise in demand for watches will raise not only the cost and price of watches, but also the cost and price of instruments, optical goods, and so forth—all products that use the same kind of labor as watchmaking. Conversely, as workers leave the garment industry and begin to enter other fields for which they possess the necessary skills, the wage rates, production costs, and product prices in those fields will begin to decline.

The question we want to ask is: what *principle* determines which industries among those that employ the same kind of labor as watchmaking actually release additional labor for watchmaking, and to what extent? And which industries among those potentially capable of absorbing the labor released from the garment industry actually absorb it, and to what extent? To arrive at the answer, we must realize that at the higher prices of the various goods that use the same kind of labor as watches, the consumers will reduce their purchases of those goods. It is these decisions of the consumers to restrict their purchases, that determine which of the industries release labor for watchmaking and to what extent. For example, if the consumers decide to go on buying an unchanged quantity of optical goods at their higher price, but a reduced quantity of jewelry and various instruments, none of the labor will come from the optical goods industry, and all of it will come from the jewelry and instrument industries. Obviously, the labor will come from these various industries in accordance with whatever proportions the consumers decide to curtail their purchases of the various products at their respectively higher prices.

Clearly, what occurs in this case is an indirect bidding for the use of labor between the buyers of wristwatches and the buyers of all other products employing the same kind of labor. The buyers of wristwatches, in effect, bid up the price of the wider category of labor that produces both wristwatches and all the other products I have named. In the face of this intensified bidding, the buyers of these other products—jewelry, instruments, optical goods, and so forth—must either match the bids of the watch buyers or restrict their purchases. To the degree that they restrict their purchases, they release labor to the watch industry and make possible its expansion.

Now to the extent that the consumers are rational, the products whose purchase they discontinue at the higher prices will be the *least important* among the ones they previously purchased. That is, the consumers will discontinue their previously *marginal purchases*. For each consumer who buys these various products will cut back his purchases in the way that hurts him least in his context and in his judgment. Thus, if he needs eyeglasses, he will certainly go on buying a pair of eyeglasses, but perhaps forgo the purchase of a telescope for his hobby, say. If he was previously in a position to buy several pairs of eyeglasses and a telescope and some jewelry, then, when he is confronted with higher prices for all of them, he may decide to go ahead with the telescope but cut back on an extra pair of sunglasses and some jewelry. The effect on the quantities demanded of these goods in the whole economy is, of course, simply the aggregate of all such individual decisions. In this way, it can be seen that in a free economy the labor released for watchmaking will come from its previously marginal employments—that is, from the employments where all the various individual consumers in the market judge they can best spare it.

By the same token, the labor released from the garment industry will be absorbed in those employments which are the most important of the employments for which the supply of that type of labor did not previously suffice; that is, it will be absorbed in the most important of its previously submarginal employments. This conclusion follows from the fact that the workers released will be seeking to earn the highest incomes they can and that these incomes will be found in producing those goods for which the consumers are willing to allow the highest prices over and above the allowance for the other costs entailed in producing them. The displaced garment workers will enter whatever fields can absorb them with the least fall in wage rates. These are the fields whose products the consumers are willing to buy in additional quantities at the least fall in prices. They offer the displaced garment workers the highest wages now available to them. I have not attempted to enumerate these other employments because the skills involved are so common that the labor released would probably be absorbed to some degree in a vast number of industries. For example, some of the former garment workers might end up as office workers, taxi drivers, metal workers, or who knows what.

Everything we have seen concerning the source of labor for additional watches applies in principle to the source of any factor of production in limited supply for an expansion of the production of any good. Always, the process is essentially one of an intensified bidding for the use of the factor by the consumers of one or more of its particular products against the consumers of its other products. This bidding drives up the price of the factor, the costs of using it in production, and the prices of all of its various products. Supplies of the factor are always released, in accordance with the choices of the consumers, from the production of its previously marginal products—from the products where the consumers decide they can best spare it. In the same way, everything we have seen concerning the absorption of labor released from the garment industry applies to the absorption of any factor in limited supply released from any industry. Always, the factor is absorbed in the most important of its employments previously unprovided for, in accordance with the judgment of the consumers, as manifested in what they are willing to pay the most for.

The identical reasoning that we have applied to changes in the demand for a factor of production in limited supply applies to changes in the supply of such a factor. If the overall supply of a factor should increase, the addition goes to provide for the most important of the employments of the factor previously unprovided for. For example, an increase in the supply of wheat in the present-day United States would be used to expand the production of such things as wheat-fed meat and aged whiskey. If the supply of a factor should decrease, the reduction is taken out on the least important of the employments previously provided for. In the case of wheat in the context of the present-day United States, this would mean a reduction in the production of such things as wheat-fed meat and aged whiskey. In other words, an increase in the supply of a factor goes to the most important of its previously submarginal employments; a decrease is taken out on its previously marginal employments.

The principle that emerges from this discussion is that *in a free market if a factor is in reduced demand or additional supply, the portion of it that becomes newly available is channelled to the most important of its previously submarginal uses; if the factor is in additional demand or reduced supply, the portion of it that is no longer available is taken from the least important of its previous uses, that is, from its previously marginal uses.* In other words, as stated, every change in the demand or supply of a factor of production in a free market is dealt with in a way that maximizes gains and minimizes losses; which is to say, it is dealt with in the most rational and efficient manner possible.

A Rational Response to the Arab Oil Embargo

The above principle has major application to the Arab oil embargo. It enables us to understand in yet another respect how a free market would have minimized the impact of any reduction in the supply of oil that the Arabs might have been able to impose on us.

If we had had a free market, the price of crude oil and the production costs and prices of all oil products would have risen during the embargo. The consumers would have decided where the reduction in the use of crude oil was to be effected and to what degree by the extent to which they cut back on their purchases of the various oil products at the higher prices. Where the use of an oil product was important, consumers would have paid the higher price, and oil would have continued to be used for that purpose. Only where the use of an oil product was not worth its higher price, would the use of oil have been cut back or discontinued. For example, consumers would have paid a higher price for the gasoline required to drive to work and for the heating oil required to keep them warm. They would not have been as ready to pay higher prices for the gasoline required for extra shopping trips or for heating oil to keep their garages warm.

The crucial point is that in a free market the more important employments of oil would have outbid the less important ones, and the reduction in the supply of oil would have been taken out exclusively at the expense of the *marginal* employments of oil—that is, at the expense of the least important employments for which the previously larger supply of oil had sufficed.

But, of course, we did not have a free market. We had price controls. Price controls prevented the more important employments of crude oil from outbidding the less important employments. They prevented the most vital and urgent needs for oil from outbidding the most marginal. For example, during the oil shortage one could read stories in the newspapers about truck drivers not being willing to deliver food supplies to southern Florida for fear of being unable to obtain fuel for the return trip up the length of the Florida peninsula. There was even a story about the operation of oil rigs off the Louisiana coast being threatened as the result of an inability to obtain supplies of certain oil products needed for their continued functioning.

Now it is simply insane that such vital activities should suffer for a lack of oil—that even the production of oil itself should be threatened. In a free market, it could never happen. Such vital uses of oil would always be able to outbid any less urgent employment for all the oil they required. But under price controls even these most vital employments are prohibited from outbidding any other employment that can pay the controlled price.

Price controls simply paralyze rational action. In effect, they bring together at an auction for the use of oil a trucker needing fuel to deliver food supplies and a housewife needing gasoline to take an extra shopping trip to the supermarket, and they prohibit the trucker from outbidding the housewife. They bring together oilmen needing lubricants for their wells and homeowners seeking oil to heat their garages, and they prohibit the oilmen from outbidding the homeowners. In a word, price controls make it *illegal to act rationally.*

### 5. The Economic Harmonies of Cost Calculations in a Free Market

We can now understand even more fully than was possible in Chapter I how in a free market the production of each good is carried on in a way that is maximally conducive to production in the rest of the economic system. For we are now in a position to understand how the concern with costs of production promotes the production of other goods every time it leads to the substitution of a lower priced factor of production in limited supply for a higher priced one, such as the use of unskilled labor where skilled labor was previously required, or the use of a less expensive quantity of aluminum where a more expensive quantity of copper was previously required, and so on. All we have to do is realize that the less expensive factor in limited supply *is* less expensive, because the importance of its marginal products to the consumers is less. To substitute a less expensive factor for a more expensive one, therefore, is to make it possible for the consumers to obtain products to which they attach greater marginal importance at the expense of products to which they attach smaller marginal importance. For the more expensive factor is released to uses of greater importance than those from which the less expensive factor is withdrawn.

The fact that in a free market production is carried on at the lowest possible cost that businessmen can achieve means that the production of each thing is carried on not only with the least possible amount of labor, but with *those specific types of labor and other factors of production in limited supply whose use represents the least possible impairment of the satisfaction of alternative wants.*

We can observe the operation of this principle in every cost calculation that businessmen make. To take some examples, let us assume that a railway company is contemplating the extension of its line across a body of water or that an electric company is contemplating the construction of additional generating capacity. In these cases, and in practically every other case, alternative methods of production are possible. The railway could build a bridge across the water, it could tunnel under the water, build a ferry, or, perhaps, detour around the body of water. In each instance, a variety of further alternatives are possible, such as where to construct the bridge, what materials and design to use, and so on. In the same way, the electric company could build a coal-powered plant, a water-powered plant, an oil or gas-powered plant, or an atomic-powered plant. Again, major variations are possible in each of these alternatives.

Now each method of production and each variant of any given method requires some different combination of factors of production in limited supply. Each of these factors of production has its own alternative uses in various other employments. For example, the bridge requires workers with the special skills required to build bridges. These workers could be employed in building bridges elsewhere or in building skyscrapers, or, of course, in a variety of lesser jobs. The tunnel requires the special skills of sandhogs. These men may first have to be trained, and a long period of time will go by during which they are unavailable to produce a different variety of goods than the bridge builders. Again, different methods require different combinations of materials that may themselves be in limited supply or require different combinations of labor skills or limited materials in their own production.

The point here is that the selection of any given method of production has its own unique impact on the rest of the economic system in terms of withdrawing factors of production from possible alternative employments. The fact that businessmen select the lowest-cost methods of production means that they try to produce each good with the least overall impairment of the production of alternative goods. Because to produce at the lowest cost means to use that combination of factors of production in limited supply that has the lowest total marginal significance in alternative employments.

Not only is the production of each good harmoniously integrated with the production of all other goods in a free market, but so too is the consumption of each good. As we have seen, insofar as any good is produced by factors of production in limited supply, its price reflects the competitive bidding of the consumers of all the products of those factors. For example, the price of bread in a free market reflects the competitive bidding of the consumers of all wheat products for the use of wheat; the price of gasoline in a free market reflects the competitive bidding of the consumers of all oil products for the use of crude oil; and so on. The consumer buyers of any of these products, therefore, when they take account of their prices, are led to pay the same regard to the rest of the economic system as businessmen when they make cost calculations.

More on the Response to the Oil Embargo

The above facts about the harmonious integration of the production and consumption of each good into the rest of the economic system also have application to how a free market would have responded to the Arab oil embargo.

If we had had a free market, the response to the reduction in the supply of oil would have been based on the exercise of the intelligence and judgment of each and every individual businessman and consumer in the economic system.

As the price of oil and oil products rose, each individual businessman and consumer would have decided where and to what extent to cut back on the use of oil by consulting his own individual circumstances. Those businessmen would have cut back who had lower-cost alternatives available. For example, businessmen with the alternative of switching to coal or shipping by rail or barge instead of truck would have done so. And more and more would have done so, more and more rapidly, as the price of oil rose higher, because the comparative savings in doing so would have become greater. In the same way, some firms might have concentrated their production in fewer days to conserve fuel. Some might have concentrated production more heavily in plants in warmer parts of the country. Some might have reduced or stopped production entirely, because of an inability to sell as many goods at the higher prices necessitated by higher costs of fuel and transportation. The point is that there would have been as many *individual* responses as there were separate business firms and even subunits within business firms. The response in each case would have been based on a consideration of costs and alternatives in the individual case.

Similarly, each individual consumer would have decided where and to what extent to cut back on the basis of the individual circumstances confronting him. What would have decided in each case was the importance of the particular oil product, as determined by the individual consumer's personal needs and desires dependent on that product, and the extent of his wealth. For example, no one to whom time was essential would have been forced to reduce his driving speed. Nor would a wealthy person have been forced to give up driving his Cadillac. By the same token, no one whose only means of getting to work was an automobile would have gone without gasoline. He would have chosen to go without other things first and to spend the money he saved from somewhere else, to buy the necessary gasoline. Anyone in such a position would have been assured of all the gasoline he required, because he would certainly have been willing and able to pay more for gasoline for the purpose of getting to work than most other people would have been willing to pay for it for any lesser purpose. To obtain gasoline for getting to work, one would merely have had to outbid other people seeking gasoline for pleasure trips, marginal shopping trips, and so on.

More broadly, since more gasoline can always be produced from crude oil made available by producing less of other oil products, an individual needing gasoline to get to work would merely have had to outbid other people seeking the use of *crude oil* for any lesser purpose than one comparable to that of getting to work. For example, he would have been able to obtain it by outbidding even people far richer than himself who previously used oil to heat their swimming pools, or, perhaps, who previously consumed vegetables or flowers grown in hothouses with the aid of large quantities of oil.

The specific ways in which oil would have been economized are too numerous to name. It is impossible even to learn them all. They would have depended on an enormous number of individual circumstances, in many cases known only to the individuals directly involved, whoever and wherever they might have been.

The essential fact is that oil would have been economized in ways that affected each individual as little as possible. Each individual—businessman and consumer—would have dealt with the problem in the way best suited to his own business or personal context, and at the same time his efforts would have been harmoniously integrated—through the price of oil and oil products—with the like efforts of everyone else. Each would have acted on the basis of the price of oil and oil products, and the circumstances and judgments of each would have determined just how high those prices would have had to go before the quantity of oil and oil products demanded was levelled down to equality with the reduced supply of crude oil available. In other words, *in a free market, the oil crisis would have been met by the conscious planning of each individual harmoniously integrated with that of every other individual.*

Of course, this is not what occurred—because of price controls. All considerations of individual context were dropped. The intelligence and planning of the individuals were paralyzed, as we have already seen. The government's solution was a sledgehammer approach that disregarded all individual circumstances and context. It arbitrarily curtailed the use of oil and oil products for whole categories of employments. For example, it declared that the airline industry would operate on 80 percent of its previous year's fuel, that farmers would have to make do with so much less propane, and that everyone would have to drive at no more than fifty-five miles per hour and set his thermostat at no more than sixty-eight degrees. This absurd approach simply ignored which industries and which specific firms and individuals could really afford to cut back on oil, and just where. It disregarded such elementary facts as that lower truck speeds would require proportionately more trucks and man-hours to haul the same amount of freight, so that to arbitrarily save a few gallons of gasoline, whole trucks and untold manhours to operate them would be wasted. It disregarded the fact that thermostat settings of sixty-eight degrees in some places and for some people can be tantamount to freezing and cause pneumonia. But more of such consequences of price controls soon enough.

# Price Controls and Shortages
## III

### 1. Shortages

We have seen that the free market constitutes a rational, ordered system of social cooperation; indeed, that it is a truly awe-inspiring complex of relationships in which the rational self-interest of individuals unites all industries, all markets, all occupations, all production, and all consumption into a harmonious, progressing system serving the well-being of all who participate in it.

All of this is what price controls destroy.

The one consequence of price controls that is the most central and the most fundamental and important from the point of view of explaining all of the others is the fact that *price controls cause shortages.*

A shortage is an excess of the quantity of a good buyers are seeking to buy over the quantity sellers are willing and able to sell. In a shortage, there are people willing and able to pay the controlled price of a good, but they cannot obtain it. The good is simply not available to them. Experience of the gasoline shortage of the winter of 1974 should make the concept real to everyone. The drivers of the long lines of cars all had the money that was being asked for gasoline and were willing, indeed, eager, to spend it for gasoline. Their problem was that they simply could not obtain the gasoline. They were trying to buy more gasoline than was available.

The concept of a shortage is not the same thing as the concept of a scarcity. An item can be extremely scarce, like diamonds, Rembrandt paintings, and so on, and yet no shortage exist. In a free market, as we saw in the last chapter, the effect of such a scarcity is a high price. At the high price, the quantity of the good demanded is levelled down to equality with the supply available, and no shortage exists. Anyone willing and able to pay the free-market price can buy whatever part of the supply he wishes; the height of the market price guarantees it, because it eliminates his competitors. It follows that however scarce a good may be, the only thing that can explain a shortage of it is a price control, not a scarcity. It is a price control that prevents the price of a scarce good from being raised by the self-interest of the buyers and sellers to its free-market level and thus reducing the quantity of the good demanded to equality with the supply of the good available.

Of course, if a price control on something exists, and a scarcity of it develops or grows worse, the effect will be a shortage, or a worsening of the shortage. Scarcities can cause shortages, or worsen them, *but only in the context of price controls*. If no price control existed, the development or worsening of a scarcity would not contribute to any shortage; it would simply send the price higher.

It should be realized that a shortage can exist despite a great physical *abundance* of a good. For example, we could easily develop a severe shortage of wheat in the United States with our present, very abundant supplies, or even much larger supplies. This is because the quantity of wheat demanded depends on its price. If the government were to roll back the price of wheat sufficiently, it would create a major additional demand—not only a larger export demand, but a larger demand for raising cattle and broilers, making whiskey, and perhaps for many other employments for which one does not presently think of using wheat, because of its price. In other words, no matter how much wheat we now produce or might produce in the future, we could have a shortage of wheat, because at an artificially low price we could create a demand for an even larger quantity.

It should be held in mind, therefore, that shortages are not a matter of scarcity or abundance. Scarcity need not cause them; abundance is no safeguard against them. Shortages are strictly the result of price controls. Price controls are the only thing that allows scarcities to cause shortages; and they create shortages even when there is no scarcity, but abundance.

Indeed, the true relationship between scarcities and shortages is the *reverse* of what is usually believed. While scarcities *per se* do not cause shortages, *shortages cause scarcities*. That is, no matter how abundant are the supplies with which we begin, we have only to impose price controls, create shortages, and we will soon bring about growing scarcities. As an example of this, consider the fact I pointed out in the last chapter that in the oil crisis oilmen needing oil products to keep their wells running were prohibited from outbidding homeowners needing oil to heat their garages. It is obvious what such a situation is capable of doing to the subsequent supply of oil.

The fact that it is shortages that cause scarcities will be a recurring theme in the remainder of this book.

In a free market shortages are a virtual impossibility. The closest thing that exists to them is that sometimes people may have to wait in line for the next showing of a popular movie. The typical case in a free market is that a seller is in a position to supply more than his present number of customers. There are very few stores or factories in a free market that are not able and eager to do more business. Even goods and services in limited supply are priced in such a way that the sellers are usually able and willing to do more business. For example, the wine shops have some reserve inventory of the rare wines. Landlords have a certain number of vacancies. There is even some limited degree of unemployment in most occupations. This is because, in a free market, the prices of goods and services in limited supply are set somewhat above the point that would enable the sellers to sell out entirely and the workers to be 100 percent employed. The reason prices are set in this way is because the sellers, including the workers, believe that by waiting before they sell, they can find better terms. They are holding out, waiting for the right customers or the right job.

## 2. Price Controls and the Reduction of Supply

The preceding discussion showed how price controls create shortages by artificially expanding the quantity of a good demanded. To the degree that the controlled price is below the potential free-market price, buyers judge that they can afford more of the good with the same monetary wealth and income. They judge that they can carry its consumption to a point of lower marginal importance. In this way, the quantity of the good demanded comes to exceed the supply available, whether that supply is scarce or abundant.

Price controls also reduce supply, which intensifies the shortages they create.

### a. The Supply of Goods Produced

In the case of anything that must be produced, the quantity supplied falls if a price control makes its production unprofitable or simply of less than average profitability.

It is not necessary that a price control make production unprofitable or insufficiently profitable to *all* producers in a field. Production will tend to fall as soon as it becomes unprofitable or insufficiently profitable to the highest-cost or *marginal* producers in the field. These producers begin to go out of business or at least to operate on a smaller scale. Their place cannot be taken by the more efficient producers, because the same price control that drives them out of business restricts the profits of the more efficient producers and deprives them of the incentive and also the capital required for expansion. Indeed, the tendency is eventually for even the most efficient producers to be unable to maintain operations and to be driven out of business.

For example, the price controls on oil have held down the supply of oil. They have not yet totally destroyed the supply of oil, but they have discouraged the development of high-cost sources of supply, such as oil from shale rock and even from the continental shelf in some instances. They have also made the more intensive exploitation of existing oil fields unprofitable, which, it is estimated, could be made to yield from one-third to two-thirds more oil over their lives by the adoption of such methods as thermal or chemical flooding, sometimes known as "tertiary recovery." At the same time, in restricting the profits from the lower-cost oil deposits, price controls have held down both the incentives to discover and develop new such deposits and the capital necessary to the oil companies for expanded oil operations of any type.

Rent controls on housing that has already been constructed provide a similar example of the destruction of supply. As inflation drives up the operating costs of housing—namely, such costs as fuel, maintenance, and minor repairs—more and more landlords of rent-controlled buildings are forced to abandon their buildings and leave them to crumble. The reason is that once the operating costs exceed the frozen rents, continued ownership and operation of a building become a source merely of fresh losses, over and above the loss of the capital previously invested in the building itself. This destruction of the housing supply starts with the housing of the poor and then spreads up the social ladder. It starts with the housing of the poor because the operating costs of such housing are initially so low that they leave relatively little room for further economies. For example, there are no doormen to eliminate and therefore no doormen's salaries to save. Also, the profit margins on such housing (i.e., profits as a percentage of rental revenues) are the lowest to begin with, because the land and the buildings are the least valuable and therefore the amount of profit earned is correspondingly low. As a result, the housing of the poor is abandoned first, because it provides the least buffer between rising operating costs and frozen rents.

*b. The Supply of Goods in a Local Market*

A price control reduces supply whenever it is imposed in a local market and makes that market uncompetitive with other markets. In such a case, the local market is prevented from drawing in supplies from other areas, as was the Northeast and the United States as a whole during the Arab oil embargo.

The Natural Gas Crisis of 1977

In exactly the same way, in the winter of 1977, price controls on natural gas prevented areas of the United States suffering freezing weather from bidding for additional supplies from the producing regions in the South and Southwest. Natural gas shipped across state lines was controlled by the Federal Power Commission at a maximum of $1.42 per thousand cubic feet. Natural gas sold within the states where it was produced, and thus outside the jurisdiction of the FPC and free of price controls, was selling at $2.00 per thousand cubic feet, with lower costs of transportation besides. It was therefore much more profitable to sell natural gas in the states where it was produced, such as Texas and Louisiana, than in such states as New Jersey or Pennsylvania.

Indeed, in the absence of government controls over the physical distribution of supplies, price controls would have resulted in still less gas being shipped outside the producing states and more being sold inside, in accordance with the difference in price and profitability. This process would have gone on until enough additional gas was retained within the markets of the producing states to make its price in those markets actually fall below the controlled interstate price by an amount equal to the costs of transportation; only at that point would it have paid producers to ship their gas out of state. The shortage in the rest of the country, of course, would have been correspondingly more severe. As I say, government controls over the physical distribution of natural gas prevented this outcome; the government simply forced the gas producers to sell a major part of their output in the interstate market. But the government's allocation formulas did not take into account the extremely cold winter of 1977, and its allocations proved inadequate to keep people from the threat of freezing. Price controls then prevented the people of the affected regions from obtaining the additional supplies they urgently needed.[1]

The Agricultural Export Crisis of 1972-73

A price control not only prevents a local market from drawing in supplies from elsewhere, but it can also cause a local market that normally exports, to export excessively. In this case, as supplies are drawn out, the price control prevents the people in the local market from bidding up the price and checking the outflow.

This phenomenon occurred in this country in 1972 and 1973. Our price controls on wheat, soybeans, and other products made possible an unchecked exportation that jeopardized domestic consumption and led to an explosion of prices each time the controls were taken off, in President Nixon's succession of on-again, off-again "phases."

In this instance, the fall in the value of the dollar in terms of foreign currencies played a critical role. When President Nixon imposed price controls in August of 1971, he also took steps to devalue the dollar by 10 percent. Over the following two years, the dollar continued to fall in terms of foreign currencies and in 1973 was formally devalued a second time. The fall in the dollar's foreign exchange value meant a lower price of dollars in terms of marks, francs, and other currencies. Since the prices of our goods were frozen, a lower price of dollars meant that all of our goods suddenly became cheaper to foreigners. As a result, they began buying in much larger quantities—especially our agricultural commodities. As they began buying, domestic buyers were prevented by price controls from outbidding them for the dwindling supplies. As a result, vast accumulated agricultural surpluses were swept out of the country, and domestic food supplies were threatened, which is why prices skyrocketed each time the controls were taken off.

Price Controls as a Cause of War

The fact that price controls jeopardize supplies in markets that export leads to embargoes against further exports, as occurred in this country in the summer of 1973, when we imposed an embargo on the export of various agricultural commodities. In addition, price controls in markets that must import make such markets helpless in the face of embargoes imposed by others, as we were made helpless in the face of the Arab oil embargo. It follows that in degree that countries impose price controls, they must fear and hate each other. Each such country must fear the loss of vital supplies to others, as the result of excessive exportation, and the deprivation of vital supplies from others, as the result of their embargoes and its helplessness to cope with them. Each such country makes itself hated by its own embargoes and hates the countries that impose embargoes against it. Our embargo on agricultural products in 1973 did not endear us to the Japanese. And there was actual talk of military intervention against the Arabs. Simply put, price controls breed war. A free market is a necessary condition of peace.

c. *The Supply of Goods Held in Storage*

A price control reduces supply whenever it is imposed on a commodity of the kind that must be stored for future use. The effect of a price control in such a case is to encourage a too rapid rate of consumption of the commodity and thus to reduce supplies available for the future. As we have seen, buyers are led to buy too rapidly by the artificially low price, and sellers are led to sell too rapidly, since the fixity of the controlled price does not enable them to cover storage costs and earn the going rate of profit in holding supplies for future sale.

If the buying public is unaware of the impending exhaustion of supplies, the effect of sellers placing their supplies on the market right away is to depress the current market price below the controlled price. This process tends to go on until the current market price falls far enough below the controlled price, so that once again it has sufficient room to rise in the months ahead to be able to cover storage and interest costs. The resulting structure of prices guarantees the premature exhaustion of supplies.

An elaboration on the example of the deficient wheat harvest will make these points clear.[2] Assume that in a year of normal wheat supplies, the price of wheat begins at $1.00 per bushel in the harvest month, when supplies are most abundant, and then rises a few cents per month, to cover the costs of storage and interest, and reaches a peak of $1.20 in the month immediately preceding the next harvest. Now assume that when the harvest is one month's consumption below normal, the price of wheat should begin at $1.30 in the harvest month and gradually ascend to something over $1.50 in the month preceding the following harvest, in order to reduce the quantity of wheat demanded to equality with the smaller total supply available. Assume further that a price control limits the price of the deficient wheat crop to no more than $1.20 in any month. In this case, when the deficient crop comes in, its value cannot remain even at $1.20 for very long, because it has no prospect of ever getting above $1.20; as a result, it will be sold more heavily. It will tend to be sold until the price in the harvest month is driven down to $1.00, and from there the price will gradually ascend in the succeeding months toward $1.20. This structure of prices will encourage the same rate of consumption as prevailed in years of normal supplies, and will threaten famine conditions at the end of the crop year.

Hoarding and Speculation Not Responsible for Shortages

Under conditions such as those described above, the buying public sooner or later becomes aware of the fact that supplies will run out. At that point, demand skyrockets, as the buyers scramble for supplies. As soon as this occurs, and it may be very early, the larger supplies that sellers are encouraged to place on the market under price controls are not sufficient to depress the market price below the controlled price, because they are snapped up by the speculative buying of the public, which is aware of the shortage to come. (In our example of wheat, the whole supply would tend to be carried off at the controlled price of $1.20 per bushel as soon as the public becomes aware of the inevitable shortage of wheat to come.) The consequence of the speculative buying of the public is that the item disappears from the market right away; it is hoarded.

The hoarding of the buying public is not responsible for the existence of shortages. The public hoards *in anticipation* of shortages caused by the price controls. The public's speculative demand cannot even be blamed for hastening the appearance of a shortage. That too must be blamed on price controls, because in the absence of the controls the additional demand of the public would simply raise prices; at the higher prices, the rise in the quantity of goods demanded would be cut back; prices would rise to whatever extent necessary to level down the quantity demanded to equality with the supply available.

Speculation on the part of the suppliers of goods is likewise blameless for the existence of shortages. Contrary to popular belief, price controls do not give suppliers a motive to withhold supplies, but, as we have seen, an incentive to unload them too rapidly.

There is, of course, an important exception to the principle that price controls give sellers an incentive to sell their supplies too rapidly. This is the case in which the sellers are able to look forward to the repeal of the controls. In this case, a price control makes it relatively unprofitable to sell in the present, at the artificially low, controlled price, and more profitable to sell in the future, at the higher, free-market price. In this case, sellers do have a motive to withhold supplies for future sale.

Even in this case, however, it is still the price control that is responsible for the existence of any shortage that develops or intensifies. In this case, the price control discriminates against the market in the present in favor of the market in the future; it prevents the market in the present from competing for supplies with the market in the future. Furthermore, in the absence of a price control, any build-up of supplies for sale in the future would simply be accompanied by a rise in prices in the present, which would prevent the appearance of a shortage, as we have seen repeatedly in previous discussion.

Finally, it should be realized that the withholding of supplies in anticipation of the repeal of a price control does not imply any kind of antisocial or evil action on the part of the suppliers. Price controls, as we have seen, lead to inadequate stocks of goods; in many cases, it is probable that the build-up of stocks in anticipation of the repeal of controls merely serves to restore stocks to a more normal level. Even if the build-up of stocks does become excessive, its effect later on, when the stocks are sold, is merely to further reduce the free-market price in comparison with what that price would otherwise have been. In any event, any ill-effects that may result are entirely the consequence of price controls.

Rebuttal of the Accusation that Producers Withhold Supplies to "Get Their Price"

The preceding discussion applies to the accusation that producers withhold supplies in order to "get their price." This accusation was levelled against the oil companies during the oil crisis and, again, during the natural gas crisis.

Once more, the fact is that price controls generally cause sellers to sell too rapidly, and not to hold even normal stocks. Where the anticipation of controls being removed does lead to the withholding of supplies, the fault is not that of the sellers, but of the existence of controls in the present. It is simply absurd to tell producers that soon they will be permitted to sell at the free-market price while for the present they must pay fines or go to jail if they attempt to sell at as good a price. Responsibility for the withholding of supplies in such a case lies with those who impose price controls and whose support of price controls makes their imposition possible. For no other result can be expected. To blame the producers in such a case is comparable to blaming the laws of physics for the damage done by a delinquent who throws rocks against windows.

Although this did not happen in the oil or gas crisis, and is unlikely ever to happen where big business is involved (because of the fear today's big businessmen have of the government), it would be perfectly proper if sellers really did withhold supplies to "get their price"—i.e., not merely to take advantage of the higher free-market price they expect to follow the government's removal of controls, but to withhold supplies in a deliberate attempt to force repeal of the controls. Such a withholding would be a kind of strike; more correctly, it would be a refusal to work under conditions of forced labor. By putting an end to price controls, it would be an action in the public interest in the true sense of the term.

It should be realized in connection with this discussion, that in a free market the speculative withholding of supplies is not a means by which sellers can arbitrarily enrich themselves. It is not possible, as widely believed, for sellers arbitrarily to raise prices by withholding supplies and then to sell the supplies they have withheld at the higher prices they themselves have caused. Any attempt to do this would necessarily cause losses to the sellers who tried it. First of all, when these sellers put their supplies back on the market, they would push prices back down by as much as they had first increased them, and in the meanwhile they would have incurred additional costs of storage and have had to forgo the profits or interest they could have earned by selling sooner. In addition, so long as the high prices lasted, other sellers would be encouraged to place on the market whatever stocks they could spare, so that when the first set of sellers returned to the market they would find their normal market already partly supplied, and thus would end up having to sell at prices lower than they could have received had they not attempted to raise prices in the first place. The only way the speculative withholding of supplies can be profitable in a free market is when it takes advantage of a prospective rise in price that is independently caused, i.e., not caused by the speculators themselves.[3]

In the specific case of the oil crisis the withholding of supplies turned out to be entirely mythical. Reports of large numbers of fully loaded tankers standing offshore to "get their price" had no more foundation in fact than the stories about full tank farms and storage depots.[4] As concerns the natural gas crisis, the charge has now been withdrawn by one of the principal original accusers, Interior Secretary Cecil D. Andrus. According to *The New York Times*, the secretary "said today that a series of studies had produced no evidence that oil companies were withholding natural gas from offshore leases. . . . The interior secretary insisted today that he had had no part in raising those charges and contended instead that they were initially leveled by reporters. . . . Mr. Andrus also made it clear today that the question of withholding was now closed. 'I'm not going to continue to chase a rabbit,' he said."[5]

Price Controls and the "Storage" of Natural Resources in the Ground

Price controls have a peculiarly destructive effect on the supply of natural resources. Unlike products, natural resources in the ground are imperishable and have zero storage costs. This means that it is possible to consider reserving their use to much more remote periods of the future than is the case with regard to products. The consequence is that under price controls a tendency exists to withhold natural resources from current exploitation even though their current exploitation might be profitable. The reason is that their future exploitation—following the repeal of price controls—is expected to be sufficiently more profitable to justify waiting. In this way, price controls on natural resources act to bring about a twofold restriction of supply: they prevent the development of high-cost deposits by making them unprofitable and they postpone the development or exploitation of low-cost deposits by making their development or exploitation in the present less profitable than it will be in the future.

The question may be raised of why price controls would not encourage the more rapid exploitation of low-cost natural resources if the controls were expected to exist permanently. To answer this question, it is only necessary to realize what "permanently" would have to mean in this context. "Permanently" would have to refer to a period of at least a decade and, more probably, at least a generation. For suppose the effect of a price control is to hold the value of a resource to half of what it would be in the absence of controls. This means the owners of the resource can look forward to the prospect of a doubling of its value whenever controls are repealed. Since they incur no storage costs of any kind by waiting, even if they had to wait *twenty-five years* for price controls to be repealed, their gain would work out to something on the order of three percent per annum compounded. Such a rate of return, in *real terms* (i.e., adjusted for losses in the purchasing power of money), is by no means insignificant in a period of inflation. It might pay to wait even for the prospect of a considerably lower rate of return. Of course, if price controls undervalue a resource less severely, the inducement to postpone exploitation is less powerful. But it does not take very much undervaluation to make the owners of the resource prefer to wait five or ten years for the repeal of a control if they have to.

It follows that it is highly probable that the repeal of the present price controls on crude oil and natural gas would be followed by a substantial increase in the supply of low-cost oil and gas as well as by additional supplies available only at higher costs.

## d. The Supply of Particular Types of Labor and Particular Products of a Factor of Production

A price control reduces supply if it is applied to the wages of any particular occupation or to the wages paid by any particular industry while wages in other occupations or industries are left free. In these cases, the workers in the controlled occupation or industry simply leave to take better-paying jobs at uncontrolled wages elsewhere; and new workers do not enter the occupation or industry. The controlled occupation or industry is made uncompetitive and loses its labor force. For example, if the government were to control just the wages of steel workers, say, the effect would be that steel workers would start going into other industries in response to higher, uncontrolled wages in those industries. Young workers would stop becoming steel workers. Exactly the same would happen if the government controlled just the wages of carpenters, say.

A price control reduces supply whenever it applies to some products of a factor of production, but not to other products of that factor. In this case, the production of the controlled products is curtailed, because it is more profitable to use the factor of production to produce the uncontrolled products. For example, if the price of milk is controlled, but cheese is not, then the production of cheese will be more profitable than the production of milk. As a result, raw milk will be used more heavily to produce cheese, and less milk will be available for drinking. In other words, the supply of milk for drinking will fall.

## e. Price Controls and the Prohibition of Supply

Sometimes, the question is raised as to what argument one could give to a consumer to convince him to be against price controls; especially what argument one could give to a tenant to convince him to be against rent controls. Our discussion of how price controls reduce supply indicates a very simple argument to give to any consumer against any price control. That is that if he wants something, he must be willing to pay the necessary price. It is a natural law—a fact of human nature—that a good or service can only be supplied if supplying it is both worthwhile to the suppliers and as worthwhile as any of the alternatives open to them. If the price is controlled below this point, then it is equivalent to a prohibition of supply. To command, for example, that apartments be supplied at rents that do not cover the costs of construction and maintenance, and the going rate of profit, is equivalent to commanding that buildings be built out of impossible materials like air and water rather than steel and concrete. It is to command construction in contradiction of the laws of nature. In the same way, to command that oil be sold less profitably in New York than in Hamburg, say, or that natural gas be sold less profitably in Philadelphia than in Houston, is equivalent to commanding that these materials become drinkable and that water become burnable, for it is no less an act in contradiction of the nature of things.

Now it is simply absurd for a consumer who wants a good, to support a measure which makes its supply impossible. And that is what one should tell him. That is what the consumers themselves should tell all the legislators who are busy enacting price-control laws for their alleged benefit. These would-be benefactors of the consumers are prohibiting the consumers from making it worthwhile for businessmen to supply them. They are destroying the businessmen. In effect, they are destroying the consumers' ability to find agents to act on their behalf. They are reducing the consumers to the point where if they want anything, they will have to produce it themselves, because price controls will make it unprofitable for anyone to supply it to them. Already, rent control has "benefitted" tenants to the point that it is becoming increasingly necessary if one wants an apartment to own it oneself: one must buy a "co-op" or a condominium. Price controls have made it increasingly difficult, and at times absolutely impossible, to buy oil or natural gas. If the legislators are to go on "benefitting" the consumers long enough with their price controls, they will benefit them all the way back to the economic self-sufficiency that was the leading characteristic of feudalism.

## The Destruction of the Utilities and the Other Regulated Industries

It may be thought that price controls on genuine monopolies, such as government-franchised electric utilities, are an exception to the principle that price controls reduce, indeed, prohibit, supply. In fact, they are not. On the contrary, they are currently an excellent illustration of it.

In the absence of inflation, or when inflation is proceeding very moderately, these controls are largely without effect, for then they do not actually impose below-market prices. At such times, they are set at a level that, if anything, is almost certainly higher than would have prevailed in a free market. This is the case because they are set high enough to provide the going rate of profit, and then some, to legally protected monopolists, whose costs of production are almost certainly above the costs of production that would prevail in a free market. But in a period of more rapid inflation, such as has characterized the last decade, the price controls on these monopolies begin to operate as genuine price controls. This occurs because inflation drives up the production costs of the monopolies, while the regulatory authorities either refuse to allow rate increases or allow only insufficient rate increases. In this way, the utilities, and all the other regulated industries, become unprofitable. At first, they merely cease to grow rapidly enough, because their reduced profitability throttles their ability to generate additional capital—that is, they lack the profits to plow back and they lack the profits to provide an incentive to the investment of sufficient additional outside capital.

When the reduced profitability of these industries is understood to be permanent, or when the policy of the regulatory agencies inflicts actual losses on them in terms of making it impossible for them to replace worn-out equipment at the higher prices caused by inflation, then these industries go into an actual decline. They do not have the means of replacement, and their owners withdraw capital to whatever extent they are able in the form of taking dividends.

We are already very far along in this process. Areas such as New York City, for example, have been skirting for several years on the edge of power disasters. Every summer there is a question of whether generating capacity will be adequate to meet the demand in such places. That things were not much worse in the summers of 1975 and 1976 than in previous summers was due only to the recession, which sharply cut back the growth in demand for power. The summer of 1977 finally witnessed a major blackout in New York City.

This situation of an inadequate supply of power is the result of nothing but the restricted profitability of the utilities, compounded by the ecology movement's policy of harassment of energy producers: both have prevented the construction of sufficient additional generating capacity to keep pace with demand.

At the present time, in the lapse of all-round price controls, the traditionally regulated industries, such as the electric utilities, the telephone company, and the railroads. are the principal victims of price controls, along with rental housing and the oil and natural gas industries. All these industries are literally being destroyed by price controls. And, since the rest of the economic system is vitally dependent on them, their destruction implies disaster for the entire economy.

Let us pause for a moment and consider what we can already see ahead if inflation and price controls continue. What must lie ahead in that case is the specter of power shortages—shortages that will grow worse as the electric utility industry declines. These shortages will mean an inability to operate electrical appliances, and a need to resort to more primitive methods of production that substitute human muscle power for machinery driven by electric power. They will mean periodic brownouts, then blackouts, as whole areas are put on reduced power and then totally deprived of power at specified intervals. Telephone service will collapse, as it already briefly did in New York City a few years ago. The railroad network will disintegrate. The oil and natural gas industries will be destroyed—already, domestic production has been declining for several years, and the winter of 1977 witnessed the closing of thousands of factories due to a lack of fuel. All of these industries will be reduced to the level of rent-controlled housing in the slums of New York City. The only difference will be that they will carry down with them the rest of the economic system.

It must be stressed as strongly as possible that none of this destruction is necessary or inevitable. If it happens, all of it will be the result of ignorance and irrationality. For there is a simple way to prevent these results. It includes three measures. One: the repeal of all price controls, and, in the case of the monopolies, such as the electric utilities, the repeal of exclusive government franchises as well; this latter would deprive them of their monopoly character and of the ability to set monopoly rates. Two: the establishment of a full gold standard and thus an end to inflation. Three: an end to the harassment of energy producers by the ecology movement.

Many people will call these measures impractical, because it would be very difficult or even impossible to gain widespread public support for them in the foreseeable future. Such an accusation is totally confused, however. The measures are perfectly practical, because they actually would succeed in saving our economic system. It is the current state of public opinion which is impractical: it expects that men can live in a modern economic system while destroying the foundations of that system. Given this state of public opinion, the measures I suggest still serve as a *standard* for political action. Those in favor of a rational economic policy should try to convert public opinion to support these measures, and, so long as that is not yet possible, they should use their power and influence to try to move government policies *in the direction* of these measures. If we do not yet have the power immediately to repeal the existing price controls, we do have the power at least to see that they are relaxed or applied less stringently. If we do not yet have the power immediately to establish a gold standard and stop inflation, we do have the power at least to remove some of the legal obstacles in the way of gold and to make inflation go slower. And the same is true of the harassments imposed by the ecology movement. We have this much power, at least, simply by voting for less bad political candidates and by intelligently voicing our opinions.

### 3.  Ignorance and Evasions Concerning Shortages and Price Controls

The fact that price controls are the cause of shortages has been known to all economists at least since the time of Adam Smith. Nevertheless, this elementary knowledge is either unknown or simply evaded by almost all of our presumably educated political and intellectual leaders.

These people do not have any idea of the connection between price controls and shortages. In their view, shortages are the result of some kind of physical deficiency in the supply or of an innate excess of needs. They simply do not have any knowledge of the role of price in balancing demand and supply. As a result, it is common to hear them blame shortages on such things as poor crops, an alleged depletion of natural resources, even that old standby the "greed" of consumers. Their level of knowledge is typified by a provision of the rent control law that governed New York City for many years. According to this law, rent controls could not be lifted until the vacancy rate in apartments had first climbed to a certain substantial level. In other words, only when the shortage that rent controls created and maintained was over, could rent controls be lifted.

The same point of view was expressed by New York's Mayor Beame when he was still in office. When asked to comment on an economic regeneration plan for New York City that had urged the repeal of rent control, he "refused to endorse the rent control proposal, saying, 'we still have a vacancy rate of less than 5 percent, and we still have a housing shortage.' "[6]

To find a parallel for this kind of reasoning, one would have to find a badly overweight person, say, who was firmly resolved to go on a diet just as soon as he lost twenty pounds, or an alcoholic who was firmly resolved to stop drinking just as soon as he sobered up. Of course, these are not perfect analogies, because the overweight person and the alcoholic at least know the causal connections and are evading them. In the case of the government officials and the intellectuals responsible for rent control, most of them don't even know the causal connection. They are too ignorant even to be guilty of evasion in this particular instance.

The confusion of our public officials extends to the point that when they are confronted with the fact that the repeal of a price control would actually end a shortage, they then deny the very reality of the shortage: they view the shortage as "artificial" or "contrived." For example, during the natural gas crisis Governor Milton Schapp of Pennsylvania declared before television news cameras that if price controls were lifted and the gas shortage came to an end through the appearance of additional supplies, the very appearance of the additional supplies would prove that the shortage had been "contrived." The governor simply did not know that a higher price increases supply by enabling a local market successfully to compete for supplies with other markets, and, of course, that it leads to an expansion of the total supply by making production more profitable. He also did not know that the supply available for vital purposes can be increased by enabling those purposes to outcompete marginal purposes.

Inflation and the Appearance of High Profits

In an important respect, the ignorance that surrounds the effect of price controls is made possible by the fact that inflation raises the apparent or, as economists say, the nominal rate of profit that businesses earn. It does not increase the real rate of profit—the rate in terms of the actual physical wealth that business firms gain—(in fact, quite the contrary), but it does increase the rate of profit expressed in terms of the depreciating paper money.

To understand what is involved, it must be realized that the costs which enter into the profit computations of business firms are necessarily "historical"—that is, they are incurred prior to the sale of the products. This follows from the fact that production always takes place over a period of time. Materials and labor must usually be bought weeks or months before the resulting products are ready for sale, and sometimes even further in advance. Machinery and factory buildings are bought many years, even decades, before their contribution to production comes to an end. Thus the costs of business enterprises in producing their products represent outlays of money made weeks, months, years, or even decades earlier.

Now to whatever extent inflation occurs, the sales revenues of business firms are automatically increased: the greater spending that inflation makes possible is simultaneously greater sales revenues to all the business firms that receive it. Since costs reflect the given outlays of earlier periods of time, the increase in sales revenues caused by inflation necessarily adds a corresponding amount to profits.

A slightly different way to grasp the same basic idea is to realize that the total outlays business firms make for productive purposes at any given time are a reflection of the quantity of money in existence at that time, while the sales revenues they will subsequently take in for the products resulting from those outlays will be a reflection of the quantity of money in existence later on. It follows that the more rapidly the quantity of money grows, the greater must be the ratio of sales revenues to costs of production and to capital previously invested. This, of course, implies a corresponding rise in the general rate of profit on capital previously invested. The rate of profit in the economy automatically rises the more rapidly the quantity of money, spending, and sales revenues rise.

It cannot be stressed too strongly, however, that the rate of profit that rises is purely nominal, i.e., strictly in terms of money. All that is happening is that the more rapidly money is increased, the faster is the rate at which *money* is gained. If there are different monies, increasing at different rates, then the nominal rate of profit is higher in the monies that increase more rapidly. For example, it is higher today in U. S. dollars than in Swiss francs, and higher in Argentine pesos than in U. S. dollars. (The same principle and example apply to interest rates, since the most important determinant of interest rates is the rate of profit that can be earned by investing borrowed money in business.)

The rise in the nominal rate of profit does not imply any increase in the *real* rate of profit, because the same rise in spending that raises sales revenues and profits in the economy also raises the level of prices. The extra profits are almost all necessary to meet higher replacement costs of inventory and plant and equipment, and the rest are necessary to meet the higher prices of consumers' goods that the owners of businesses were previously able to buy in their capacity, say, as stockholders receiving dividends. A good illustration of these facts is the case of a hypothetical merchant who normally buys $100 worth of goods on January 1 and sells them the following December 31 for $110. If total spending in the economy rises by 10 percent over the year, this merchant will tend to sell his goods for $121 instead of $110. Consequently, his nominal profit will be increased from $10 to $21. However, the merchant is in no way better off as a result of this. For if he wants to stay in business, he will have to use $10 of his additional profits to replace his inventory at higher prices, i.e., for $110 instead of $100, and the consumers' goods which he previously could have bought for $10 will now cost him $11. Thus, his entire additional profit is used up without his being able to buy any additional goods whatever.

Indeed, this example of the merchant can show how businessmen are actually made *worse off* as a result of earning higher nominal profits. Assume that our merchant must pay over a part of his profits as taxes, say, 50 percent. Thus, initially, when he made $10 in profit, he paid $5 in taxes and had $5 left to himself, which he could either consume or use to expand his business. When his profit rises to $21, his taxes rise to $10.50. Of the $10.50 left after taxes, fully $10 are required to replace inventory at higher prices. Thus, our merchant is left with a mere 50 cents for his own consumption or for expansion of his business, and even these 50 cents do not go as far as 50 cents did before.

Exactly the same principles as apply to the profits of our hypothetical merchant apply to the profits of all real-life merchants, and to the profits of businessmen in general, because the same kind of increase in nominal profits as occurs on inventories also occurs in the case of depreciable assets, such as buildings and machinery.

If the reader looks at Table 2, he will see the following example. We assume that a machine (or a building, or any form of fixed capital) initially costs $1 million. For the sake of simplicity, we assume that it lasts 10 years. The most common accounting method is to spread the cost of such a good evenly over its life. In this way, we arrive at an annual depreciation cost of $100,000 per year. This $100,000 a year is supposed to be recovered out of the revenues of each year—that is, out of the sales receipts, rents, or whichever that the firm takes in—and when saved up over ten years should suffice for the purchase of a second, replacement machine.

In the left-hand column of the table, the column labeled "Calculation of Profits Without Inflation," I show a hypothetical income statement of the firm, which describes its annual operations on the assumption of no inflation. I assume that each year the firm has sales revenues of $1,000,000 and operating costs of $850,000. These operating costs are costs of labor, materials, fuel, advertising, and so forth—for the most part, they are outlays made in

Table 2
*The Effect of Inflation on the Nominal Rate of Profit*
A machine (or building, or any form of fixed capital) initially costs $1,000,000
and lasts 10 years. Its annual depreciation, therefore, is $100,000.

|  | Calculation of Profits Without Inflation | Calculation of Profits With Inflation |
|---|---|---|
| Sales Revenues | $1,000,000 | $2,000,000 |
| Operating Costs | 850,000 | 1,700,000 |
| Gross Profit | 150,000 | 300,000 |
| Depreciation | 100,000 | 100,000 |
| Net Profit Before Taxes | 50,000 | 200,000 |
| Pre-tax Rate of Profit | 10% | 40% |
| Tax on Profit (50%) | 25,000 | 100,000 |
| Net Profit After Taxes | 25,000 | 100,000 |
| Necessary Provision for Replacement of Machine at Higher Price | None | 100,000 |
| Net Profit After Provision for Replacement at Higher Price | 25,000 | None |

the current year to keep on producing, given the fact that the firm already
owns the fixed capital. When we subtract operating costs from sales revenues, we arrive at "gross profit." And when we subtract depreciation from
gross profit, we arrive at "net profit before taxes"—the profit remaining
after all costs but taxes have been deducted. For the moment we will ignore
taxes.

In our example, as we see, gross profit is $150,000 per year, and net
profit is $50,000 per year. The *rate* of profit in our example is 10 percent.
We arrive at this figure by dividing the $50,000 amount of net profit by
$500,000, which is the *average* amount of capital invested in the machine
over its ten-year life. (A million dollars is invested in the machine only at
the beginning of the first year. Thereafter, as depreciation is recovered, the
amount of capital invested in the machine is steadily reduced. At the end
of year five, only half a million remains invested, and at the end of year ten,
nothing remains invested. The average investment, taking the balance of all
the years, is only half a million dollars. Hence, the rate of profit is 10
percent.)

Let us assume that this 10 percent rate of profit is normally a very good
rate and is competitive or even more than competitive with the rate of profit

in industry generally. So far, then, all is fine for the particular industry concerned.

But now let us observe the effects of inflation, and then of the government's attempt to keep the industry's profit at this initial rate.

For the sake of simplicity, let us imagine that sometime after the firm has bought its machine and before it must buy a replacement machine, inflation brings about a doubling of all prices and wages. We could imagine this doubling to take place gradually, over a period of years, or all at once. In either case, we reach the income statement on the right-hand side of the table, labeled "Calculation of Profits With Inflation."

In that income statement, sales revenues are doubled—because the firm sells its goods at twice the price. Operating costs are also doubled—because the firm must pay twice the wages and twice the prices for materials, fuel, and so forth. With a doubling of both sales revenues and operating costs, gross profit, too, is necessarily doubled—it is now $300,000 instead of $150,000.

However, there is one vital magnitude that has not doubled, but has remained the same, namely, depreciation. That cost is based on the initial cost of the machine, not its replacement cost. Inflation doubles the price of a new, replacement machine, but it does not act retroactively to double the price already paid for the firm's present machine. Hence, depreciation cost, which is based on the price actually paid for the machine, in the past, remains unchanged.

Because depreciation cost remains unchanged while gross profit increases, the effect is a disproportionately large increase in net profit. In our example, net profit quadruples, going from $50,000 to $200,000. The rate of profit, therefore, also quadruples—going from 10 percent to 40 percent, as the quadrupled amount of profit is divided by the same capital base.

Now this 40 percent rate of profit is in fact no greater in terms of benefit to the firm's owners than was the initial 10 percent rate of profit. For if they want to stay in business and replace their machine, they have to devote most of their extra profit to saving up for a replacement machine at a higher price. Since they ultimately will require $2 million to buy a replacement machine, what this means is that they must use at least $100,000 a year of their additional net profit for this purpose. Consequently, while their net profit appears to give them a gain of $200,000 a year, actually they dare not consume more than $100,000 a year without impairing their ability to stay in business. And because all prices have doubled, a consumption of $100,000 does not enable them to buy any more goods than $50,000 previously bought. In this way, the $200,000 profit with inflation is really no greater than was the $50,000 profit without inflation. And thus the 40 percent rate of profit with inflation in reality signifies no more than did the 10 percent rate of profit without inflation. It is purely a nominal rise, not a rise in the real rate of gain to the firm.

Indeed, in this case too, the firm actually has to be worse off as the result of the rise in its nominal profits, because it must pay additional taxes on them. If the reader looks at the table, he will see that the firm's after-tax profit—assuming a 50 percent tax rate—goes from $25,000 to $100,000. However, in order to replace its machine, the firm would have to have such profits for the full ten years and use the *whole* of them to accumulate a replacement fund. Observe. Initially, without inflation, the firm could replace and had $25,000 left over for expansion or for its owners' consumption. Now, with the $100,000 profit, it has nothing available for expansion or for its owners' consumption without impairing its ability to replace. I show this by entering an additional item, below "Net Profit After Taxes." That is the item "Necessary Provision for Replacement of Machine at Higher Price." Without inflation, this item is "None." With inflation, it is $100,000, and, as a result, the real profit of the firm is "None."

In the light of these examples, consider the consequences of the attitude that profits are "too high" and that the old rate of profit is "good enough." Our examples show that in the context of inflation even the highest rates of profit that firms can earn are not good enough. Even these rates represent a decline in real profits and, quite possibly, a total elimination of real profits.

In such circumstances, to argue that because a rate of profit is high by historical standards it is high in any meaningful sense, is to display the utmost ignorance. To limit an industry's profits in any way in such circumstances is simply to invite its destruction.

But precisely that is what is being done today to the electric utilities, the phone company, the railroads, and the oil and natural gas industries. And it is what has been done to the rental housing industry in New York City for over thirty-five years. Until quite recently, for example, the government of New York City was proud of the fact that it guaranteed to landlords under rent control the right to earn a 6 *percent* rate of return on their initial investments, made, in most cases, before World War II. Six percent, reasoned the city officials, was a "fair" rate of return. What honest landlord could want more? The city officials neglected the fact that since the landlords' original investments were made, replacement costs had increased many times over and that a 6 percent return on the construction costs of a generation or more earlier had to represent a disastrously losing proposition.

Amazingly, when landlords began to stop keeping up their properties as a result of such loss-making conditions, *they* were the ones accused of "milking" their properties—as though the city or the tenants had originally constructed the buildings and the landlords were now trying to squeeze out of them whatever they could. (And then, as punishment, the city refused to grant rent increases even when called for by its own criterion of providing a 6 percent return.) The simple truth is that the city government of New York, with the support and participation of hundreds of thousands of ignorant tenants, has milked the rental housing industry to the point of totally destroying vast segments of it. The same fate now awaits other, more important industries in this country that are suffering from price controls.

The Destructionist Mentality

What is at root in these cases of wholesale industrial destruction is not ignorance alone, but a mentality that makes itself ignorant. It is a mentality that shows up in the cavalier assumption that the problems an industry experiences as the result of price controls, rising costs, mounting taxes, and harassment by the ecology movement are all somehow the result of "its own inefficiency." This mentality is unaware that inefficiency is itself an inevitable consequence of government interference. If an industry is deprived of the prospect of profits, if its operations are encumbered with endless bureaucratic regulations, then it has no incentive or even possibility to be efficient.[7] It is absurd to blame an industry's inefficiency on anything but government interference; in a free economy, profit and loss incentives and the freedom of competitin operate steadily to increase efficiency.

The ignorance that underlies the destruction of our economic system is made possible by a protective shell of envy and resentment. People take the attitude that somehow the utilities, the landlords, the oil industry, or whoever, are "already rich enough," and that they'll be damned if they'll let them get any richer. So, on with the price controls. That is the beginning and the end of their thinking on the subject, and they just don't care to think any further. They are eager to accept high nominal profits as a confirmation of their view that the industries concerned are "rich enough," and to let it go at that.

However, the simple fact is that none of these industries is rich enough, and in preventing them from becoming richer, or even staying as rich as they are, people foolishly harm themselves. None of these industries is rich enough for the simple reason that we really do not have enough power plants, enough good apartment buildings, or enough oil wells and oil refineries. Speaking for myself, *as a consumer*, I must say that I would like Con Edison, the landlords of New York City, the oil industry, and so on, all to be worth many more billions than they are presently worth. I would benefit from that fact. If Con Ed had more power plants, my supply of electricity would be assured. If the landlords had more and better buildings, I would have a better apartment. If the oil industry had more wells and refineries, I would have a more abundant and secure supply of oil products.

If one thinks about it, I believe, nothing could be more absurd than consumers in a capitalist economy attacking the wealth of their suppliers. That wealth serves *them*—they are the physical beneficiaries of it. All of the wealth of the utilities, the landlords, the oil companies—where is it? It is in power plants and power lines, apartment buildings, oil wells and oil refineries. And whom does it actually, physically, serve? It serves the consumers. It serves *us*—all of us. We have a selfish interest in the preservation and increase of that wealth. If we deprive Con Ed of a power plant, we deprive ourselves of power. If we deprive our landlords of more and better buildings, we deprive ourselves of apartments. If we deprive the oil industry of wells and refineries, we deprive ourselves of gasoline and heating oil.

This harmony of interests between the consumer and the producer under capitalism is one of the great, profound insights of von Mises.[8] Because of it, even if businessmen become cowardly and do not fight for their own interests, we, as consumers, must fight for them, and thereby for ourselves. For we have a selfish interest in being able to pay prices that make it profitable for businessmen to supply us. It is to our self-interest to pay utility rates, rents, oil prices, and so on, that enable the producers in these fields to keep their facilities intact and growing, and that make them want to supply us. And I must say, in view of the principles we have learned in the earlier chapters of this book, that we do not have to worry about being charged unfairly in a free market, because any high profits that might be made from us are simply the incentive and the means to an expanded supply, and are generally made only because of special efficiency on the part of the producers who earn them.

A Defense of Supermarket Repricing

In early 1974, when inflation was proceeding more rapidly than now, supermarkets began to raise the prices of the goods already on their shelves, which had initially been marked with lower prices. Because the stores had purchased those goods at prices which had not yet risen, it was assumed that it was some kind of monstrous injustice for them to charge higher prices. The higher prices, it was argued, merely bloated the profits of the supermarkets and were the cause of a higher cost of living for consumers.

What those who spread this argument chose to ignore was that the *replacement* costs of the merchandise had risen and that if the supermarkets had not raised their prices, they would not have had the means of replacing their inventories. They would have been in exactly the same position as our hypothetical merchant if he had not raised his prices.[9] Assume that our merchant held to his old prices and thus continued to take in only $110, while his replacement cost rose from $100 to $110. His nominal profit that year, based on historical cost, would have remained at $10 and, after paying taxes, he would still have had $5. The only problem would have been that even if he allowed absolutely no dividend for his own consumption, he would have had no more than $105 available for replacing his inventory, while the sum he required for replacement was $110. He would have had to reduce the size of his operations. Exactly this would have been the position of the supermarkets if they had been unable to raise their prices in anticipation of higher replacement costs.

It follows that the consumers who wanted cheap goods at the supermarkets' expense would have gotten fewer goods and, if this process were kept up long enough, eventually no goods at all. And, paradoxically, at whatever point the control on the nominal rate of profit was finally abandoned, they would have had to pay higher prices than if the control had never been imposed, because prices would then have had to rise on the basis of a decrease in supply as well as on the basis of an inflation-caused increase in demand.

The Campaign Against the Profits of the Oil Companies

In early 1974, every release of a quarterly earnings report by an oil company was an occasion for *The New York Times* to run a story headlined as a staggering increase in oil company profits. Day after day, one would read a headline in that newspaper that the profits of oil company X were up 60 or 70 percent or more over the same quarter the year before. This rise in profits was constantly mentioned in conjunction with the rise in the price of gasoline and other petroleum products, which had also risen on the order of 60 or 70 percent over the same period of time. It was constantly implied—by *The New York Times*, by *Time* magazine, and by a host of television news commentators—that the rise in oil company profits was responsible for the rise in the price of oil products. And because the rise in these prices was presented as the cause of practically the whole problem of inflation, the impression was created that the oil companies were out to destroy the country with their insatiable greed for profits. By the same token, of course, the oil companies were depicted as eminently deserving to be throttled with price controls.

The evasions, distortions, and misrepresentations in this case were enormous. I think they are worth going into because they are a classic illustration of how the supporters of price controls argue and what they are capable of.

First of all, the supporters of controls evaded two facts that should have been known to everyone: They evaded the fact that the rise in the price of oil products in the United States was the result of a rise in the world price of crude oil brought about by the Arab embargo and the Arab-sponsored cartel, i.e., that it was the result of a rise in the oil companies' *costs* of obtaining imported oil. In addition, they evaded the fact that since August of 1971 the prices of oil and oil products produced or sold in the United States were already totally controlled by the United States government, and were currently controlled at levels far below the world-market prices of these goods; indeed, at levels which, until the end of the crisis period, did not even allow the oil companies to pass on more than a part of the higher cost of imported oil. The truth is that our price controls made the importation of foreign oil highly *unprofitable*, which is one of the major reasons we suffered from a shortage of oil at the time. Furthermore, while *The New*

*York Times* and the other news media were spewing headlines about the enormous rise in oil company profits, they neglected to mention that the profits of the oil companies on oil production within the United States increased only on the order of about 6 percent during the crisis period. This was in line with the increase in the physical volume of domestic production in the period. Profits on domestic production did not and could not have increased any more than that because the selling prices of the oil companies were all rigidly controlled by the government, in line with their costs of production.

The real facts, therefore, are that during the oil crisis the American market was a very unprofitable market for the importation of foreign oil and a not very profitable market for the production of domestic oil or oil products. Nevertheless, the news media constantly pointed to a sharp rise in oil company profits and claimed that it was responsible for the rise in prices.

To be sure, there was a substantial increase in oil company profits *on a percentage basis.* Technically, the media were correct in reporting profit increases of 60 and 70 percent or more. But in representing these profit increases as the cause of higher American oil prices, the media committed four distinct acts of dishonesty or misrepresentation.

First, the media neglected to inform the public that these higher profits were not earned on the production or sale of oil or oil products *in the United States.* In many cases, over half the rise in profits came from inventory profits on stocks of oil and oil products held abroad, where price controls did not apply, and from profits on foreign-exchange holdings. The inventory profits were the same in principle as the jump in profits of our hypothetical merchant or of the supermarkets that raised prices in anticipation of higher replacement costs. These inventory profits earned abroad reflected nothing more than that the oil companies possessed some inventories acquired before the rise in the world-market price of crude oil, and were able to sell the inventories at the higher prices corresponding to the higher replacement price of crude oil. The extra profits earned on the inventories merely served to enable the oil companies to maintain their level of operations, just as was the case with the supermarkets.

The profits on foreign-exchange holdings were similar. The oil companies are largely international and hold such currencies as Swiss francs and German marks, as well as U. S. dollars. During the oil crisis, the price of the dollar fell in terms of these currencies. This meant that the francs and marks held by the oil companies were suddenly equivalent to a larger number of U. S. dollars. This increase in the dollar value of their foreign-exchange holdings was included in the reported profit gains of the oil companies.

The rest of the increase in oil company profits was the result of higher profits on foreign operations other than profits on inventory or currency holdings, and higher profits on other lines of business, such as the chemical business, in which a number of oil companies are involved and which had a good year at the time. All of these facts about the sources of the higher profits were simply ignored.

The second dishonesty of the media was that they did not point out that even with the 60 or 70 percent increase—from whatever sources—the profits of the oil companies were only restored to the same level in relation to sales revenues at which they had existed in 1968. It was not pointed out that the intervening years had been poor ones for the oil industry and that the sharp percentage increase in its profits was largely the result of measuring the increase against an unusually low base. I remember one case in particular, in which the headline in *The New York Times* blared "2-Month Earnings Soar at Occidental."[10] It turned out, if one read the article very, very carefully, and did some arithmetic that the reporter and the editor had not bothered to do, that the soaring earnings represented an increase in profits from about *seven-tenths of one percent of sales revenues to about 5½ percent of sales revenues*, which latter figure was still below normal for the oil industry in previous years. Of course, with this type of misrepresentation, it would be possible to write headlines about infinite increases in profits. All one would need would be to find firms that earned some profits in the current period but which had earned zero profits or incurred losses in the period with which it is compared. The percentage increase would be infinite.

Closely related to this kind of dishonesty was a further misrepresentation. In all of the countless times that the news media mentioned 60 to 70 percent increases in profits in conjunction with 60 or 70 percent increases in product prices in the petroleum industry, they never once, to my knowledge, mentioned that profits are only a small percentage of prices—5 percent, 10 percent, rarely much more than 10 percent. This applies both to the petroleum industry and to practically every other industry. Accordingly, it was never pointed out that any given percentage increase in profits must necessarily represent a much smaller percentage increase in prices. If profits are initially 10 percent of a price, a 70 percent increase in profits does not equal a 70 percent increase in price, but only a 7 *percent* increase in price. If, as in the case I mentioned, profits are initially seven-tenths of one percent of the price, even a 1,000 percent increase in profits would not mean some kind of fantastic increase in price, but a rise merely on the order of a few percent. Thus, even if the oil companies had earned their higher profits in the United States, which they did not, and even if those higher profits had been the cause of a rise in prices, which they were not, they could not have been of any significance as a cause of higher prices. Nevertheless, by the news media's constant conjunction of their roughly equivalent percentage increases, it was made to appear that the rise in profits of the petroleum industry is what accounted for the rise in the prices of petroleum products.

Finally, just as the media regularly associated the percentage increases in profits with the percentage increase in the price of oil products, they just as studiously avoided ever mentioning the rate of profit on capital in connection with the rise in the consumer price index. Such a connection would have shown that the oil industry was far from being very profitable in real terms. The reasons are as follows. During the oil crisis, the consumer price level was rising at an annual rate of 13 percent, while the world's most profitable, most successful major oil company was earning only 18 percent a year on its capital. This meant that while $100 invested in that company would grow to $118 in a year, it would take $113 at the end of the year to buy what the $100 had bought at the beginning of the year. This meant that the real rate of gain of the owners of that company was less than 5 percent a year—it was $5 divided by $113. A real rate of profit of less than 5 percent for the most profitable, most successful major oil company is quite low. And, of course, most oil companies were earning substantially lower real rates of profit. Any oil company whose nominal rate of profit was below 13 percent, say, 8, 10, or 12 percent, was actually losing money in real terms! But, as I say, one never found the media dealing with the real rate of return of the oil companies.

It may be asked where I obtained my knowledge of the facts I have cited. The answer, strangely enough, is the general news media themselves, especially *The New York Times*. The facts appeared there. They simply received no stress, or they weren't integrated. They were buried in a mass of articles whose headlines and general tenor created exactly the opposite impression. Or they appeared at different times, in different stories. For example, as I have indicated, figures were reported showing dollar totals of profits and sales revenues; it was simply left to the reader to perform the necessary long division in order to compute profits as a percentage of sales revenues. Likewise, while the percentage increase in profits over the previous year was carried in headlines, only occasionally, in an almost offhand reference, would one find a mention of the actual nominal rate of profit on capital invested. And, while the rate of increase in the consumer price level was featured prominently, it was never mentioned in connection with nominal profit rates, so that one would know what to make of those rates.

One would also read statements, buried deep in articles denouncing oil company profits, that, according to oil company officials or other sources, the rise in profits was largely the result of inventory profits earned abroad and gains on foreign-exchange holdings. The statements were never disputed. They were simply ignored, as being of no significance. And, of course, it was certainly reported in the press that all of the prices charged by the oil companies were controlled by the government and that the Arabs had brought about a radical increase in the world price of crude oil, which, of course, meant higher costs to the oil companies. Yet, these two facts of fixed prices and radically higher costs, facts which were obviously incompatible with the oil industry being very profitable, were simply ignored in the articles reporting the profit increases, as I discussed earlier.

The kind of distortions committed in the media's treatment of the profits of the oil companies will almost certainly be committed in the future, in attempts to impose or continue controls on other industries. The reader should be on guard against them and should hold in mind, in addition to the need for nominal profits to allow for the replacement of assets at higher prices, such further important matters as the source of the alleged profits under attack, their size in relation to sales revenues, the basis of comparison used in showing their change, and the relation between percentage changes in them and percentage changes in selling prices.

How the U. S. Government, Not the Oil Companies, Caused the Oil Shortage

Let us try to keep in mind all that we have learned about shortages, and look further at the ignorance and evasions displayed during the oil shortage. I am concentrating on the oil shortage in this book, because it had such a dramatic effect on practically everyone in the United States and is so illustrative of all of the problems associated with controls, including the kind of inappropriate mental attitudes that are connected with them.

There were two very popular explanations of the oil shortage that went around at the time, both of which tried to blame it on the oil companies rather than on price controls. According to one of these explanations, the oil companies had created the shortage in order to be able to obtain permission to build the Alaskan oil pipeline, which had been delayed for many years by the lawsuits of the ecology movement. According to the second explanation, the oil companies had created the shortage in order to eliminate the independent gas stations, to which they were reportedly observed denying supplies.

The first observation which must be made against both of these claims is that they do not see that shortages can only result from a price that is too low and must disappear as the price rises. To repeat once again, no matter how physically limited is the supply of a good or how urgent the demand for it, no shortage can possibly exist at the price established in a free market. For the free-market price will be high enough to level the quantity of the good demanded down to equality with the supply that exists—all the while, of course, acting to expand the supply that exists. Even if one could establish—which one certainly cannot—that the oil companies had conspired to reduce the supply of oil, still, one could not blame them for the shortage. Had they reduced the supply of oil, they would have sold it at a higher price, and at the higher price there would have been no shortage. In order to blame the oil companies for the *shortage*, one would have to show that the oil companies *deliberately charged too low a price for their oil*. That would be the only conceivable way that they could have caused the shortage. But that is absolutely absurd. It was not the oil companies that were responsible for too low a price, but the government, with its price controls. The government stood ready to fine or possibly even imprison anyone selling oil or oil products at prices that would have eliminated the shortage.

The interests of justice, however, require that I show not only that the oil companies could not have caused the shortage, but also that they were not responsible for anything acting to raise the price of oil in the absence of price controls.

Observe. The oil companies were not responsible for the nationwide and worldwide increase in aggregate demand that has acted to drive up all prices, including, of course, the price of oil. Nor were the oil companies responsible for any decrease in the world supply of oil. Both were exclusively the result of government actions. All governments, that of the United States included, are bent on reckless expansions of the money supply that act to raise the demand for everything and the price of everything. And it was governments that were responsible for the restriction in the supply of oil—not only the governments that are members of the international oil cartel or that participated in the Arab embargo, but the U. S. government.

The U. S. government, acting largely under the influence of the ecology movement, restricted the supply of oil in the following ways: 1. It delayed the development of the Alaskan oil fields for years. 2. It prevented the development of offshore wells on the continental shelf. 3. It stopped the construction of new refineries and of harbor facilities for handling supertankers. 4. It imposed price controls on oil. 5. It acted to further restrict oil company profits, and thus oil industry investment, by punitively increasing their rate of taxation through first reducing and then totally abolishing the customary depletion allowance on crude oil. (It follows from the uniformity-of-profit principle that a measure such as the depletion allowance, or any form of reduced rate of taxation, does not enable an industry to earn a permanently above-average rate of profit; such a measure results in an expansion of the industry until the point is reached where only the going rate of profit is earned. Reduction or abolition of the depletion allowance, or any other long-term tax advantage, produces exactly the opposite effects: it cuts the rate of profit and requires a cutback in the size of the industry to restore the going rate of profit.) 6. It has deterred investment in the oil industry through threats of antitrust actions forcing the breakup of existing companies, and through threats of nationalization.

In addition, the U. S. government has been responsible for an enormous artificial increase in the demand for oil, over and above the increase caused by its policy of inflation. It has caused an artificial increase in demand in the following ways: 1. Since the mid-1960s, it has controlled the price of natural gas, thereby undermining the growth of that industry. The demand for fuel that normally would have been supplied by natural gas has therefore overflowed largely into an expanded demand for petroleum, which is its closest substitute for most purposes. 2. Under the influence of the ecology movement, the government has prevented the construction of atomic power plants and restricted the mining of coal. In these ways too, it has forced the demand for fuel to rely more heavily than necessary on oil supplies. 3. Again under the influence of the ecology movement, the government has forced electric utilities to shift from the burning of coal to the burning of oil and it has forced automobile manufacturers to produce engines requiring far higher gasoline consumption per ton-mile.

In sum, the government and the ecology movement have done everything in their power to raise the demand for and restrict the supply of oil.

It should be realized that it is only these actions of the U. S. government that have made possible the dramatic rise in the price of oil. The U. S. government bears a far greater responsibility than the Arab cartel. *It* is the party that has made it possible for the cartel to succeed. All that the cartel has done is to take advantage of the artificial increase in demand and restriction of supply brought about by the U. S. government. Had the government not restricted the expansion of the domestic petroleum industry and forced up the demand for oil, the supply reductions carried out by the cartel would not have been able to have such a significant effect on the price. Because in that context, such supply reductions would have been at the expense of far less important wants than actually turned out to be the case. With the larger domestic supply of oil and competing fuels that a free market would have produced, the marginal significance of any given amount of oil would have been far less. The loss of any given amount of oil by virtue of the supply reductions carried out by the cartel would therefore have been far less serious. As a result, the cartel would not have been able to raise the price nearly as much by virtue of any given amount of supply reduction. In such circumstances the cartel members would probably not have found it worthwhile to reduce the supply at all.

Furthermore, in the absence of our price controls, any rise in the price of oil achieved by the cartel would have worked to the advantage of the American oil industry at the expense of the oil industry in the countries belonging to the cartel. This alone would have been enough to frustrate the plans of the cartel. For in this case, the effect of the cartel's restriction of supply would have been to hand the American oil industry the profits and the capital required for an expansion of supply. The cartel would then either have had to allow the price of oil to fall or else it would have had to restrict its own production still further, which would have meant that the American oil companies would have earned the high price of oil on a larger volume of production and have had still greater profits available for expansion, thereby creating still worse problems for the cartel in the future.

It should be obvious that it is impossible for any cartel to succeed that is confronted with a major competitor able to profit from its policies and expand his production. The Arab cartel can succeed only because the U. S. government does its utmost to prevent the cartel's competition—the U. S.

oil industry—from earning high profits and expanding. In the absence of the government's destructionist policies, the Arab cartel would probably never even have been formed in the first place, because the conditions required for its success would have been totally lacking.

In sharpest contrast to the actions of the U. S. government, at each step of the way the oil companies have sought to expand the production of crude oil and oil products in order to keep pace with the growing demand for oil. They have consistently sought to develop new sources of supply, such as the Alaskan and offshore fields, and to construct new refineries and improved harbor facilities. In other words, they have done everything in their power to keep the price of oil and oil products as low as economically possible. Any other policy would have been against their interests.

This last point must be stressed. In a free market, the oil companies' *profit motive* is tied to maintaining as great a supply and as low a price as possible. Consider first the interests of the firms that are predominantly petroleum refiners. Their capital is invested primarily in refineries, pipelines, tankers, delivery trucks, and the like, rather than in deposits of crude oil in the ground. These firms clearly have an interest in the greatest possible supply and lowest possible price of crude oil. For the price of crude oil is their *cost*. These firms have the same interest in an abundant supply and low price of crude oil that every producer has in an abundant supply and low price of his raw material.

By the same token, consider the interests of the producers of crude oil. Their interests lie with the greatest possible efficiency of refining operations and the lowest possible price of refined petroleum products. Because the lower the prices of refined products, the greater the quantity of them demanded and therefore the greater the quantity demanded of crude oil: the price of crude oil can benefit by part of any cost savings in refining. This mutual tension between the interests of refiners and producers of crude oil makes it necessary for each group to try to improve its own production. If the existing producers of crude oil lag behind, they can expect competition from the refiners, who can develop their own supplies of crude oil or expand their existing crude oil operations. If the existing refiners lag behind, they can expect competition from the producers of crude oil, who, for their part, can undertake refining operations or expand their existing refining operations.

In addition, both groups can expect competition from total outsiders if they fail to exploit any significant opportunity for improvement. And, of course, within each group, whichever individual firm succeeds in improving production ahead of its rivals will almost certainly gain at their expense. For example, if one particular refiner improves his efficiency and cuts his costs, he will have higher profits and will thus be able to accumulate additional capital. It will almost certainly pay him to use his additional capital to expand his production, and to create a market for his additional production by lowering his prices. His lower costs will still enable him to have high profits even at lower prices, and his lower prices will both attract new customers to the industry and take away some customers from rivals who cannot afford to sell at such low prices.

Any refiner who does not strive to cut his costs and expand his output merely creates an opportunity for someone else to do so—whether another existing refiner, a crude oil producer, or a total outsider—and thereby risks making *himself* the rival who cannot afford to sell at the market price; that is, he risks the destruction of his firm. In the same way, every producer of crude oil has similar profit as well as loss incentives to cut his costs and develop new supplies at lower prices.

For these reasons, it was no accident, but logically necessary, that the oil companies have all along sought to expand their production. It was the operation of these very principles that brought the oil industry into existence in the first place and developed it from virtually nothing into the productive giant it is today.

To argue, therefore, that the oil companies were responsible for the oil shortage is an absurdity compounded by a triple injustice. It is an absurdity in that, as we have seen, it implicitly accuses the oil companies of charging too low a price for their oil. This is something they would never do. And the critics of the oil companies, who constantly accuse them of seeking to charge prices that are too high, should have a sufficient respect for logic not to accuse them simultaneously of causing shortages by charging prices that are too low. (Of course, the critics do not know that they are guilty of a contradiction, because they have no idea either of what causes shortages or what determines the price of oil.) The accusation embodies a triple injustice in that it evades: 1. The fact that it was the government's price controls that kept the price too low and so created the shortage. 2. The fact that the government and the ecology movement did practically everything they could to restrict the supply and expand the demand for oil. 3. The fact that by the nature of the profit motive the oil companies have always worked to expand the supply of oil and reduce its price.

To argue in addition that the oil companies created the shortage for the purpose of being able to build the Alaskan pipeline is to pile on still further absurdities. The obvious truth—given the price controls—is that the construction of the pipeline would have mitigated the shortage somewhat, had it not been so long delayed. To argue that its construction was the *motive* for the shortage is not only to display the utmost ignorance about the causation of shortages and callous indifference to the most elementary questions of justice, it is also to display a lack of comprehension of the law of causality in relation to the physical world. Because according to this argument, the pipeline was something that only the oil companies wanted; the consumers of oil products, allegedly, could have gotten along quite well without the pipeline. Oil products, according to the mentality behind this argument, simply come from oil companies. The oil companies, it is believed, are perfectly capable of producing oil products without oil fields or oil pipelines. The oil companies desire oil fields and oil pipelines, one gets the impression, not because they are necessary to production—production is causeless—but in order to disturb the reindeer and the grizzly bears and to pollute the air.

This denial of the elementary physical connection between products and the means of producing them, I must point out, is not an isolated phenomenon confined to the arguments about the pipeline. It is simply a further manifestation of the same mentality we have already encountered in consumers who denounce the wealth of their suppliers—consumers who will be damned if they'll let the utility that supplies them own the power plants necessary to do so, or their landlord own a decent building. This mentality pervades the whole ecology movement. It is the mentality of all of its members insofar as they both prevent the development of energy supplies and denounce the producers of energy for not producing enough.

Let us turn to the second version of the argument that the oil companies were responsible for the shortage: the claim that they created it for the purpose of eliminating the independent gas stations by denying them supplies.

It may very well be the case that the oil companies did cut off or discriminatorily reduce supplies to the independents, as widely reported. My own personal experience does not confirm this, but I am willing to believe it—not because it was reported in the press, but because it would have been a logical consequence of the shortage. Given the existence of the oil shortage, every oil company that owned gas stations had the following choice: either it could reduce supplies to its own gas stations, where its own capital was invested and stood to suffer loss if the stations had to close or restrict operations; or it could reduce supplies to gas stations owned by others, where it was other people's capital that was invested and would suffer loss. Naturally, if an oil company—or anyone else—is confronted with the choice of having to lose its own capital as a result of some absurd government action, or allowing the loss to fall on the capital of someone else, it will choose the latter. And there is no moral reason why it should not. It is no one's moral obligation to offer up his wealth to the government's destructionist policy so that he may suffer his "fair share" of the damage it inflicts.

I must point out that if it were not for the controls and the shortage, the oil companies and the independents would have enjoyed a perfectly harmonious, mutually profitable relationship, as they always did in all the years before the controls and the shortage. An oil company *benefits* from the existence of independent stations willing to sell its gasoline, and has absolutely no reason to try to undermine them, but every reason to try to promote them. Its benefit is that it can sell more gasoline without having to supply the capital necessary to buy or build gas stations. Even if the oil company owns some of its own gas stations, it still benefits from selling to independents—in just the same way that a company like Howard Johnson's or Schrafft's benefits by being able to sell its ice cream through retail outlets it does not own. The benefit is wider marketability of the product. An oil company benefits by selling to independent stations even if they are in direct competition with stations it owns, because it is better that *it* supply the competing stations than that some other oil company do so—if that happened, it would still have the same competition, but it would sell less gas. In the absence of price controls, even the physical scarcity of oil would not have stopped the oil companies from selling to the independents. They would have been glad to sell whenever an independent was in a position to pay a price sufficiently high to compensate them for the profits they had to forgo by being unable to sell through their own gas stations.

The Conspiracy Theory of Shortages

I cannot help noting that this whole argument about the oil companies being out to eliminate the independents (or even just being out to build the Alaskan pipeline), and allegedly staging a nationwide, worldwide crisis to do it, introduces a strange element into the discussion. That is the element of alleged secret plots, dark conspiracies, evil forces, and all the rest of that syndrome.

Strange to say, this kind of argument is much more prevalent than one might imagine. It is present in implicit form whenever anyone asserts that a shortage, whether of oil or anything else, is "contrived." This view of things is not only ignorant of all the consequences of price controls, but it implies the existence of a secret conspiracy. It assumes that price controls themselves create no problems, but that the problems are created by the evil of private firms who combine together secretly and arbitrarily to produce the consequences we have seen can result only from price controls.

In view of all that we have proved about shortages in general and about the oil shortage in particular, I believe I am justified when I say that these arguments really deserve no greater intellectual respectability than the fear some unfortunate people have of Martians or the evil eye. Certainly, they should not be taken seriously by the media or by public officials, as, unfortunately, they have been. It is the intellectual and moral responsibility of the media and the public officials to stop engaging in slander based on ignorance and fear, and to acquire the enlightenment provided by economic science.

Rebuttal of the Charge that Private Firms "Control" Prices

A rather vicious argument has been advanced as a justification for the imposition of price controls. This is the argument that private firms already "control" prices, only they "control" them in their own selfish interest. Instead, it is urged, the government should control prices, for it will do so in the "public interest."

This argument was repeatedly presented in television commercials during the campaign for the 1976 Democratic presidential nomination by one of the leading contenders, Representative Morris Udall. Representative Udall repeatedly asserted that he believed that instead of the price of oil being "controlled" by the oil companies, in their selfish interest, it should be controlled by the president (i.e., Morris Udall), in the public interest.

The reason that Representative Udall and others believe that private firms "control" prices is that they can observe the producers of manufactured or processed goods, and also retailers and many wholesalers, engaged in the *setting* of prices. For example, these businessmen can be observed sending out price catalogs and price lists, and also posting prices on signs and writing them on tags. To set prices in this way is, according to Representative Udall and others, to "control" prices. The essential characteristic of a controlled price, on this view, is that someone sets it. It is considered secondary and inconsequential *who* sets it—whether a private businessman or a government official. Indeed, since prices do not create themselves, it is difficult to understand how, on this view, any price can avoid being described as "controlled."

The distinction seems to be that a price is not considered controlled if it is formed in markets so broad—like the organized exchanges for common stocks and commodity futures—that it is difficult to trace from precisely whom any given price quotation emanates; such price quotations have the appearance of being formed independently of any definite individual. If, on the other hand, price quotations emanate regularly from the same, easily identifiable source—such as a steel mill's published price at which it stands ready to ship steel, or a candy store's sign announcing the price at which it stands ready to sell candy bars—the price is declared to be "controlled." (Often, the word "administered" is used as a synonym for "controlled.") The supporters of this idea rarely mention the fact that they believe candy stores and barbershops and the like are engaged in "price control"—they confine their attacks to large firms, like steel companies and oil companies, where they can count on envy and the existing hostility to big business—but that is the logic of their position.

The viciousness of this doctrine is that it evades and seeks to obliterate the fundamental and radical distinction between private action and government action.[11] Private citizens, and this, of course, includes private corporations, have no authority to resort to physical force against other people. If they do, they are in violation of the law and will be punished. Private action, therefore, is essentially voluntary in character—that is, it can only occur by peaceful means, with the mutual consent of all involved. Government action is totally different. The government has legal authority to resort to physical force—e.g., to arrest, fine, imprison, and even execute people. All government actions rest on this authority. There is no such thing as a law (or a ruling, edict, or decree) that is not backed by the threat of physical force to assure compliance.

Let us see what difference these facts make to whether prices are set by private firms or by the government. When prices are set by private firms, they are set with regard to the mutual self-interest of the buyer and seller, including the need to take into account the threat of competition or potential competition. Thus, a seller must ask prices that are not only high enough to enable him to stay in business and make the best possible profit he can, but, simultaneously, that are low enough to enable his customers to afford his goods and too low for other sellers or potential sellers to try to take away his market.

When the government sets prices, its prices are backed by the threat of physical force, and are necessarily against the mutual self-interests of buyers and sellers. The government invariably tries to sacrifice either the seller to the buyer (by imposing prices that are too low), or the buyer to the seller (by imposing prices that are too high). In the one case, it succeeds in destroying the sellers, leaving the buyers without suppliers. In the other case, it succeeds in destroying the buyers, leaving the sellers without customers (or the workers without employers).

This is the difference that is made by whether prices are set by private firms or by the government. This is the difference that Congressman Udall's usage of the term "price control" evades and seeks to obliterate.

Private firms do not and cannot control prices because they have no power to resort to physical force. Only the government can control prices—i.e., only the government can use force to set prices in violation of the mutual self-interests of buyers and sellers. Price control means not the setting of prices, but the setting of prices *by the government*.

Rebuttal of the Charge that a Free Economy Lacks Freedom of Competition

A further fallacy—a corollary of the doctrine that private firms control prices—must be unmasked. This is the doctrine that freedom of competition in a free economy is impaired by the fact that large sums of capital are required to enter many lines of business, such as the automobile, steel, or oil business.

This doctrine evades and seeks to obliterate the fundamental and radical distinction that exists between two sorts of obstacles to the achievement of a goal or desire: "obstacles" constituted by the ordinary facts of reality and obstacles constituted by the government's threat to use physical force. For example, by the nature of things, it is impossible for me to square circles, walk through walls, or be in two places at the same time. It is also not possible for me, in the actual circumstances of my life, to win the Nobel Prize in Chemistry or the Academy Award for Best Actor of the Year, or to enter the automobile or steel business. Absolutely none of these facts constitutes a violation of my freedom, a denial of my rights, or anything of the kind. In order for a violation of freedom to exist, it is not sufficient merely that someone be unable to achieve what he desires. What is necessary is that the thing stopping him be the government's threat to use force against him, specifically, its threat to *initiate* the use of force against him in response to an action on his part that does not represent the use of force.

Freedom is simply the absence of the initiation of physical force on the part of the government; only the government's initiation of force can violate freedom. For example, if I ask a girl to marry me, and she says no, my freedom is not violated. But suppose she says *yes*, and the government stops me from marrying her—say, by virtue of a law concerning marriages among people of different races, religions, or blood-types—*then* my freedom is violated. Or again, if I want to travel to California, but lack the fare and am unwilling to try hitchhiking, my freedom of travel is in no way violated. But suppose I do have the fare to go to California and want to pay it, but the government stops me—say, with a wall around my city (as in East Berlin), a passport restriction, or a price control on aviation fuel that stops the airlines from flying—*then* my freedom of travel is violated. Or once more, suppose I want to print my views in *The New York Times*, but can neither afford the advertising rates nor persuade the publisher to give me space. My freedom of the press is not violated; I am not a victim of "censorship." But suppose I do have the money to pay the advertising rates or could persuade the publisher to print my views, and the government disallows it—*that* would be a violation of the freedom of the press; *that* would be censorship.

To come to the specific issue of the freedom of competition, if I cannot enter the automobile business because I am unable to raise the money necessary to buy the equipment that would enable me to produce and sell cars as cheaply as Ford or General Motors, my freedom of competition is not violated. But suppose I *can* raise the money to enter the automobile business—suppose I am backed by a major steel company or oil company or foreign automobile producer, or even by one of the existing domestic auto firms—and the government stops me; then, and only then, would my freedom of competition be violated. Only the government can violate the freedom of competition, the freedom of entry, or any other freedom.[12] And the government is, in fact, constantly engaged in violating the freedom of competition—for example, by means of its antitrust laws. In prohibiing such things as acquisitions and mergers, these laws continuously exclude from entry into industries and market areas the very firms which do have the necessary capital and other abilities required to enter them.[13] Recently, Congress contemplated proposals to deny the oil companies freedom of entry into the coal and uranium industries. It will probably do so again.

# Further Effects of Price Controls and Shortages
## IV

1. Consumer Impotence and Hatred Between Buyers and Sellers

Once price controls result in shortages, their destructive effects are greatly increased. The combination of price controls and shortages not only deprives the consumer of the power to make it profitable for sellers to supply the goods he wants, but of all economic power of any kind over the seller. Instead of being a valued customer, whose patronage or lack of patronage makes a difference to the seller's profit or loss, the buyer is reduced to the status of absolute insignificance, totally at the seller's mercy. His position is much worse, in fact, than if he were dealing with a protected legal monopolist.

Consider. If a shortage exists, and a buyer is dissatisfied with his supplier, he dare not leave him, because he has nowhere else to go. In a shortage, even if there are many other suppliers of the same good, each of them has his own waiting line or waiting list, and, as a result, the dissatisfied customer of any one supplier cannot count on actually being supplied by any other supplier. The other suppliers, therefore, do not represent a real alternative for him in a shortage. Consequently, no matter how many sellers of a good there may be, price controls and shortages place each of them in the position of being the only one. In addition, just as in the case of a protected legal monopolist, these sellers are immune from potential competition. (The threat of potential competition, in a free market, would keep in check the occasional sellers who were in the position of being sole suppliers.) Potential competition is ruled out because the industry is forced to operate at a rate of return that is not competitive, and perhaps even at an outright loss. As a result, no outside firm would want to enter such an industry.

The situation for the customer is actually much worse than if he were dealing with a protected legal monopolist, because under price controls and shortages, the seller who surpasses a customer's limits of tolerance and succeeds in driving him away *does not lose anything by doing so*. This is because for each customer who is driven away, there is a multitude of others eager to take his place. The seller simply sells to someone else who otherwise would not have been able to buy or not buy as much as he desired. This goes beyond the conditions faced by a protected legal monopolist, for such a monopolist does not have a reserve of unsupplied potential customers willing to buy on just as good terms as his present customers. If such a monopolist drives away his present customers, he can find new ones only at lower prices. A protected legal monopolist who has any sense, therefore, will not do this. He will value his customers, because he knows that he cannot afford to lose them without harming himself. But under price controls and shortages, the seller is free to regard his customers as absolutely valueless—as being instantaneously replaceable by others drawn from waiting lines or waiting lists without any loss to himself.

By the nature of the case, shortages lead sellers to regard customers not only as valueless, but as a positive nuisance—as a source of trouble and expense, not a source of livelihood. This occurs because, in fact, under a system of shortages and waiting lines, that is just what customers become. Under such a system, when a seller renders a customer some service or goes to some expense on his behalf, he is no longer doing it for the sake of gaining or keeping the customer's business and thereby earning his own livelihood, because having the customer's business no longer depends on performing the service or incurring the expense. The seller can have the customer anyway, or, if not that customer, then any one of ten or a hundred or a thousand other customers. If the seller is to continue to provide the service or incur the expense for the sake of the customer, he can only do so out of a sense of altruistic duty, not out of the sense that in serving the customer he serves himself.

Thus, price controls and the shortages they create take the profit out of serving the customer and the loss out of not serving him. They break the harmonious union of the self-interest of buyer and seller that prevails in a free market and replace it with an altruistic relationship between the two. In this relationship, the customer is reduced to impotent pleading for the customary service and customary quality that the seller no longer has any economic motive to supply. Indeed, all of the seller's motives, both economic and noneconomic, now work in the direction of reducing the quality of his product and the service associated with it.

The seller's economic motive lies with reducing quality and service because by doing so he reduces his costs and perhaps his own labor, and he does not have to fear any reduction in his revenues. For the same reason, employees feel free to work less hard in serving customers. Their poor performance no longer threatens their employer's revenue, and so he is no longer motivated to make them produce high quality products and to treat customers properly. (Thus, even under price controls, there is a tendency for customers to get what they pay for. To the extent that they pay prices below the potential free-market prices, they tend to receive products that are below the level of the products they would have received in a free market.)

The fact that price controls inflict actual harm on the sellers, and the fact that this harm is inflicted for the avowed purpose of benefitting the buyers, introduces a noneconomic element into the attitude of many sellers. They see themselves as being sacrificed for the benefit of their customers, and they may actually come to hate their customers as a result of it. In some cases it is possible that they may derive actual pleasure from the reduction in quality and service that they impose on their customers.

Price controls and shortages, in fact, launch a spiral of mutually reinforcing hatreds between buyer and seller. The buyer arbitrarily demands the quality and service he is accustomed to, even though he is not paying the necessary price any longer. The seller has no economic reason to comply with these demands, but, on the contrary, has both economic and psychological reasons not to. The buyer then views the seller as an omnipotent tyrant whom he must beg for favors or threaten with reprisals in order to obtain what he wants. The seller views the buyer as a hysterical petty chiseler seeking values without payment. In degree that the accustomed quality and service are not forthcoming, the buyers become more shrill and insistent in their demands, and the sellers become correspondingly more resistant.

This principle—of deterioration of quality and service accompanied by mutual hatred between buyer and seller—was illustrated to some extent in the gasoline shortage of early 1974. Suddenly, service station attendants who had always cleaned windshields and eagerly volunteered to check under the hood ceased to do so. Whereas before they had always been courteous and polite, seeking to encourage as much repeat business as possible, they now became surly and rude. The customer, who had always been king at the gas station, as everywhere else, suddenly became a useless pest waiting in line to have his tank filled and causing unnecessary labor to gas station attendants. The breakdown of the normal harmony of interests between buyer and seller, and its replacement with open hostility, was strikingly illustrated in *The New York Times*' "Quotation of the Day" for February 5, 1974: (I quote first the statement quoted by *The Times* and then its description of the person and circumstances surrounding the quotation. I omit the individual's name, in order to spare him possible embarassment.) " 'If he's that stupid, he waits in line an hour and doesn't know the rules, I let him get to the pump—and then I break his heart.'— . . . a service station attendant in Elizabeth, N. J., where gasoline rationing rules went into effect yesterday." For the benefit of readers who may be unfamiliar with the circumstances, what the attendant let unsuspecting motorists wait in line an hour to find out was that they were there on the wrong day: their license plates ended with an odd number when they should have ended with an even number, or *vice versa*.

The shortage of gasoline did not last long enough to make hatred between motorists and service station attendants become a regular feature of life. Today, normal relations have been restored, and the conditions of early 1974 have largely been forgotten. A more enduring and, therefore, probably more significant example is afforded by the relations between landlords and tenants in places like New York City, which has had almost continuous rent control since early in World War II. In New York City mutual hatred between landlords and tenants is commonplace. It has become the norm. Nothing is more frequent than complaints about things landlords do not do, unless it is complaints about things they are trying not to do. For example, depending on the particular circumstances, landlords do not provide, or are trying to avoid providing, such services as doormen, painting, repairs, and even heat. Tenants regard all of these things as theirs by right, and hate the landlords for not supplying them or trying not to supply them. Landlords, on the other hand, often regard the tenants as people who want to live without paying the proper rent. And, in many cases, while they watch the real value of their investments shrink to zero, they observe tenants able to afford expensive automobiles and adopt a style of life that is above their own—made possible by the low, controlled rents they pay. In such circumstances, there are landlords who derive positive enjoyment from such things as providing no heat, as well as save money by it.

Of course, it should be realized that there are also many cases—and undoubtedly a far greater number—in which the controls simply make it impossible for a landlord to provide many things, even if he wants to for the sake of keeping up his building, such as a new boiler or wiring system or any major repair or improvement. The controls often make these things impossible by leaving the landlord with too little capital to make the necessary investments. In the long run, controls must produce a progressive elimination of services even if landlords have the best will in the world.

How Repeal of Rent Controls Would Restore Harmony Between
Landlords and Tenants

The hatred between landlords and tenants would disappear in a rental market that was free of controls. Such a market would restore economic power to the tenants: it would give tenants the power to make landlords serve them out of self-interest.

Consider how a free market would bring this about.

The first effect of the establishment of a free rental market would be a jump in the previously controlled rents. This jump in rents would eliminate the shortage of rental housing. Immediately, even before any increase in the supply of rental housing could occur, the rise in rents would level the quantity of living space demanded down to equality with the limited supply that exists. In fact, the quantity of living space demanded would be reduced to a point somewhat below the supply that exists: landlords would have some vacancies on their hands at free-market rents. Precisely these vacancies are what would restore to tenants their economic power over landlords. At free-market rents, each tenant would be able to choose from a large number of apartments available in his price range. If he did not like the service his present landlord gave him, he would simply move when his lease expired. He would not be in the position of having to regard his present apartment as the only one in the world, and feel obliged to stay no matter how bad conditions in it became. By the same token, his landlord would no longer be able to count on easily replacing him. At free-market rents, his landlord would not have a waiting list of potential tenants, but vacancies on his hands. If he were to act in such a way as to make too many tenants move, he would either be unable to replace those tenants or he would have to reduce his rents below the general market in order to attract replacements. In this way, a landlord who did not satisfy his tenants would suffer financial loss. The landlord's self-interest would once again make him want to gain and keep tenants. Landlords would once again begin to compete with each other in terms of improved quality and service. They would have to, because they would need tenants once again, while tenants would no longer need any particular one of them.

## 2. The Impetus to Higher Costs

A major consequence of price controls and shortages is that they increase costs by means of creating various inefficiencies.

For example, in those cases in which goods come in a variety of models and price ranges, such as television sets, cars, lawn mowers—most goods—they create an incentive for producers to eliminate the more economical models, while cutting corners in the production of the more expensive models. The reason this occurs is that, on the one hand, the buyers are able and willing to pay the higher prices of the more expensive models rather than do without the good altogether, and, on the other hand, corner-cutting can generally be carried out more easily and with less serious results on the upper end of a product line than on the lower end. The process is actually a disguised way of raising prices and restoring profits. But it is a very uneconomic way of doing so, because, as a result of it, many buyers end up having to pay more for more expensive models that they don't really need or want than they would have had to pay in a free market for the models they really do want. For example, someone seeking a sixteen-inch black and white television set may end up having to buy a nineteen-inch color set, because that's all that's available. At the same time, the buyers who do want the better models find they are not as good any more.[1]

This process is a corollary of the decline in quality and service discussed in the previous section. And as soon as a shortage becomes severe enough, quality and service are cut to the point that buyers are offered models that would never appear in a free market in any price range. What happens is that sellers are led to cut corners in order to make relatively small savings to themselves and which have a great impact on the buyers. For example, situations can exist in which it is advantageous to a seller to save a few cents in manufacturing costs that later imposes many dollars in repair costs on the buyer. The harm inflicted on the buyers does not cause the sellers any economic loss, because at the controlled price there is a surplus of buyers eager to buy even a very inferior product.

In the same way that price controls and shortages make it impossible for a consumer to select his model on the basis of cost, they also make it impossible for a businessman to select his *methods of production* on the basis of cost. For one or more of the factors of production he requires may simply be unobtainable, because a price control has created a shortage of it. Under price controls, businessmen must select those methods of production for which the means happen to be available, and not necessarily those which have the lowest costs. The inability to find the right factors of production, of course, also frequently results in a decline in the quality of products as well, and should be viewed as a further and major cause of declining quality. The very deterioration of quality and service is itself a powerful source of higher costs both to businessmen and consumers, as I have already indicated. If, for example, a machine is produced or serviced in an inferior way, then even if its price remains the same, it will cause higher costs of maintenance and repair and may have to be replaced sooner. The same obviously applies to many consumers' goods. If a television set lasts only half as long and has to be repaired twice as often, it is a lot more expensive to own, even though its price remains the same.

Shortages of supplies and the mere threat of shortages themselves directly raise the costs of production. The effect of a shortage of a factor of production is to delay production. This causes the capital invested in all the other, complementary factors of production that depend on it, to have to be invested for a longer period of time than would otherwise be necessary. For example, a shortage of building-nails causes capital to be invested in half-finished houses and in piles of lumber for an unnecessary period of time. Since interest must be paid on capital for the full time it is invested, the effect of all such delays is to raise the interest cost of production. Similarly, the mere anticipation of shortages of supplies leads businessmen to hoard supplies of all types. This requires that production be carried on with a larger capital investment—in the additional stocks of supplies and in facilities for storing them. And this, of course, in turn, means extra interest costs and extra costs on account of the storage facilities. Finally, there is the loss of the valuable time of executives in searching for sources of supply and in performing all the paperwork required to comply with the government's price controls and any associated regulations, such as rationing.

It should be noted that shortages and the threat of shortages also directly raise costs to consumers. Consumers too suffer effects analogous to wasted investment and the need for more investment. For example, consumers who could not obtain gasoline could not use their cars or enjoy their country homes until such time as they could obtain gasoline. To that extent, the money they had spent for these complementary consumers' goods represented a kind of wasted investment. In addition, of course, consumers too are led to hoard supplies and thus to tie up larger sums of money in stocks of goods and, quite possibly, incur additional costs on account of acquiring extra storage facilities—for example, extra home freezers, if there should be the threat of a food shortage. Finally, one must mention the wasted man-hours spent in waiting lines during every shortage, which, while not a money cost, are nonetheless a real hardship and burden and can well be at the expense of actual working time.

To some extent, the rise in production costs that price controls and shortages bring about may come out of profits. But it certainly does not always do so—as, for example, when it is a case of concentrating on the production of more expensive models that have correspondingly higher controlled prices. Moreover, it is possible for most or even all of the rise in costs not to come out of profits—at least, not out of nominal profits. For the government may very well follow a policy of allowing prices to rise insofar as the producers can prove a rise in costs. This was the case to a large extent in World War II. During World War II, most defense contracts were written on a cost-plus basis—that is, the government paid defense contractors their costs plus a percentage of their costs as profit. The same principle seems often to have been applied in setting the price controls on civilian goods. This procedure, it should be realized, is tantamount to the positive encouragement of extra costs, because it makes the incurrence of extra costs the way to raise profits. It thereby totally perverts the profit motive from being the driving force of greater efficiency to being a driving force of greater inefficiency.

By their very nature, price controls pervert the operation of the profit motive. One must charge to their account not only all of the actual inefficiencies they create, but all of the potential improvements in efficiency they prevent. Price controls create a situation in which it is no longer necessary to reduce costs or improve quality in order to raise profits. In a free market, the price every firm receives is the very best it can obtain under the prevailing state of the market. A firm has the legal right to ask a higher price than this in a free market, but does not ask such a price because it would drive away too many customers: its customers would turn to competitors, and new competitors would probably appear; or, even if there were no close competitors, its customers would simply buy too much less of its type of product to make a further rise in price worthwhile.

Thus, in a free market, a firm must accept the fact that its price is limited by forces beyond its control. In order to increase its profits, it cannot simply raise its price—it must reduce its costs of production or improve the quality of its products to attract new buyers. That is final. There is simply no other choice. But under price controls, the price a firm receives is not something that is imposed upon it by an unyielding external reality, to which it has no choice but to adapt its own conduct. The price it receives can be changed in its favor—if only it can prevail upon the officials in charge of the price controls to relax them, or if it can find ways of evading them. Thus, the firm's focus necessarily switches. Instead of being focused on reducing costs and improving quality as the ways of increasing profits, it becomes focused on ways to have the price controls relaxed or to evade them. This alone represents a radical change in the way a firm directs its talents and energies.

Furthermore, as we have seen, firms lose the incentive to reduce costs or improve quality. Price controls and the shortages they create place *these things* beyond a firm's power. Even if it wanted to, a firm has no power to reduce its costs or improve its quality when shortages prevent it from obtaining the appropriate means of producing its products or cause the quality of those means to deteriorate. But, of course, even if it had the power, there is simply no reason under price controls and shortages for a firm to reduce its costs or improve the quality of its products. There is no reason to improve the quality of its products, because its customers will snap up goods of lower quality than it now offers. It has no reason to reduce its costs (except at the expense of quality) in an environment in which customers are eager to pay prices that would cover substantially higher costs and in which, besides, it has little or no prospect of profiting from any cost reductions it might achieve.

This last is the situation of every price-controlled firm in a period of inflation, insofar as its suppliers are still free to raise their prices. Inflation will raise the costs and destroy the profitability of such a firm no matter what it does to control its costs. To the extent that it succeeds in retarding the rise in its costs, the price-control authorities will use that very fact to deny its need for a price increase. The only effect of cutting costs in such a situation is to postpone the day that one is permitted to obtain relief by raising one's prices. In other words, cost reductions simply cease to pay, even if they are still within the firm's power to make.

In sum, price controls and shortages thoroughly pervert or destroy the operation of the profit motive. In place of profit incentives to improve quality and reduce costs, they make it possible to profit by means of reducing quality and allowing costs to rise. For they destroy the resistance of buyers to declining quality and to higher prices to cover higher costs. Indeed, they often necessitate declining quality and positively encourage higher costs.


The Administrative Chaos of Price Controls

It should be realized that the willingness of the government to allow higher controlled prices on the basis of higher costs of production introduces a significant complication into the administration of price controls. The complication arises because different parts of the supply of the same good will have different costs of production. As a result, the government must set a *number* of controlled prices on the identical good, depending on the particular cost of production incurred to produce the particular batch of goods in question. This procedure is generally accompanied by further procedures, all of which help to make price controls an administrative nightmare.

What the government does is to allow producers to sell to distributors (or to further processors) at varying prices, corresponding to their varying costs. The distributors, however, are required to sell to the ultimate consumers at a *uniform* price, based on an average of the varying costs to them as a group. By itself this procedure would threaten some distributors with financial ruin while offering other distributors the prospect of correspondingly higher profits. For all distributors must sell at the same price, while their costs may be significantly above or below the average on the basis of which that price is set. In order to deal with this problem, the government must assign to each distributor his "fair share" of low-cost and high-cost goods, or force the distributors to agree to some scheme of mutual compensation.

This sort of situation exists today in the oil industry. Those firms that are supplied mainly with so-called "old" oil at $5.25 a barrel are forced to compensate the firms that must rely mainly on "new" oil, which is controlled at a much higher price, or on imported oil, which is not subject to controls at all and sells for about $14.50 a barrel. This is because all firms must sell at essentially the same prices to consumers, and the consumer prices are based on an average of the prices of old, new, and imported oil. Under this arrangement, some oil companies are forced to turn over hundreds of millions of dollars, called "entitlements," to other oil companies.

The entitlement system is not only administratively chaotic, but actually represents an expropriation of the wealth of American oil companies for the benefit of the Arabs. Under it, the profits that are made by refiners that buy "old" oil at $5.25 a barrel are transferred largely to those refiners that buy Arab oil at $14.50 a barrel. This means that money that should have gone to purchase American oil is instead used to finance the purchase of Arab oil It is literally a system for keeping money out of the hands of American producers and putting it into the hands of the Arabs.

### 3. Chaos in the Personal Distribution of Consumers' Goods

In Chapter II, we saw that, in a free market, consumers' goods in limited supply are distributed to the individual consumers in accordance with a combination of their relative wealth and income, on the one side, and the relative strength of their needs and desires for the goods, on the other. Price controls and shortages totally disrupt this principle of distribution. What they substitute is not another principle, but merely the rule of the random, of the arbitrary and the accidental—the rule of chaos.

One should think back to the gasoline shortage and consider what determined the distribution of gasoline. It was a matter of luck and favoritism. Gasoline went to those who happened to be on the spot when deliveries were made to gas stations, or who had the time to waste waiting hours in line or following gasoline delivery trucks around. It went to those who happened to be friendly with service station owners or the employees of service stations. Both the wealth and the needs of the buyers were made irrelevant. The country's most productive businessmen were placed on an equal footing with welfare recipients: the value of their higher incomes was simply nullified. It was just a question of who arrived first or who had the right friends. By the same token, people whose very livelihood depended on gasoline were in no better position to obtain it than people wanting it for the most marginal purposes. Again, it was just a question of who got there first or who had the right friends.

Rent-controlled apartments are distributed in just the same way. If meat were placed under price control, it would not be long before it too was distributed in this way. The distribution of any good subjected to price controls becomes chaotic just as soon as the controls produce a shortage.

### 4. Chaos in the Geographical Distribution of Goods Among Local Markets

We already know that price controls prevent an area that has an urgent need for a product from obtaining it by bidding up its price in competition with other areas. When price controls are joined by shortages, a further major element of chaos is introduced. Under the combination of price controls and shortages, not only is the price of a good prevented from rising, but also, paradoxically, it is prevented from *falling*.

Where a shortage exists, an increase in the supply of a good, or a decrease in the demand for it, does not reduce the price; *it merely reduces the severity of the shortage*. Where a shortage exists, an additional supply merely makes it possible for someone to buy at the same—controlled—price who previously could not do so; likewise, a decrease in demand merely means a reduction in the number of those contending for the supply who must go away empty-handed. The price does not fall in such circumstances because it is already too low, as a result of price control.

The significance of the fact that prices can neither rise nor fall is that if price controls and shortages exist in various local markets, a broad range of *indeterminacy* is introduced into the distribution of a good among them. Because of shortages, producers are in a position to sell a larger quantity in every such market without any reduction in the price in that market or, therefore, in the profitability of sending supplies to it. All that they have to do is find an additional supply of the good to send. What this situation makes possible, in essence, is that producers can send their goods practically anywhere, in widely varying proportions, and it doesn't matter to them. If they send too little to some areas, the price controls in those areas prevent prices and profitability from rising and halting the drain. Meanwhile, in the areas into which they are sending too much, shortages prevent prices and profitability from falling and stemming the inflow. In a word, the geographical distribution of a good simply becomes random and chaotic, disconnected from the consumers' needs and purchasing power.

Consider the following case, based on the experience of the gasoline shortage. The price control on gasoline created a shortage in the whole northeastern region of the United States. Almost every state and locality in that region had its own individual shortage. In this context, it largely ceased to matter to the oil companies how their gasoline was distributed among the various areas in the region. Suppose, for example, that they sent a million gallons less a month to New Jersey and a million gallons more a month to Connecticut. It didn't matter to them. The price of gasoline in New Jersey and the profitability of sending it there could not rise even if New Jersey received hardly any gasoline at all. Price controls prevented it. At the same time, the price of gasoline in Connecticut and the profitability of sending it there could not fall—until the shortage in Connecticut was totally eliminated. Of course, just the reverse could have occurred. A million gallons less a month could have been sent to Connecticut, and a million gallons more a month could have been sent to New Jersey. Price control would have prevented any rise in the price and profitability of sending gasoline to Connecticut; and, so long as it existed, the shortage would have prevented any fall in the price and profitability of sending gasoline to New Jersey.

This indeterminacy introduced by price controls explains how some areas can suffer relatively mild shortages, and other areas very severe shortages, and how their positions can easily be reversed. The significance of this is that price controls not only create shortages, *but make it a random matter how the burden of those shortages is distributed*. In the gasoline shortage, for example, it would have been possible for the various areas to share the burden of the overall shortage in any proportions. All might have suffered more or less equally, or some particular areas might have borne almost the entire shortage, while others suffered almost none at all, or any intermediate situation might have existed. The actual chaos that did exist fully accords with this principle.

Precisely how the burdens are distributed is the result of accident. In the gasoline shortage, the main accidental factor was that the Northeast happened to be the region most heavily dependent on imports, and so it bore the far greater part of the nationwide burden. Within the Northeast, further accidental factors played a role, such as the very time of the year when the controls were imposed. To understand this last point, imagine that the controls are imposed in the summertime. In the summer, there is a large demand for gasoline in many resort areas. As a result, the wholesale price of gasoline in these areas is at a seasonal high in relation to the wholesale price in many city areas. It is high enough to cover such special summertime costs as may be entailed in having to bring in supplies from more distant refineries than is necessary at other seasons, when the local demand in the resort areas is smaller. The imposition of controls freezes this seasonal price relationship and carries it forward to the fall and winter, when there is a different pattern of demand, and when there should be a different set of gasoline price relationships to reflect it. Given the perpetuation of the summertime price relationships, what happens is that gasoline continues to be heavily supplied to the summer resort areas—perhaps to the point of pushing the price there somewhat below the level permitted by the controls. As a result, no shortage whatever exists in these resort areas. The entire shortage is concentrated in the cities. If the controls are imposed in the wintertime, instead of the summertime, then, of course, the reverse situation develops.

Further chaos in distribution can be caused by such things as small bureaucratic adjustments in the price controls. For example, it is quite possible that after the controls are imposed, the officials in charge may make some minor adjustments here and there, such as for the purpose of rectifying the kind of seasonal problems I have just described. In doing this, they can unleash major movements in supply which they may not be aware of causing. Imagine, for example, that they decide to permit, say, a penny a gallon rise in the price of gasoline in one particular major city. If this small rise makes this particular city a relatively more profitable market than other markets, the various distributors will want to sell more heavily in this city; and as long as a shortage exists in the city, they can do so without any reduction in the newly increased price and profit margin. The effect will be that this particular city will tend to be supplied very heavily, perhaps to the point of totally eliminating its local shortage, while supplies will simply disappear from other markets to the same extent.

Frankly, it is impossible to know all the different factors that might suddenly unleash major movements in supply. The essential point is that under price controls and shortages, movements in supply have no effect on price and profitability until a local shortage is totally eliminated, at which point the local price and profitability will begin to fall and the further movement of supplies to that area will stop. Short of that point, massive movements of supply are possible in response to very small differences in profitability. Anything that can create such differences can cause such movements.

### 5. Chaos in the Distribution of Factors
### of Production Among Their Various Uses

The discussion of random geographical distribution applies equally to the distribution of factors of production in limited supply among their various uses. If a shortage exists of all the different products that a factor of production is used to produce, then there is a ready and waiting market for more of each such product. More of each such product can be sold without causing any reduction in its price or profitability, until the shortage of that particular product is totally eliminated. All that it is necessary for producers to do is find a way of getting more of any such product to the market.

In this situation, the allocation of a factor of production among its various uses becomes utterly chaotic. A factor of production can be withdrawn from the production of any of its products and added on to the production of any other of its products. The price and profitability of the product in reduced supply cannot rise to halt the decrease in supply. The price and profitability of the product in expanded supply cannot fall to stop the increase in supply.

Again, the oil shortage provides an excellent illustration of the principle. During the oil shortage there was a shortage of all the different oil products: gasoline, heating oil, jet fuel, propane, kerosene, etc. In these circumstances, it essentially ceased to matter to the oil refineries what they produced. If they took a million barrels of crude oil away from the production of gasoline and added it on to the production of heating oil, they could sell the additional heating oil with absolutely no reduction in its price or profitability, because of the shortage of heating oil. And if they did the reverse—if they took a million barrels of crude oil away from the production of heating oil and added it on to the production of gasoline—they could sell the additional gasoline with absolutely no reduction in its price or profitability, because of the shortage of gasoline. Of course, the price and profitability of the product being cut back could not rise—it was controlled.

The result was that the production of the various oil products was made random and chaotic. Practically any combination of products was possible. The only limits were those set by the possible total elimination of particular shortages. For example, gasoline production might have been expanded at the expense of heating oil production up to the point where the gasoline shortage came to an end and any further increase in the supply of gasoline would have forced a reduction in its price. At that point, the whole burden of the combined shortage of gasoline and heating oil would have been borne by heating oil. Or, of course, the reverse could have occurred. Heating oil production might have been expanded at the expense of gasoline production up to the point of eliminating the shortage of heating oil and throwing the whole burden of the combined shortage on gasoline production.

Either of these extremes or any intermediate situation was possible, and not just with regard to gasoline and heating oil, of course, but with regard to the entire list of oil products. Any of them might have been produced up to the point of no shortage, or any of them might have suffered a drastic reduction in production. Moreover, the position of the various products could suddenly have been reversed—with the relatively abundant ones suddenly becoming short, and the short ones suddenly becoming relatively abundant. Furthermore, if we add in the existence of geographical chaos, the situation could have been different in different parts of the country at the same time—for example, a severe shortage of gasoline and little or no shortage of heating oil in New Jersey and just the opposite in Connecticut.

The chaos that existed during the oil shortage fully accords with this description. And the same kind of random, accidental factors determined what actually did occur as in the case of geographical chaos. For example, the time of the year when the controls happened to be imposed played an important role in determining to what extent the overall oil shortage fell on heating oil or on gasoline. Controls imposed in the summertime tend to cause relatively abundant supplies of gasoline and a severe shortage of heating oil. This is because they impose the freeze at a time when the price of gasoline is high in relation to the price of heating oil, with the result that it is profitable to go on producing gasoline and not profitable to step up the production of heating oil even after the summer ends.

Conversely, controls imposed in the wintertime tend to cause a relatively abundant production of heating oil and a severe shortage of gasoline. Since our controls were originally imposed in August of 1971, it is not surprising that the first major petroleum product to develop a shortage was heating oil, which occurred in the late winter and early spring of 1973, months before the Arab embargo. (Subsequently, the government took special steps to assure the supply of heating oil, and thereafter the burden of the oil shortage fell more heavily on gasoline and the other petroleum products.)

As in the case of geographical chaos, bureaucratic adjustments in the controls can cause sudden major shifts in supply among the various products of a factor of production. By making the production of any one particular product of a factor of production somewhat more profitable than the others, for example, the officials administering the controls can bring about a sudden expansion in its production up to the point of totally eliminating its particular shortage, while, of course, correspondingly worsening the shortages of other products of the factor in an unpredictable way. And if they suddenly reduce the profitability of a particular item, they can make the supply of it disappear and other items show up in its place, again, in an unpredictable way.

*Anything* that produces even slight changes in the relative profitability of the various products of a factor of production, whether a bureaucratic change in the price-control regulations, or anything else, can produce major changes in supply when shortages exist. As just one example, imagine that the uncontrolled price of some of the chemical additives used to make gasoline changed. If the prices of these chemicals rose, the profitability of gasoline might suddenly be reduced below that of other oil products. Since the price of gasoline could not rise as its supply was cut back, while the price of other oil products would not fall as their supply was increased, it would now pay to shift as much crude oil as possible away from gasoline production to the production of all other oil products. Conversely, if the price of the chemical additives fell instead of rose, then gasoline production would suddenly become more profitable, and a massive increase in gasoline production would probably occur at the expense of the production of all other oil products.

A principle that emerges from this discussion is that *price controls and shortages create tremendous instability in supply*. The supply of everything subjected to controls is subject to sudden, massive, and unpredictable shortages.

Hoarding

The chaos in supply caused by controls has a further important consequence, one that I have already noted in other connections, but which deserves some additional elaboration and stress here. This is the fact that shortages and the fear of shortages cause hoarding. If a person cannot count on being able to buy something when he wants it, because, overnight, it may disappear from the market, then he had better try to buy it when he can, so that he will have it available when he needs it. The effect of this is that price controls and shortages artificially expand the demand for everything even more. Price controls not only expand the quantity of goods demanded by virtue of artificially holding down prices, but also by virtue of creating shortages and then the need to hoard, to cope with the shortages. The demand price controls create for the purpose of hoarding is a demand that does not exist even potentially in a free market—i.e., it is not even a submarginal demand—because it would serve no purpose whatever in a free market. But under price controls and shortages, hoarding becomes a matter of survival and greatly adds to demand.

The effect of this is that the irrationality of price controls goes beyond even what I have previously described. In Chapter II, I explained how price controls prevent the most vital and urgent employments of a factor of production from outbidding its most marginal employments. I explained, for example, how they prevented truckers delivering food supplies from outbidding housewives wanting gasoline for marginal shopping trips; how they prevented the operators of oil rigs needing oil products from outbidding homeowners seeking oil to heat their garages. Actually, the situation is even worse. Under price controls, the most vital and urgent employments of a factor of production are prevented from outbidding not only its most marginal employments, but, from the standpoint of a free economy, employments that could not even qualify as submarginal; that is, employments for hoarding purposes.

Under price controls and shortages it is entirely possible for people to be unable to get to work, to be without food, or even to freeze to death, not only because they are prohibited from outbidding the marginal employments of the oil, or whatever factor of production it may be, but because products are being hoarded by other people in fear of this very kind of possibility happening to them. The consequence is that price controls and shortages not only sacrifice men's well-being and very lives to the unearned, fleeting gains of other men, but, very largely, to a hoarding demand created by price controls themselves. In effect, men are sacrificed to the controls themselves.

### 6. Shortages and the Spillover of Demand

*The effect of a shortage of any particular commodity is to cause the unsatisfied demand for that commodity to spill over and add to the demand for other commodities.*

We have already had a glimpse of this principle earlier in this chapter, in our discussion of people ending up having to buy more expensive models of goods as the result of the unavailability of less expensive models. For example, as we saw, the man who wants a sixteen-inch black and white television set may end up having to buy a nineteen-inch color set, because there is a shortage of the sixteen-inch sets and he cannot obtain one; so he settles for this substitute.

This principle applies not only to close mutual substitutes, such as different models of the same good, but also to goods which are totally dissimilar in their nature and function. For example, if our prospective buyer of a television set cannot find any model television set that satisfies him, he will eventually decide to buy some other kind of good. He may decide to buy a suit or to apply the sum he wanted to spend for a television set to the purchase of a better car or to any one of thousands of things or combinations of things. In this way, the money that price controls prevent from being spent in one channel is diverted to another channel.

This diversion of demand, it should be realized, takes place almost immediately. For example, even if our prospective television set buyer decides to add the price of the set to his savings, in the hope of being able to find the set later on, still, the demand for other things will rise almost immediately. This is because he will almost certainly deposit his savings in a bank, which will lend them out. As a result, a borrower will be put in the position of being able to buy something with the money our man had wanted to use for a television set.

The effect of this diversion or spillover of demand depends on whether or not price controls apply to the second-choice goods that people turn to. If these goods too are controlled, then the effect tends to be a worsening of the shortages of these goods. I will not elaborate on this consequence, however, until we begin our discussion of universal price controls, in the next chapter. If price controls do not apply to the second-choice goods, then the effect of the spillover of demand is simply to drive the prices of uncontrolled goods still higher and to make the profitability of their production in comparison to that of the controlled goods still greater.

This principle concerning the effects of the spillover of demand in a partially price-controlled economy has a number of important implications.

Why Partial Controls Are Contrary to Purpose

First, it shows that "selective" or partial price controls, that is, price controls imposed merely on certain goods only, are contrary to any rational purpose the government might have in imposing them.[2] The government imposes controls on the goods which it believes are the most vital. It imposes the controls because it believes they will enable people to obtain these goods who otherwise could not have obtained them because of too high a price. The government leaves uncontrolled those goods whose production it considers to be relatively unimportant. The effect of this policy, however, is to destroy the production of the very goods the government regards as vital, while encouraging the production of the goods it considers unimportant. This occurs because the price controls restrict or altogether destroy the profitability of producing the controlled goods. At the same time, the shortages the price controls create cause demand to spill over into the markets for the uncontrolled goods and thereby make their production still more profitable.

For example, the government might control the price of milk on the grounds that it is a vital necessity, and leave uncontrolled the price of ice cream and soft drinks on the grounds that they are trivial "luxuries," not worthy of its attention. The effect of this policy is to reduce the profitability of milk production in comparison with these and all other uncontrolled goods. As a result, it brings about a fall in the production of milk; this, together with the increase in demand for milk resulting from its too low price, creates a shortage of milk. The effect of the shortage of milk is to cause the unsatisfied demand for milk to spill over into the markets for uncontrolled goods, including, of course, ice cream and soft drinks, whose relative profitability is then further enhanced. The effect of the government's action, therefore, is to destroy the production of milk, which it regards as necessary and vital and wants people to have, and to promote the production of such goods as ice cream and soft drinks, which it considers unimportant.

Clearly, it would be less illogical if the government imposed controls on the things it considered unimportant and whose production it did not mind seeing destroyed, and left free the production of goods it considered vital. Nevertheless, governments do not do this, and again and again—in the early stages of a war, for example—they impose controls that undermine the production of necessities, while the so-called "ash-tray industries" and the night clubs and the cabarets flourish. For temporarily at least, these lines of business are left uncontrolled, on the grounds of being unimportant, and are therefore able to benefit from the spillover of demand caused by the shortages of necessities.

### How Price Controls Actually Raise Prices

A second implication of the principle that shortages cause a spillover of demand and a rise in the prices of uncontrolled goods is that selective or partial controls cannot hold down the general price level. The expectation that they can is based on the erroneous belief that the problem of inflation consists in the rise of this or that group of prices and can be solved by prohibiting a particular group of prices from rising. The fact is that such controls hold down the prices of some goods only by making the prices of other goods rise all the more.

Indeed, the effect of partial price controls is actually to *raise* the general price level. Partial controls have this effect, because while they leave aggregate demand and spending unchanged, they reduce the efficiency of production and, therefore, the aggregate amount of production and thus supply. We have seen that they destroy vital industries, such as the electric power industry and the oil industry, on which the production of all other industries depends. In the course of destroying an industry, they reduce the quality of its products and the service associated with them, thereby raising maintenance and replacement costs for the buyers of the products. We saw also that controls cause resort to unnecessarily expensive models and methods of production, and lead to a system of cost-plus pricing. And we have seen that they create utter chaos in the geographical distribution of the products of a controlled industry and in the combination of the various products that such an industry produces; this disrupts all subsequent production that depends on these industries, and thus reduces aggregate supply. In all these ways, therefore, partial controls actually raise the general price level.

The Absurdity of the Claim Price Controls "Save Money"

A third, closely related implication is that the supporters of price controls are badly mistaken in claiming that any particular price control "saves people money," and in arguing that the repeal of any given control will "cost" people this or that amount of money. This may be true in the short run for some individuals, who are lucky enough to obtain the goods they desire at below-market prices. But it is never true in the aggregate. In the aggregate, a control saves people money only in the sense of making them spend less for the controlled goods. At the same time, it makes them spend more for the uncontrolled goods. In the aggregate, they do not spend any less money. They do, however, receive fewer goods. Clearly, whatever saving or gain some buyers may have by virtue of controls is always at the expense of a greater loss to other buyers.

Indeed, in view of the fact that controls tend to destroy the controlled industries, the only kind of long-run "saving" they can achieve for anyone, including the people who might temporarily gain from them, is a rather bizarre one. It consists in preventing a person from spending the money he wants to spend for the goods he wants to buy. In this sense, the drivers who could not obtain gasoline at the controlled prices "saved money" on gasoline. Instead of having the gasoline they desperately wanted and which they valued far above the controlled price, they had money left over to spend on other things which they wanted much less. Such savings are obviously absurd and contrary to purpose. They are comparable to making a person save money by not buying food or medicine, or anything he values more, so that he may have money for something he values less—if he is alive to spend it. Yet this is the only kind of "saving" that controls can achieve in the long run, and it is the only kind of saving they achieve right from the very beginning for whomever suffers from the shortages they create.

As will be shown in the next chapter, total or universal controls—price controls on all goods—may be said to "save people money" in an even more bizarre way than partial controls. By virtue of creating a shortage of everything, and thus making money simply unspendable, universal controls enable people to save money in the sense of having it available for such purposes as papering their walls or lighting their fires with it. And as production declines under universal controls, and the volume of spending that can take place at the controlled prices accordingly drops further, the money that people "save" in this absurd way grows greater.

It follows from our discussion that in the aggregate the repeal of price controls would not cost people anything. If universal controls exist and are repealed, people would spend more money, but this greater spending would represent an exchange of otherwise useless paper for valuable goods, whose production would be greatly increased as a result of the repeal of the controls. If partial controls exist and are repealed, then the effect is a shift in the pattern of spending away from the previously uncontrolled goods to the newly uncontrolled goods. The prices of the former would tend to drop while the prices of the latter would tend to rise. But since the effect of the repeal is an increase in total production and supply, the general price level must tend to fall. For the same total demand with a larger total supply means a lower price level. The repeal of any partial control, therefore, must always tend to *reduce* the general price level by virtue of its effect of increasing production. It is only the repeal of a control, therefore, not the imposition of a control, that can truly be said to save people money.

How Rent Controls Raise Rents

The principle that shortages cause the unsatisfied demand for controlled goods to spill over into the market for uncontrolled goods and to raise their prices applies to rent controls as they have existed in recent decades in places like New York City.

Such rent controls are partial price controls in an even more restricted sense than we have considered up to now. They are partial controls not only in the sense that they apply only to specific goods, but also in the further sense that they apply only to part of the supply even of these goods. For example, in New York City all housing completed since January 1974 is totally exempt from rent controls. Prior to August 1971, all housing completed since February 1947 had been free of controls, and certain still earlier housing, considered "luxury housing," had also been exempted. (All this previously uncontrolled housing is now subjected to controls in the form of government limitations on annual rent increases.) Perhaps even more important has been the fact that while rents have been controlled in New York City, they were generally uncontrolled in the surrounding suburban counties and in most of the rest of the country. Nor were the prices of houses controlled anywhere.

As a result of the fact that rent control has had only partial application, large numbers of people in New York City were able to escape its effects. Those who could afford them were able to find uncontrolled apartments or, in many cases, buy houses, co-ops, or condominiums in the city. Those who could not afford to live in New York City were able to find places to live outside the city.

Before considering the effects of this diversion of demand caused by partial rent controls, it will be well to project the consequences of controls applied to all of these alternatives. In other words, let us project the consequences of a fully price-controlled housing market on a regional and national scale. We will see that some of the potentially most disastrous effects of rent controls have been avoided because of the relatively limited scope of the controls.

If the entire housing market were controlled, housing would be artificially cheap in all of its forms and everywhere. The quantity demanded of all types of housing would therefore exceed the supply. This would be true all across the country. As a result, there would be a shortage of living space and no way around it. People would simply be unable to find space in New York City, and they would be unable to find it in the surrounding counties or anywhere else in the country. There would be people desperate for living space with absolutely no way to obtain it. They would need apartments and houses but with no better chance of finding them than they had of finding gasoline at the height of the gasoline shortage.

What might happen in such circumstances? The answer is two things worth thinking about: *The government would contemplate the assignment of boarders to private homes and apartments. And it would contemplate the restriction of the internal freedom of migration.*

On the first point, the argument would be made that people cannot be left to sleep in the streets and that in the "housing emergency," or whatever it might be called, it was necessary for those fortunate enough to have space, to share it with those not fortunate enough to have space. As to the second point, it would soon become obvious that in the circumstances of a pervasive housing shortage, the influx of additional people into any area would have the effect of making the local housing shortage worse. Each area would therefore become anxious to keep out as many new arrivals as possible on the grounds of their worsening the local housing shortage. Each area would try to set up barriers to in-migration and try to prevail upon the federal government to keep people where they were.

This state of affairs actually exists in many countries. For example, it is no accident, but precisely for reasons such as these, that the Russian government deliberately restricts the number of inhabitants of its various cities and controls the internal movement of the Russian population. The communist sympathizers and apologists who boast about how inexpensive housing is in the communist countries—extremely limited and wretched housing, it should be noted—do not realize that precisely this is what creates a nationwide housing shortage in those countries. They do not realize that the low rents they are so proud of virtually necessitate restrictions on the internal movement of people—even apart from all other factors working in the same direction in the communist countries. In addition, of course, families cannot take their privacy for granted in the communist countries. Millions of families are forced to live in communal apartments. Often, two families must share a single room, separated from each other only by a curtain—just as depicted in the movie *Ninotchka*.

Fortunately, in the areas of the United States where rent control has existed, such as New York City, people have been able to escape such disastrous effects, because the controls have been confined to a very limited part of the overall housing market. But, even so, the consequences have been severe.

Let us pass over quickly the consequences as they affect the part of the housing supply actually subjected to controls, and then focus on the consequences as they affect the part of the housing supply that is left free of controls.

We know that controls create a shortage of the housing to which they apply because people scramble for apartments at artificially low rents. We know that this fact, coupled with the lack of capital on the part of landlords that results from restricted profits, causes the quality of such housing to decline, in the process unleashing a spiral of mutually reinforcing hatreds between tenants and landlords. Ultimately, as the costs of operating buildings continue to rise, because of inflation, the effect of rent control is to cause widespread abandonments of buildings by their owners. Such abandonments have been going on for some years now in New York City, at the rate of tens of thousands of apartments per year. As a result of rent control, there are growing areas in New York City—in the South Bronx, for example—that have been reduced to the status of a primitive village, with people living without electricity and having to fetch their water from public fire hydrants. (Such facts are reported every so often in *The New York Times*.)

As for the uncontrolled housing, we know from the present chapter that the shortage of housing that is under controls causes the unsatisfied demand for such housing to spill over and enlarge the demand for uncontrolled housing. This phenomenon and its consequences must be examined more closely.

The controls on rents bring space within the reach of people who otherwise could not have afforded it. That is their purpose and that is what they achieve. But to whatever extent the controls make it possible for some people to obtain space who otherwise could not have obtained it, they simultaneously *reduce* the space that is available for other people, who could have afforded to rent that space in a free market. These other people, of course, must then direct their demand for space into other channels, with the result that rents on uncontrolled space in the area rise.

As far as the market is concerned, *partial rent controls are equivalent to a reduction in the supply of rental housing*. They take part of the housing stock off the market by giving it to people who could not afford the market rents. This leaves less of a supply of housing for the market and, consequently, increases rents on the diminished supply that is available for the market.

Perhaps the best and clearest way to understand these points is to think once again of the conditions of an auction. So imagine that an auctioneer is holding up two units of the same good. Imagine further that there are three bidders for these units. One bidder, imagine, is willing to bid a maximum of $300 for one of these units, if necessary. Another bidder is willing to go as high as $200, if necessary. The third bidder, assume, can afford to bid no more than $100—that is his maximum limit in the bidding. In a free market, the price at which these two units will be sold will be above $100 and below $200. The price will have to be above $100 to eliminate the weakest bidder. It will have to be below $200, in order to find buyers for both units. It will tend to be the same for both buyers because there is usually no way to discriminate between them. Let's assume the actual price turns out to be $150: too high for the weakest bidder, yet low enough for both of the other bidders.

The weakest bidder has been excluded from this market. What must happen if we begin to feel sorry for him? Suppose people begin to feel so sorry for him that they get a law passed that orders the auctioneer to give him one of the units of the supply at a price he can afford—say, $50. In that case, he gets his unit at $50. But now, as a result of this, instead of the auctioneer having two units to auction off in the market, he has only one; the supply available for the market has fallen. And this one unit will now have to sell at a price somewhere above *$200* and below $300—say, $250. It has to be high enough now to eliminate *the middle bidder* instead of the weakest bidder. All that has happened is that one party has gotten part of the supply at an artificially low price and has caused the price on the re-maining supply to go high enough to eliminate another party. The party eliminated could have afforded the market price if it were determined by the full available supply. But he cannot afford the market price *as deter-mined by the artificially reduced supply.*

This auction example does not differ in any essential respect from the case of partial rent controls. Partial rent controls give part of the supply of housing to some people at below-market rents. To whatever extent these people could not have afforded as much space in a free market as they obtain under rent control, they leave that much less space available in the uncon-trolled market. Consequently, rents in the uncontrolled market must rise that much higher—in order to level down the quantity demanded to equality with the reduced supply that is left for the market. For example, if the total housing supply in a city is one million rooms, and we give half of those rooms to people who could not have afforded them at free-market rents, then we are correspondingly depriving other people of those rooms who could have afforded them at free-market rents. In the process we make the rents on the uncontrolled half-million rooms rise so high that that dimin-ished number of rooms is all that people will be willing and able to rent in the uncontrolled segment of the market. In other words, we make the open-market rents balance demand and supply at a supply of half a million rooms instead of a million rooms. People are eliminated from the market who could have afforded market rents *as determined by the full supply of rental housing.* These people cannot afford market rents *as determined by the artificially diminished supply of rental housing that results from rent con-trol.*

The fact that partial rent controls act to raise rents on the uncontrolled part of the housing supply is reinforced by the fact that they increase the *costs* of providing rental housing. This occurs because the existence of controls on some housing today implies that the housing that is presently free of controls may later on be brought under controls. The threat of being brought under rent controls in the future makes it necessary for landlords of presently uncontrolled buildings to recover their investments more rapidly. For example, instead of looking forward to recovering their investments over a fifty-year period, say, the threat of rent control being imposed may make them want to recover their investments over a ten-year period, or even a five-year period, to be safe. This represents a great jump in the costs of providing new rental housing, and it explains why high rents on uncontrolled buildings do not result in corresponding new construction.

Insofar as rent control comes to be regarded as a regular institution, to be imposed at any future time the government may desire, the effect is to make today's tenants in uncontrolled buildings pay for the spoils of tomorrow's prospective beneficiaries of rent control. This artificial increase in the costs of new housing, it should be realized, is one of the reasons why today's so-called "luxury housing" is often inferior in many respects to housing constructed in earlier decades. The reason is that it is not genuine "luxury housing," but rather cheap housing that must be rented at luxury rates in order to offset the prospective losses that are expected to be caused by rent controls in the future.

Even if rent controls were not expected to be extended, partial rent controls would prevent the premium rents on uncontrolled housing from being eliminated. In a free market, rents tend to equal the costs of constructing and maintaining housing plus only as much profit as is required to yield the going rate of profit. Under partial rent controls, the rents on the uncontrolled portion of the market tend to permanently exceed this level, and exceed it the more, the larger is the proportion of the housing stock under controls. The reason for this is that if the supply of uncontrolled housing were increased to the point that the rents on such housing were no higher than costs plus an allowance for the going rate of profit, the danger would exist that if rent controls were ever repealed, rents in the open market would then be driven below cost plus the going rate of profit. For the repeal of rent controls would throw back on the market all of the housing diverted from the market to tenants paying below-market rents. If open-market rents were already no more than equal to cost plus the going rate of profit, this increase in the supply available for the market would drive them below that point.

Obviously, the greater the stock of housing presently under rent controls and therefore capable of being added to the supply available for the market, the greater is the potential reduction in open-market rents. The implication of this is that the larger the proportion of the housing stock under rent controls, the more must rents on the uncontrolled housing stock exceed costs, because the greater is the potential fall in open-market rents.

Thus, so long as they are in force, partial rent controls raise rents on uncontrolled housing, whether landlords expect them to be extended to the uncontrolled housing or to be removed from the housing to which they presently apply.

It follows from the preceding discussion that when partial rent controls are repealed, not only do rents in the open market fall, but the construction of new housing becomes much more profitable at any given level of open-market rents. For the repeal of the partial controls reduces the threat of new housing later on being subjected to controls, and thus extends the period of time over which investments in housing can be recovered. At the same time, the repeal eliminates any fear hanging over the market concerning the possible adverse effects of repeal on profitability. Thus, unless the decline in open-market rents is quite drastic, the effect of the repeal of partial rent controls is not only lower open-market rents, but also a surge in the construction of new housing at those lower rents.

The Case for the Immediate Repeal of Rent Controls

The fact that partial rent controls increase the rents on uncontrolled housing is not recognized by the general public. The result is that the higher partial controls drive rents, the more necessary people believe rent controls to be; the more desperately do they cling to the existing controls and the more eager they are to urge the extension of the controls. They fear that the repeal of the existing controls would raise all rents to the level of the presently uncontrolled rents, and they believe that the uncontrolled rents are enormous because they are not controlled.

Our discussion shows that the best solution to the problems created by rent controls would be the *immediate* and total abolition of rent controls, accompanied by constitutional guarantees against their ever being reimposed. This would both immediately reduce rents in the open market and bring about the greatest and most rapid possible increase in the supply of rental housing.

Calling for the immediate abolition of rent control raises the question of what is to become of many of the people who are presently living in rent-controlled apartments and who would have to move if rent control were all at once repealed. (In order to have some term to describe these people, let us refer to them as the "beneficiaries" of rent control—provided it is understood that they are beneficiaries in a short-run sense only, and not genuine beneficiaries.)

Our previous discussion provides the answer to the question of what would happen to these people. In essence, the answer is that *they would simply have to change places with an equally large but generally unrecognized class of victims of rent control.*

*Two* facts about the immediate repeal of rent control must be kept in mind: not only would it raise rents to the beneficiaries of rent control, but also, as we have seen, it would simultaneously reduce rents in the open market, because the space presently occupied by the beneficiaries of rent control would be added to the supply in the open market.

What would happen in response to these changes in rents is two related sets of developments, the one affecting the beneficiaries of rent controls, the other the victims. Let us consider the effects on the beneficiaries first.

In the face of a jump in their rents, some of the beneficiaries of rent control might have to share apartments or even single rooms with other people, in order to economize on rent. Others might have to move in with relatives. Still others might decide to move to remoter areas of the city, where rents were cheaper, or to leave the city altogether. It should be observed that none of the former beneficiaries of rent control would have to sleep in the street; they would simply have to occupy less space or live in less favorable locations. These points must be stressed, in view of the hysteria that is often evoked in projecting the allegedly dire fate of these people.

Now consider the fact that the apartments vacated by the former beneficiaries of rent control would not remain empty, but would practically all be occupied. For the rents on those apartments, though too costly for the rent-control beneficiaries, would represent a decline in the rents charged in the open market, and would thus come within the reach of new tenants. To use the same figures as in our auction example,[3] assume that initially a beneficiary of rent control was paying a controlled rent of $50, while rents in the open market were $250. Now, with the repeal of rent control and the addition of the previously controlled apartments to the supply available in the market, rents in the market fall from $250 to $150. A rent of $150 is too expensive for the former rent-control beneficiaries. But it represents a reduction in rents in the open market and brings apartments within reach of people who could not afford them at the $250-a-month rents caused by partial rent controls.

Let us focus on the new tenants who would occupy the previously controlled apartments. Let us try to figure out who they would be and where they are now. These are people who could afford their own apartments in the city at $150 a month, but not at $250 a month. At $250 a month, they find it necessary to share apartments (or single rooms), to live with relatives, or to live in remote areas of the city or out of town altogether. In other words, they find it necessary to do all of the things the beneficiaries of rent control might have to do if rent control were repealed. Perhaps some readers of this book may know some of these victims of rent control, though they probably have not thought of them in that light before. The victims are young people who must live with roommates, young couples who must live with in-laws, families that cannot afford to live in the city, and so on. These people represent the class of rent-control victims, though they are almost all unaware of that fact and see no connection between rent controls and their own plight. They are fully as numerous as the class of rent-control beneficiaries, and they are already suffering as much hardship as the rent-control beneficiaries would suffer if rent control were repealed.

In fact, these victims of rent control are suffering vastly *more* hardship than the beneficiaries of rent control would suffer. For if rent control were repealed, the total supply of housing would quickly begin to expand and its quality would improve. In places like New York City, the supply would increase almost overnight, because the abandonment of buildings would cease, and many previously abandoned buildings would be restored. The hardship of the former beneficiaries of rent control would be temporary, because rental housing would once again become an expanding, progressing industry. As time went on, more and more of the former beneficiaries of rent control would be better off than they ever could have been under rent control. In the long run, everyone would be better off. The real answer to the question of what would happen to the present beneficiaries of rent control, if rent control were repealed, therefore, is this: In the short run and at the very worst, they would suffer no more, and probably less, than the victims of rent control have already been suffering for many years. In the long run, what would happen to them is simply more and better housing.

Furthermore, it should be stressed that in the long run, the very idea of someone being a beneficiary of rent control is a self-contradiction. The gains of the beneficiaries of rent control are made possible by the consumption of their landlords' capital. The tenant who is able to afford a better car, say, or an extra vacation, because of the artificially low rent he pays, is buying that car or vacation at the expense of part of a new apartment building somewhere, and ultimately he is buying it at the expense of the upkeep of the very building in which he lives. The day comes when he wants to move and finds no decent place to move to, because he and millions of others like him have consumed the equivalent of all the new apartment buildings that should have been built. For they have consumed their landlords' capitals and destroyed the incentives for building. Finally, the day comes when they have consumed the equivalent of a new boiler or wiring system or plumbing system that their own building needs, and their landlord has neither the means nor the incentive to try to replace it. Then they live in cold, in darkness, and without running water. This is already the fate of tens of thousands of people in Harlem and in the South Bronx, as I have indicated. There is no reason why it could not happen to all controlled housing in the country, given further inflation and more time. The only "gains" from rent control are the gains of consuming the capital invested in housing and then being left without housing. People do it because the housing belongs to the landlords, not to them. But in the long run, the loss is theirs, because they are the physical beneficiaries of the stock of housing. When they destroy the property of the landlords, they destroy the property that serves them.

How Repeal of Our Price Controls on Oil Would Immediately Reduce the
Price Received by the Arabs

A further application of the principle that partial controls raise prices of
goods that are free of controls concerns oil prices. It follows from this principle that our price controls on oil raise the price received by the Arabs,
and that their repeal would immediately divert billions of dollars a year
away from the Arab oil industry to our oil industry, at relatively little cost
to American consumers.

At the time of writing, domestically produced crude oil in the United
States is controlled at an average price of approximately $8.75 per barrel.
Imported crude oil is uncontrolled; it is currently selling at about $14.50
per barrel, which is the price the Arabs receive. The prices of the various
oil products produced in the United States, such as gasoline, heating oil,
and so forth, are controlled on the basis of a weighted average of the price
of imported oil and domestically produced oil. For example, since about 45
percent of our crude oil is imported and 55 percent is domestically produced, the present cost base can be taken as $14.50 × 45 percent plus $8.75
× 55 percent, which is equal to about $11.34 per barrel. Eleven dollars and
thirty-four cents per barrel of crude oil can be taken as the present cost
base on which the prices of oil products are set.

In order to see how this arrangement benefits the Arabs and how its
repeal would divert billions of dollars a year from their oil industry to our
oil industry, all we have to do is think through the consequences of repealing
our controls. If we repealed our controls, the effect would be that the price
of domestically produced oil would rise above $8.75 a barrel. But the effect
would also be that the price of imported oil, and, therefore, the price received by the Arabs, would fall below $14.50 a barrel. To understand just
why, imagine for the moment that the price of domestically produced oil
simply rose all the way to $14.50—the same price as the Arabs now receive.
If that happened, the cost of producing oil products would have to be based
on an average price of $14.50 a barrel rather than on the present average
of $11.34 a barrel. The prices of oil products would therefore have to be
raised correspondingly. But observe. At such higher prices, the quantity of
oil products that could be sold would be less, and, therefore, the quantity
of crude oil that could be sold would also be less. The only way to counteract
this loss in sales would be if the prices of oil products did not rise by so
much. The only way that that would be possible would be if the average
price of crude oil did not rise by so much. But this implies that the price
received by the Arabs actually *falls*. For in a free market our oil would sell
for just as much as theirs; *yet, we have just seen that their present price of
$14.50 is too high for an average cost base.* Our price cannot meet theirs
at $14.50 a barrel. Both must come together at some lower figure. Our oil
would sell for just as much as theirs, but at a price that is lower than their
present price of $14.50.

Observe further. In order for the *same* quantity of crude oil to be sold in this country as is presently sold, it would be necessary for the Arabs' price to meet ours *at $11.34 a barrel—the present average*. For any higher cost base than $11.34 would require a rise in the price of oil products, which would reduce the quantity of oil products that could be sold and which would therefore reduce the quantity of crude oil that could be sold in this country.

Indeed, one may raise the question of why the effect of repeal would not actually be to leave the price of oil products unchanged in the United States and simply reduce the price of Arab crude oil and raise the price of our crude oil to the present average price of $11.34. The reason these results would not occur is because *oil imports* into the United States would diminish. The present price of $14.50 for imported oil prevails throughout most of the world. The price of imported oil could not fall to $11.34 here while it was any higher elsewhere. What would happen is that as the price of imported oil fell in this country, in the direction of $11.34, less of it would be sent here and more of it would be sent to other markets. The result would be that the price of imported oil would settle at some amount above $11.34—say, $12 or $12.50, or wherever. And the price of our domestically produced oil would settle at the same point.

So the consequence of repeal would be some rise in the average price of crude oil in the United States and some rise in the price of petroleum products in the United States. But the rise in price to American consumers would be much less than the rise in price to American producers; much of the rise in price received by our oil companies would be financed by a fall in the price received by the Arabs and other foreign suppliers. For example, if the price of crude oil settled at $12.50 per barrel, the cost base of oil products for American consumers would be increased by $1.16 per barrel ($12.50 − $11.34), while the price received by our oil companies would be increased by $3.75 per barrel ($12.50 − $8.75). The rise in price received by our oil companies would largely be financed by a $2 drop in the price received by the Arabs and the other foreign suppliers ($14.50 − $12.50).

Furthermore, this rise in domestic prices would merely be a short-run effect. For oil production in the United States would have become vastly more profitable and American oil companies would have billions of additional dollars to invest in oil production. Domestic oil production would immediately begin to expand, even, indeed, especially, from existing wells, because it would pay to exploit them more intensively at higher oil prices. (At present, it should be noted, much of the additional output that could be obtained from existing wells, through methods such as chemical or thermal flooding, is controlled at $5.25 per barrel, because it is classified by the government as "old" oil.) In addition, of course, new wells would start to come in. As American production grew, the price of oil would begin to fall. And, as a result, oil imports would fall still further. Thus, as soon as controls were repealed, America would immediately become less dependent on unreliable foreign supplies by virtue of reducing imports, and would grow still more independent as our own production expanded.

All of the above could be achieved simply by repealing the existing price controls on oil. I refer the reader to previous discussions for what could be achieved by a more comprehensive program of freedom that would include such things as the freeing of the natural gas industry from price controls, an end to the harassment of energy producers by the ecology movement, and a reduction in the burden of taxation on energy producers that would necessarily follow an end to inflation. [4] In time, such a program would radically reduce oil prices, and go on reducing them—at least in terms of the time one had to work in order to earn the money to pay them. For, once free, the American oil industry and the other American energy producing industries would be led by the profit motive to once again strive to reduce their costs of production and improve the quality of their products—things which they presently have little incentive to do or are simply stopped from doing. This dynamic effect of repeal and the reestablishment of economic freedom would ultimately make the real cost of oil and other forms of energy in the United States lower than they had been before the oil crisis. [5]

More on the Destruction of the Oil Industry

Unfortunately, a majority of the Congress has seemed more eager to help the Arab oil industry than to promote the best interests of the United States. In the fall of 1975, the Congress actually *rolled back* the average price of domestically produced crude oil from $8.75 a barrel to $7.67 a barrel. In the process, it imposed price controls on a major portion of domestic crude oil production that had temporarily been free of controls. Prior to the fall of 1975, so-called new oil—that is, oil produced from wells that began operation after January 1973—had been freed of controls. This, of course, would have meant the progressive freeing of the oil industry, as a larger and larger proportion of oil came to be "new" oil. The Congress placed new oil under controls by retaining the control on "old" oil—i.e., oil from wells that began operation prior to January 1973—at $5.25 a barrel, and requiring that new oil be priced in such a way that the average price of old and new oil together amount to $7.67 a barrel. The effect of this legislation was to transfer billions of dollars away from our oil industry to the Arab oil industry, and to make us even more dependent than before on unreliable imports. The Congress acted in order to reduce the price of gasoline by two or three cents a gallon, and probably out of a desire to punish the American oil industry. President Ford, who talked about the goal of energy independence, did not veto the legislation.

Today, the controlled average price of domestically produced crude oil stands once again at about $8.75 per barrel, as we have seen. It has been raised from $7.67 by the Federal Energy Administration, and its successor the Department of Energy, under discretionary authority granted by Congress to increase the price by up to 10 percent per year. However, this formula provides no genuine relief to the oil industry. For if the Department of Energy does not deliberately raise the controlled average price of domestic oil, its inaction automatically implies a progressive *reduction* in the price of new oil as the proportion of old oil in domestic output drops. To illustrate this, assume that half of current domestic output is old oil selling at $5.25 per barrel. In that case, because old oil represents half the current output and is priced $3.50 below the controlled average price, it is possible for new oil to be priced $3.50 per barrel above the controlled average price. In other words, new oil can sell at $12.25 because there is enough old oil selling at $5.25. (In reality, less than half of current output is old oil, and new oil, therefore, actually sells for only about $11.45 a barrel.)

However, as time goes on, the proportion of old oil must steadily decline and that of new oil steadily rise. Eventually, all oil must be new oil. At that point, if the controlled average price of oil remains $8.75, new oil will have to sell at $8.75. As the proportion of old oil declines and that of new oil rises, the existence of a constant average price of $8.75 would imply that the price of new oil must steadily drop toward $8.75. A rise in the controlled average price of oil, therefore, is necessary to prevent the price of new oil from actually being reduced. The rise thus far has not been sufficient to prevent this from happening. For example, as of April 1978, the controlled price of new oil was actually more than 50 cents a barrel below what it had been in 1975, despite the rise in the controlled average price from $7.67 to about $8.75. This was because of the decline in the proportion of old oil. Over the same period, the price received by the Arabs rose more than $1.50 a barrel.

Consider what the government is doing to the oil industry. On the one hand, it has arranged matters so that the price of new oil will not only be controlled, but must automatically be reduced unless it chooses to take deliberate action to keep the price where it is now. On the other hand, the government prints money without restriction, so that the costs of finding and producing new oil are sure to rise, and can rise to an unforeseeable extent. Clearly, the government has the oil industry in a vise, and the oil industry is simply not going to invest much money under these conditions. As a result, as our existing wells run dry, they will not be replaced. Already, our production has been declining in every year since 1972, and we now produce about 16 percent less crude oil than we did in 1972. We will thus have to rely more and more on imports, and the Arabs will be in a position to boost the price of oil higher than ever before. And then the Arabs' wells too will run dry and not be replaced, because of the backward and socialistic nature of their economies. The destruction of the American oil industry ultimately means the destruction of the world's oil industry.

How Repeal of Controls on Natural Gas Would Reduce Gas Prices

Still another application of the principle that partial controls raise prices on uncontrolled goods concerns natural gas prices. Natural gas prices are controlled at four basic levels: gas from wells drilled subsequently to January 1, 1975, is controlled at $1.49 per thousand cubic feet (tcf) and is permitted to rise 1 cent per tcf every 3 months; gas from wells drilled between January 1, 1973, and December 31, 1974, is controlled at 94 cents per tcf and is permitted to rise 1 cent per year; gas from wells drilled before 1973 is controlled at 29.5 cents per tcf and is ultimately scheduled to be controlled at 54 cents per tcf, as are various special categories of gas already. Uncontrolled natural gas, accounting for roughly one-third of domestic output and consumption, sells for about $2 per tcf in the intrastate markets of Texas and Louisiana. Of the roughly two-thirds of domestic output under controls, about 56 percent is controlled at the 29.5 cent price, 15 percent at the 54 cent price, 16 percent at the 94 cent price, and about 7 percent at the $1.49 price.

If controls on natural gas were abolished, all of the natural gas that is presently diverted to uses that appear economic only by virtue of the artificially low, controlled prices would be made available for the market. It is not absolutely certain, however, that this alone would be enough to reduce the presently uncontrolled intrastate price, although it very well might. The reason for this is that the interstate market is today totally controlled. In that market, not only is gas diverted to users who would not be willing or able to pay $2 per tcf, but many potential users willing and able to pay more than $2 per tcf are *prohibited* from doing so, such as new factories and the buyers of new homes.

Whether the short-run free-market price following the repeal of controls would be above or below $2 depends on whether the reduction in the quantity of gas demanded in the interstate market caused by a rise to $2 would exceed or fall short of the additional demand for gas that would appear on the part of those presently closed out of the market. If it turned out that the reduction in quantity demanded caused by the rise to $2 were greater than the rise in quantity demanded at that price on the part of previously prohibited buyers, then the price of gas would settle below $2. It would fall in Texas and Louisiana as sales to the interstate market were reduced and intrastate sales correspondingly expanded. If, on the other hand, the net effect were a rise in the quantity demanded in the interstate market at a price of $2, then the short-run free-market price would be above $2, and additional gas would be shipped from the producing states to the rest of the country.

What is absolutely certain, however, is that the natural gas industry would be enormously more profitable as the result of selling its gas at a sharply increased *average* price, would therefore have at its disposal vast sums of additional capital, and would no longer labor under the threat of future expropriation through price controls. The consequence could not fail to be a large-scale increase in the supply of natural gas accompanied by a substantial reduction in the price. At that point, if not immediately, the price of natural gas in the open market would be lower than it is today. And then, of course, as a result of the dynamic effects of the unrestrained profit motive, it would resume the process of continuous long-term reduction in real terms.

*Postscript.* Since the preceding discussion was written, Congress has changed the legislation respecting natural gas prices. According to legislation enacted on October 15, 1978 (as reported the following day in *The Wall Street Journal*), the price of all natural gas, including gas sold in the intrastate market, is to be controlled for a period of six to ten years. The controlled price of intrastate gas is set at $2.09 per tcf—approximately the free-market price prevailing at the time the legislation was passed—and is scheduled to rise each year by the rise in the general price level plus about 4 percent more. In addition, the price ceiling on post-1974 gas is raised immediately to the same level and is to rise each year in the same way. Finally, the price ceilings on older gas are raised, in some cases significantly. However, gas presently selling below 55¢ per tcf—roughly 70 percent of the nation's production—is to be raised only to that price plus an allowance for the rise in the general price level since April 1977.

The long-run effect of this legislation will be to create a universal gas shortage. Although price controls on intrastate gas and probably even post-1974 gas as well are now temporarily ineffective, in that they are placed above the potential prices that would exist in their absence, it is only a question of time before they become effective.

The fact that 70 percent of the gas industry's output is still controlled at a price of 55¢ per tcf seriously undermines its ability to produce. The inevitable outcome is that the gas industry will continue to decline. As supplies of older gas diminish, the scarcity of new gas will become more severe and its price will certainly need to rise more rapidly than the rate at which prices in general rise plus 4 percent. Thus, it is only a question of time before a gas shortage develops that embraces intrastate gas along with all other gas.

A particularly absurd feature of the new legislation, which is worthy of note, is the fact that controls on intrastate gas and on post-1974 gas are scheduled to be removed on January 1, 1985; however, after six months following this date, there is to be a two-year period during which controls can be reimposed either by the President or both the House and Senate, through a concurrent resolution, for another eighteen months *if gas prices are thought to be rising too rapidly*. Since the inevitable effect of the legislation is to create a shortage of gas, it is inescapable that as soon as the controls are removed, the prices of intrastate and post-1974 gas will begin to skyrocket. At that time, the supporters of controls will undoubtedly point to the rise in gas prices as proof of the need for the reimposition of the controls. In this way, price-control legislation is made the cause of its own extension.

# Universal Price Controls and Their Consequences
## V

1. The Tendency Toward Universal Price Controls

Price controls tend to spread until all prices and wages in the economic system are controlled—i.e., partial price controls lead to universal price controls.

Universal price controls existed in Nazi Germany, and the equivalent of universal price controls exists in Soviet Russia, Red China, and the other members of the communist bloc. Universal price controls existed in the United States in World War II. They also existed very briefly under President Nixon, when he imposed a ninety-day freeze on all prices and wages in August 1971. They could easily come into existence again in this country, and this time on a long-term basis, within the next few years.

The reason partial controls lead to universal controls is their destructiveness. We have already seen how partial controls destroy the industries to which they apply, while causing the uncontrolled industries to flourish. If the government wants to prevent the destruction of the industries it initially brings under controls, it has only three alternatives: It can repeal its controls on those industries, it can subsidize their losses out of the treasury, or it can control the prices that constitute their costs of production. If the government refuses to repeal its initial controls, and if it is unable or unwilling to pay the necessary subsidies, then its only alternative is to extend its price controls to the prices that constitute the costs of the industries concerned. But then the same story repeats itself, and the government finds that it must bring under controls the prices that constitute the costs of these industries, too, and so on, with the list of controlled prices steadily lengthening.[1]

For example, consider the case of the oil industry right now. It is headed for destruction, as we have seen. In order to prevent this, the government can either repeal the present controls on oil, or subsidize the oil industry to the extent of billions of dollars a year, or extend its controls to include the prices that constitute the oil industry's costs, such as the price of steel pipeline and the wages of oil field workers. If it controls these prices, then it must go still further. It must extend its price controls not only further backwards, but in every direction. For example, if it controls the price of steel pipeline, then it must extend its controls to all other steel products, such as I-beams, steel sheet, steel cans, and so on, as well as to the price of iron ore, coke, the wages of steel workers, and so forth. If it does not, the effect of its control on steel pipeline is simply to make that one steel product less profitable than the others, and so to destroy its production.

Similarly, if the government controls the wages of oil field workers, it must control wages in other occupations, into which the oil field workers might go, or into which potential oil field workers might go. As soon as it controls wages in these other occupations, it must seek to control wages in all the fields into which workers in these occupations might go. Obviously, the government must quickly seek to control all wages, because all the different occupations are interconnected. Finally, as the government controls wages and other prices that constitute costs, it is led to extend its controls *forward* to whatever remaining products may have previously escaped controls. Otherwise, the controls on costs would merely serve to make such products more profitable and thereby encourage their production at the expense of the controlled products.

In this way, price controls have the potential to spread through the economic system like a cancer travelling through the human body's lymphatic system. All that it takes for this to occur is for controls to reach the point that the government becomes unable or unwilling either to tolerate their effects or to use subsidies to mitigate their effects.

The effects of the limited controls we have had up to now, such as rent control in New York City, could largely be tolerated by the government, because they critically affected only a small minority of people; and to the extent they could not be tolerated, the government was able to some degree to mitigate them—as, for example, through subsidized housing of one kind or another. But the effects of the destruction of the oil industry or the electric utilities will be intolerable to the government, and it may very well lack the will or the ability to subsidize these industries on the vast scale that would be necessary to save them. Hence, these controls may very well turn out to be malignant and bring about universal controls.


2. Universal Price Controls and Universal Shortages

The first point which must be understood concerning universal price controls is that they create universal shortages, in which the shortage of each good compounds the shortage of every other good. Under universal controls, a shortage not only exists of each good, but the excess demand for each good spills over and adds to the excess demand for every other good. As illustration, consider again the case of the man who wants a television set but cannot find one at the controlled price. If television sets are the only controlled good, he can find his second choice, a new suit, say. But now, under universal controls, the suit will probably be as hard to find as his television set. As a result, he must be prepared to settle for his third choice, or, indeed, for his fourth, fifth, or still lower choice, if it is all that is available to him. Eventually, in fact, he will be willing to settle for *any* good that is of greater intrinsic utility to him than the otherwise useless paper money—that is, he will be willing to settle for virtually anything at all.

It should be realized that paper money is of less intrinsic utility than the least valuable good. It does not even make good wallpaper or provide a good fire. The only reason that people do not rush to trade it in for matches or pins or any other intrinsically more useful commodity is that they expect to be able to obtain still more valuable goods for it later on—perhaps later that day, the next day, the next week, or whenever. Price controls and shortages undermine this expectation. They destroy the desire to hold money and eventually make people willing to accept virtually anything in exchange for it.

In these conditions, our man's unsatisfied demand for a television set is *simultaneously* an unsatisfied demand for a new suit and *simultaneously* an unsatisfied demand for goods of still lower choice—it is an unsatisfied demand for anything and everything. And so it is with the unsatisfied demand of everyone else. Thus, it comes about not only that there is an excess demand in the entire economic system, but that the whole of it is poised ready to strike at whatever goods may be available from any industry. The excess demand facing each industry comes to be not only the unsatisfied demand of those for whom its products are the first choice with the money in question, but also the unsatisfied demand of those for whom its products are the second, third, fourth, and still lower choices. In this way, the excess demand of the whole system comes to exert its pressure against every point in the system. In addition, this excess demand is everywhere further compounded by an enormous hoarding demand for each good.

This discussion, it should be realized, is an actual *description* of conditions in Soviet Russia. In Soviet Russia, there is a shortage of *everything*. The only exceptions are goods they manage to produce that are of negative utility, such as pots that ruin the taste of food, or clothes that shrink out of all relation to their original size. Apart from such exceptions, everything is chronically in the same state of shortage as gasoline was in this country in early 1974. A book published in 1976 called *The Russians*, by Hedrick Smith, tells of waiting lines up to a mile long; and of one, to sign up to buy rugs (a once-a-year event in Moscow), that was comprised of between ten and fifteen thousand people lined up four abreast in the winter snow and that lasted for two solid days and nights. Smith reports that Russian women normally spend fourteen hours a week waiting in line just to buy food. He writes that women normally carry shopping bags called "just-in-case bags"—meaning bags for just in case they happen to find something that is for sale and worth buying. The briefcases that Russian men are generally seen carrying serve the same purpose.[2] I cannot resist quoting one passage because it so eloquently describes the condition of a willingness to buy anything:

"Yet despite such ordeals the instinctive reaction of a Russian woman when she sees a queue forming is to get in line immediately—even before she knows what is being sold. Queue-psychology has a magnetism of its own. Again and again, I have been told by Russians that anyone's normal assumption on seeing people up front hurrying to get in line is that there must be something up there worth lining up for. Never mind what it is. Get in line first and ask questions later. You'll find out when you get to the front of the line, or perhaps they'll pass back word before then. A lady lawyer told me she once came upon an enormous line stretching all through the Moskva Department Store, and when she asked those at the end of the line what was on sale, 'they said they didn't know or else snarled at me and told me not to interfere. I walked up 20 or 30 yards asking people and no one knew. Finally, I gave up asking.' "[3]

Shortages of this type come to exist whenever universal price controls are in force for any extended period of time.


Excess Demand and Controlled Incomes

It is necessary to deal with a difficulty that many people have in understanding how excess demand can exist under universal price controls. Many people reason in the following way: The main source of demand for consumers' goods, they say, is incomes, especially wages. But under universal price controls, everybody's wages, interest, dividends, and so on are controlled. Therefore, people ask, how can demand be rising and a problem of excess demand be created?

The answer to this question is that excess demand is created by virtue of an expansion in the quantity of money, and that the limitation of incomes is irrelevant.

In order to understand this point as clearly as possible, consider the case of a hypothetical small economy with $10,000 of total spending, 1,000 units of supply, and a general price level of $10 per unit. Assume that the $10,000 of spending in this economy is the result of $10,000 of incomes. Assume further that when price controls are imposed in this economy, incomes are frozen at a total of $10,000. Nevertheless, demand in this economy can grow progressively more excessive—in the following way. Assume that the government decides to spend $1,000 out of newly created money. The price of what the government buys is controlled at $10 a unit. Consequently, the government buys 100 units of the economy's supply. This leaves 900 units of supply for the citizens. These 900 units are controlled at a price of $10 per unit. This means that the most it is possible for the citizens to spend in buying them is $9,000. Nevertheless, the citizens want to spend $10,000—their incomes. Clearly, the citizens have $1,000 of unspendable income. What has happened is that the government's spending of $1,000 out of newly created money has displaced $1,000 of spending by the citizens and has made $1,000 of the citizens' incomes back up on them as surplus, unspendable funds.

This phenomenon can grow progressively worse from year to year. We have just seen the government spend $1,000 and the citizens spend $9,000. This means that businesses have taken in $10,000 of sales revenues and in the second year are again able to pay out $10,000 of incomes. But now, these $10,000 of incomes are added on to $1,000 of surplus unspendable income from the year before. This year, therefore, the citizens would like to spend $11,000 rather than $10,000. If the government again spends $1,000 out of newly created money, the citizens will again be able to succeed in spending no more than $9,000. Thus, there will now be an excess demand of $2,000, and in the third year it will be $3,000, and so on. In this way, the shortages grow worse from year to year. It is not too long before people are ready to buy anything.

This example, incidentally, helps to show why price controls do not create severe shortages in the very moment they are introduced. When the controls are first imposed, the existing prices are the proper prices. In fact, they may even have been raised somewhat in anticipation of the controls being imposed. It takes time for these prices to become outmoded—both by continuing inflation and by all the other forces acting to bring about changes in supply, demand, and cost. The longer the controls remain in force, the more serious their consequences become, because the more out of line do the controlled prices become in relation to the potential free-market prices that would exist if the controls were repealed.

## 3. The Destruction of Production Through Shortages

The government's purpose in imposing universal price controls is to assure an adequate rate of profit to the vital industries it initially brings under controls. For this reason it imposes controls on the prices that constitute the production costs of these industries. It extends controls to the selling prices of all other industries in order to restrain their rate of profit in relation to that of the controlled industries.

It should be realized that it is perfectly possible under universal controls for all industries to be guaranteed not only approximately equal rates of profit, but rates of profit that by historical standards are relatively high in nominal terms. This is possible because the government controls all the prices that constitute costs, including wages, which are the fundamental element in costs. Nevertheless, no matter how high the nominal rate of profit the government allows, vital industries are still destroyed, and production is disrupted far more seriously than under partial price controls.

*What destroys production under universal controls is the consequences of the shortages they create.*

In the last chapter, we saw a variety of ways in which shortages disrupt production under partial controls. I will briefly recount them because all of them apply under universal controls. (It should be recalled in this recounting, by the way, that anything that acts to raise costs implies a decline in production.[4])

1. Shortages make buyers impotent and thereby remove the incentives of sellers to provide good quality and service. As a result, quality and service decline and the costs of maintenance and replacement increase.

2. Shortages of means of production, such as a material, often force sellers to reduce quality and service and make it necessary to resort to more expensive substitute methods of production.

3. Shortages encourage sellers to concentrate on the production of unnecessarily expensive models as a disguised way of raising prices.

4. Shortages create a positive incentive to using more expensive methods of production if the government allows the pass-through of higher costs and makes the incurrence of higher costs a source of higher profits.

5. Shortages result in delays in production.

6. Shortages cause hoarding and the construction of additional storage facilities.

7. Shortages cause the waste of time in searching for supplies.

8. Shortages create chaos in the geographical distribution of a good among local markets—for example, gasoline during the oil shortage.

9. Shortages create chaos in the distribution of a factor of production among its various uses in production—for example, crude oil in the production of the various oil products.

Under a system of universal price controls and universal shortages, these elements of chaos apply to all industries, instead of just a few industries. In addition, they apply more strongly to each industry than if that industry were the only industry under price controls, or if price controls were confined to it and just a few others.

First of all, the excess demand confronting each industry is far greater than under partial price controls, because it is compounded by the excess demand for all other products, as we have seen. The greater severity of the shortage of a product under universal controls creates correspondingly more severe problems in connection with that product. As just one illustration, consider the case of cotton and cotton products. If the prices of cotton and cotton products were the only controlled prices in the economic system, there would be a problem of using too much cotton to produce shirts, say, and not enough to produce other cotton products, or vice versa. Because, similarly to what we saw in the previous chapter in the case of crude oil,[5] there would be a shortage of each cotton product. Thus more of any one cotton product, such as shirts, could be produced at the expense of the others without reducing its price and profitability, until its particular shortage was totally eliminated. Yet if shirts, cotton, and the other cotton products were the only controlled goods, the increase in shirt production would be limited by the fact that people could spend their money on other goods. Beyond a point, people would only be willing to buy additional shirts at prices that made any further increase in shirt production unprofitable, however low the price of raw cotton might be controlled.

But if *everything* is controlled, and people find no other goods available on which to spend their money than shirts, there is no reason why they would not buy enough shirts to have two or three new ones to wear every day, if there were that many available. People would be willing to go on buying more shirts so long as extra shirts had an intrinsic utility greater than that of paper money. They would be willing to buy them as a source of cleaning rags, buttons, pins, or whichever, that otherwise might be unobtainable. They would buy them merely to hold as a store of value for the future, because holding them would be better than holding the otherwise unspendable paper money.

The principle that emerges is that under universal controls *it becomes practically impossible to eliminate the shortage even of an individual good by means of expanding its production*, because each good is confronted with the excess demand of the whole economic system.

There is a second reason why the elements of chaos connected with partial controls must apply more strongly under universal controls. This is the fact that *each industry must suffer the consequences of shortages in its capacity as a buyer*. Indeed, it must suffer them in everything it buys. For example, under universal controls, not only does chaos reign for the customers of the oil industry, but the oil industry itself now encounters the same chaos in its own purchases of pipeline, drilling equipment, trucks, tankers, and labor services. Whatever problems the oil industry had before are now intensified. And, of course, in accordance with the principle we just developed, the excess demand confronting the oil industry is radically expanded by the spillover of unsatisfied demand from every other fuel and chemical for which petroleum products could substitute; it is also expanded by the sheer desire of people to own any storeable physical good in preference to unspendable paper money.

Not only do universal price controls spread chaos through the whole economic system, and intensify it at every point, but they add a wholly *new dimension* to the chaos, that we have not previously encountered. Namely, *they create shortages of capital and labor*, the two factors of production required by every industry. These shortages exist because the shortages of consumers' goods create a ready and waiting employment for more capital and labor in every industry. As a result, the distribution of capital and labor among the various industries is made random. Capital and labor are made to stand in the same relation to all the different industries that we have seen crude oil or raw cotton stand in relation to their respective products. What this means is that capital and labor can be withdrawn from any industry and placed in any other industry, and there is no effect on the rate of profit anywhere. If capital and labor are withdrawn from any industry, price controls prevent prices and profits in that industry from rising. If additional capital and labor are invested in any industry, shortages prevent prices and profits in that industry from falling—all that happens is that the shortage in the industry is reduced. For example, if capital and labor are withdrawn from making paper and transferred to making pots, price controls prevent the price and profitability of paper from rising, while shortages prevent the price and profitability of pots from falling.

The consequence of this state of affairs is that production from industry to industry becomes utterly chaotic. Not only can any product of crude oil be randomly expanded at the expense of any other product of crude oil, not only can any product of cotton be randomly expanded at the expense of any other product of cotton, but any product anywhere in the economic system can be randomly expanded at the expense of any other product anywhere else in the economic system. The chaos is total.

Let us consider the significance of this. Assume the consumers would prefer to have more shoes and fewer shirts. Under price controls, they cannot bid up the prices of shoes and increase the profitability of shoe production. At the same time, as a result of universal shortages, they will not decrease their purchase of shirts, because they have no alternative use for the money. In fact, in this situation it is perfectly possible that capital and labor could be withdrawn, unchecked, from shoe production, which the consumers want more of, and added on, unchecked, to shirt production, which they want less of—that is, that the *exact opposite* of the consumers' wishes could occur. For if this perverse result did occur, price controls would prevent the price and profitability of shoes from rising to stem the withdrawal of capital and labor from the shoe industry. At the same time, the existence of a shortage would prevent the price and profitability of shirts from falling to stem the inflow of capital and labor into the shirt industry.

Indeed, this perverse result is not only possible, but fully as likely as that the consumers will get the result they want. Under universal price controls, there is no longer any connection between the consumers' preferences and business firms' profits or losses. In an economy in which there are universal shortages, the consumers are ready to buy *anything*. And that makes it possible for businessmen to produce *anything*. I leave it to the reader's imagination to think of what kind of deterioration in quality and service can take place in this kind of situation, and of all the other inefficiencies that can exist.

It should already be clear that the extent to which this perverse process can be carried, of consumers getting goods they want less at the expense of goods they want more, has no limits under universal price controls. No matter how bad the shortage of a particular good becomes as the result of a decrease in its production, price controls prevent its production from becoming more profitable. No matter how much the production of a particular good is increased, its shortage is so severe that practically no amount of additional production will eliminate it, because its shortage reflects the spillover of unsatisfied demand from the whole economic system.

In this way, universal price controls have the effect of flooding people with shirts, while making them go barefoot, or inundating them with shoes, while making them go shirtless; of giving them enormous quantities of writing paper, but no pens or ink, or vice versa; of giving them food, but no clothing, or clothing, but no food; of giving them toothpaste, but no soap, or soap, but no toothpaste; indeed, of giving them any absurd combination of goods. Moreover, at any moment, the positions of the goods can be reversed, with the relatively abundant ones suddenly disappearing, while the ones previously impossible to find suddenly appear in abundance.

These conditions are not a mere theoretical projection. They are the normal, the chronic conditions of Soviet Russia ever since the Communist Revolution. There is no connection in Soviet Russia between production and the desires of the consumers, and practically everything produced for the individual consumers in Soviet Russia is, in the words of Hedrick Smith, "simply junk."[6]

This kind of chaos in production is the source of drastic declines in production.

Merely giving consumers unbalanced combinations of goods is itself equivalent to a major decline in production, for it represents just as much of a loss in human well-being. For example, imagine that a dozen shirts represents the same physical volume of production as three new pairs of shoes, in terms of the capital and labor that must be employed to produce them. Suppose further that what a person wants each year is a dozen shirts plus three pairs of shoes. If he ends up having to settle for two dozen shirts and go barefoot, he is much worse off than if he could have gotten eight shirts and two pairs of shoes, or even just four shirts and one pair of shoes. The same overall volume of physical production becomes equivalent to a smaller volume of physical production by virtue of its being improperly proportioned among people's different wants and needs.

However, this kind of chaos in production does not merely cause chaotic

combinations of consumers' goods. It also causes chaotic combinations of
capital goods. And in so doing, it reduces the economic system's overall
physical ability to produce.

An economic system's ability to produce does not depend merely on the
quantity of its capital goods, but no less on *the proper distribution of that
overall quantity among the various specific types of capital goods*. If, for
example, the steel industry is unduly expanded at the expense of the coal
industry, say, or vice versa, the economic system's subsequent ability to
produce will be impaired: not only the extra steel mills, but part of the
*existing* steel mills may be inoperable for lack of fuel. An economy's overall
ability to produce must be thought of in terms analogous to the functioning
of an organism. It depends on the smooth coordination and adjustment of
all of its parts. Like a human body, whose total performance cannot exceed
the power of its brain, heart, lungs, or any other vital organ, the overall
performance of an economic system cannot exceed the power of any one of
a large number of vital industries. If some are unduly expanded at the
expense of others, the effect is to reduce the functioning of the whole.
Indeed, every malproportion has serious consequences.

Consider the devastating effects on production not only of disproportions
among whole major industries, like steel and coal, but of disproportions
within the output of individual industries; for example, the production of
too many trucks to haul farm products and of not enough tractors to harvest
them. Consider the effects on production of disproportions in the production
of just a few key products here and there—like ball bearings, lubricants for
machinery, spare parts, even ordinary screws, and so on. A shortage of any
one of these items, or a shortage of one special type of these items, such as
ball bearings of a particular size, must cause a widespread paralysis and the
grossest inefficiencies in production. And, of course, improper geographical
distribution of these or any other inputs has equally devastating consequences for production; for the mere existence of a thing is of no value if
the producers who need it are prevented from obtaining it. The same is
true if anything is unavailable for production because it is being hoarded.
These declines, of course, are all further compounded by the declines that
result from producers just not having to care any longer about the quality
of their products or about economies in producing them.

Again, this chaos is not a mere theoretical projection, but an actual description of the chronic conditions of Soviet Russia. In Soviet Russia, hy-
droelectric stations are built without generators and without the existence
of industries to supply; wheat cannot be harvested because the necessary
tractors have not been built, or, if they have been built, they lack spare
parts, or are in the wrong place; factories cannot operate because they lack
materials; new buildings and new machines are worthless, because of shoddy
construction due to lack of care or lack of the necessary materials.[7]

Now the declines in production resulting from all of these causes tend to be *self-reinforcing and cumulative*. For in the course of production, capital goods are physically consumed; i.e., materials and fuel are used up, and machinery and buildings wear out. If production is to be maintained, the capital goods consumed in production must be replaced. The only source of replacement, however, is production itself; i.e., the capital goods consumed in production in an economic system can be replaced only out of that system's production. But if that production declines sufficiently, because of economic chaos, then it will not be possible to reproduce the capital goods consumed in production. As a result, the stock of capital goods will fall. Once that happens, production must decline further, because it will be carried on with fewer capital goods. If the smaller supply of capital goods is used as inefficiently as was the larger supply, because of continuing chaos in production, it will not be possible to replace the smaller supply of capital goods either. Thus, once again production will decline. This process, of less production causing fewer capital goods causing less production, can go on until the economic system is carried back all the way to the level of barbarism.

To make this process more concrete, just think of the fact that in the course of production such things as steel mills, cement factories, freight cars, and so on are wearing out and must be replaced. The only way to replace them is out of the economy's current production. If that production declines sufficiently, because of economic chaos, then it will not be possible to replace them. The result will be that in the future, production will have to be carried on with fewer steel mills, cement factories, and so on. And then even the smaller number of steel mills, etc., will not be able to be replaced, because, given the continuation of chaos, the output that is obtained from them will be too low.

Special consideration must be given to the shortage of labor that universal price controls create. For the labor shortage introduces a second powerful factor making for a self-reinforcing, cumulative decline in production.

Under universal controls, every industry is eager to employ more labor, because whatever extra products it can produce with more labor will be snapped up by goods-hungry buyers. In addition, the labor shortage is intensified by the declines in efficiency that price controls create, because these declines in efficiency mean that it takes more labor on the average to produce a unit of goods. As a result of the labor shortage, employers are even led to "hoard" labor, that is, keep it on the payroll in idleness or semi-idleness in order to have it available when they need it. This, of course, only intensifies the labor shortage.

What is of special importance is that the labor shortage not only exists because of an excess demand for labor, but it also very soon becomes compounded by a *falling supply* of labor. The supply of labor begins to fall as a result of the shortages of consumers' goods. *These shortages destroy the incentive to work*. As people accumulate surplus, unspendable income, it begins to occur to them that they need not earn money they cannot spend. They lose the incentive to advance, because earning more money is useless to them. They cease to care about being fired, because not only can they immediately find another job if they wish it, but the loss of income they cannot spend does not affect them. They begin to do their jobs badly. They become willing to settle for lower-level, less demanding jobs that pay less. They quit their jobs altogether and live off their forced savings for extended periods before taking another job. All of these things represent a decline in the supply of labor. Of course, they also cause a major decline in production and thus in the supply of consumers' goods. This decline in the supply of consumers' goods resulting from the decline in the supply of labor makes the shortages of consumers' goods still worse and thereby further reduces the incentives to work, which, of course, causes even worse shortages. And so it goes, until in fairly short order production must come to a total halt.

Again, it is worth noting that the economy of Soviet Russia is characterized by a labor shortage, in which factory managers "hoard" labor in order to be sure of fulfilling their quotas under the official economic plan. The shortages of consumers' goods in Russia also contribute to the labor shortage.[8]

The Prosperity Delusion of Price Controls: The World War II "Boom"

Something that is truly remarkable about universal price controls is that, at least in their earlier stages, they can create a delusion of prosperity, even while production is becoming chaotic and on the road to collapse. The reason for this is that under universal price controls any businessman can find a ready and eager market for any merchandise, no matter how poorly it is produced. All he has to do is produce something of greater intrinsic utility than paper money. In the process, he can even make large nominal profits, simply by virtue of the government having controlled at an appropriate level the prices that constitute his costs. By the same token, the labor shortage makes it possible for any worker to obtain immediate employment in any occupation for which he is even remotely qualified. To those who confuse going through the motions of production with real production, and who confuse the earning of mere paper money with the acquisition of real, physical wealth, this situation looks like prosperity. What they see is that business is humming, everyone is employed who cares to be, and everyone is making money.

Just this situation characterized the United States during World War II. The combination of massive inflation to pay for the war, and universal price controls to hide the symptoms of the inflation, quickly produced widespread shortages, including a labor shortage. Most people mistook this situation for prosperity.

Nevertheless, despite a superficial appearance of prosperity, the real standard of living of the American people fell drastically during World War II. It fell to a level far below the worst years of the depression. In the worst years of the depression, three-fourths of the American labor force were employed, and everyone who was working could buy anything he wanted commensurate with his earnings. During World War II, *no one* could buy a new car, a new house, or a new major appliance of any kind: the government prohibited their production altogether. In addition, many of the most common, everyday goods simply became unobtainable or obtainable only with great difficulty—such as chocolate bars, chewing gum, sugar, meat, nylon stockings, gasoline, rubber tires, and so on. The goods that were obtainable badly deteriorated in quality—everyone recognized the difference between what they called "pre-war quality" and "war-time quality."

People believed they were prosperous in World War II because they were piling up large amounts of unspendable income—in the form of paper money and government bonds. They confused this accumulation of paper assets with real wealth. Incredibly, most economic statisticians and historians make the same error when they measure the standard of living of World War II by the largely unspendable "national income" of the period.

The controls did not last long enough in this country to wreck the economic system. Their effect was further mitigated by the fact that we entered the war with mass unemployment and a large amount of idle plant capacity. The absorption of these factors into production made it possible to offset much of the wastes and inefficiencies resulting from the controls. They constituted a kind of reserve fund, as it were, out of which much of the costs of the controls were met.

Also, during the war, people were highly motivated by considerations of patriotism, and were not only willing to tolerate the hardships imposed by the war, but actually to work harder and longer. Many of them reasoned that if the soldiers at the front could risk their very lives in the defense of civilization, they could do with fewer goods and put in an extra effort at work. Finally, no one regarded the controls as a permanent institution—everyone looked forward to a quick end to the war and to the opportunity to spend after the war.

Such things, however, can at best only delay the full consequences of universal controls. In the present circumstances, moreover, no such mitigating factors are present.


## 4. Socialism on the Nazi Pattern

In an effort to deal with the chaos it creates through price controls, the government adopts further measures: *it seizes control over production and distribution.*

For example, during the oil shortage a new government office—the Federal Energy Administration—was established, which had the power to tell the various oil companies how much of each of the various petroleum products they were to produce and to which industries, firms, and regions they were to distribute those products. Thus, government officials decided how much refining capacity should be devoted to producing gasoline, how much to producing heating oil, jet fuel, propane, kerosene, and so forth. In the process, government officials decided which industries dependent on the various petroleum products would obtain supplies, and to what extent. They decided the distribution of each individual petroleum product among its various uses, such as how much gasoline would go to truckers, how much to bus lines, and how much would be left for passenger automobiles. They decided which firms in each industry would get how much of the product alloted to that industry. For example, in the airline industry, they decided that each airline would get 80 percent of the jet fuel it had consumed in the previous year. They decided which geographical areas would get how much of each product. For example, they decided how much gasoline went to New Jersey and how much to New York. And they were about to decide how much gasoline and heating oil went to each individual consumer—for example, the plan to give every licensed driver over eighteen a fixed monthly ration of gasoline by issuing coupons with the picture of George Washington on them.

In addition, government officials made it their business to look into the methods of production employed by the users of oil products. For example, they began to try to force electric utilities to switch from burning oil to burning coal, in order to reduce oil consumption. (Often, these were the same utilities that only a short time before the same government had forced to convert to oil, under the influence of the ecology movement.) As part of this process, they reduced highway speed limits, which must be viewed as an interference with methods of production insofar as it applies to trucks and buses or any form of travel for business purposes.

All of these further interferences were an unavoidable response to the chaos in the oil industry, given the fact that the government was not prepared to abandon its controls over oil prices. Price controls and shortages had made the output of the oil industry and the subsequent distribution of that output utterly chaotic. The government took control of production and distribution in the oil industry in an effort to deal with this chaos.

Now under a system of universal price controls, such as existed in World War II, the government is led to seize control over the production and distribution of *every* commodity. The government thus comes to decide not only all prices and wages, but how much of each item is produced, by what methods, in what locations, and to whom it is distributed. The government fully controls all the inputs that each firm receives, how it combines those inputs, and what it does with the outputs.

There is only one appropriate name to describe this state of affairs of full government control over production and distribution. And that is *socialism*. In seizing control over all production and distribution, the government fully socializes the economic system.

The reason the system must be called socialism is because, in fact, *the government exercises all of the powers of ownership*. The meaning of ownership is the power to determine the use and disposal of property. If the government determines what a firm is to produce, in what quantity, by what methods, and to whom it is to sell its output and at what prices, then it is the government that determines the use and disposal of the firm's property. The government, therefore, becomes the real owner of the firm—the *de facto* owner. The nominal owners recognized by the law—that is, the firm's stockholders (and also the board of directors chosen by the stockholders, and the managers appointed by the board of directors)—are reduced to the status of government functionaries, compelled to carry out the government's orders. The fact that the stockholders may be allowed to continue to draw dividends is irrelevant. The status of these stockholders is essentially no different than if the government had openly nationalized their property and given them government bonds on which they received interest.

This system of *de facto* socialism, carried out under the outward guise and appearance of capitalism, in which the legal forms of private ownership are maintained, has been aptly characterized by von Mises as socialism on the German or Nazi pattern.[9] The Germans under Ludendorf and Hindenburg in World War I, and later under Hitler, were the foremost practitioners of this type of socialism. (The more familiar variant of socialism, in which the government openly nationalizes the means of production and establishes socialism *de jure* as well as *de facto*, von Mises calls socialism on the Russian or Bolshevik pattern, after *its* leading practitioners.)

It cannot be emphasized too strongly that Nazi Germany was a socialist country and that the Nazis were right to call themselves National *Socialists*. This is something everyone should know; yet it appears to have been overlooked or ignored by practically all writers but von Mises. In Nazi Germany, the government controlled all prices and wages and determined what each firm was to produce, in what quantity, by what methods, and to whom it was to turn over its products. There was no fundamental difference between the Nazis and the Communists. While the Communists in Russia wore red shirts and had five-year plans, the Nazis in Germany wore brown shirts and had four-year plans.

There is a further point that must be made about the use of the term "socialism." Socialism means *an economic system based on government ownership of the means of production*. On the basis of this definition, not only must Nazi Germany, a country usually not recognized as socialist, be categorized as socialist, but other countries, usually thought of as *being* socialist, must *not* be categorized as socialist—for example, Great Britain, Israel, and Sweden. In these three countries, the economic system is still characterized by private ownership of the means of production—not only *de jure*, but *de facto* private ownership. This private ownership, to be sure, labors under all sorts of restrictions and prohibitions, but still it is private ownership, and production in these countries is carried out primarily at the initiative of private owners for the sake of private profit. The philosophy of the dominant political parties of these countries may be socialism and socialism may be their ultimate goal, but their actual practice, up to now, has not been socialism. The correct characterization of these economies is the expression "mixed economy," and that term applies to the economy of the United States, too. What I mean by a "mixed economy" is an economy characterized both by private ownership of the means of production and by an extensive list of socialistically motivated acts of government intervention.

The only truly socialist countries in the world today are the various communist-bloc countries, such as Soviet Russia, Communist China, and their various satellites, and perhaps some of the so-called third-world countries. No other countries are in fact socialist.

# The Chaos of Socialism
# VI

1. Socialism

From this point on, our discussion of the consequences of price controls becomes a discussion of the consequences of *socialism*.

In studying the consequences of socialism, it does not matter whether we study an economy that has arrived at socialism through price and wage controls or one that has arrived at socialism openly, through the explicit nationalization of all industry. Nor does it matter whether socialism has been brought about peacefully, through lawful processes and the observance of democratic procedures, or by means of a violent revolution; it also does not matter whether the professed goal of socialism is universal brotherly love or the supremacy of a particular race or class. Economically, the system is the same in all these cases: *The government owns the means of production and it is the government's responsibility to decide how they are to be used.* Consequently, everything I will have to say about socialism will apply to all variants of socialism: to the socialism of the Nazis, to the socialism of the Communists, and to the socialism of the Social Democrats, such as the late Norman Thomas. What I have to say will apply to any economic system actually based on government ownership of the means of production. Of course, it will not apply to countries such as Great Britain, Israel, and Sweden, which up to now have not implemented socialism as their actual economic system, although it may apply to them in the future. Most importantly, it will apply to the economic system of the United States, should price controls become universal and the government seize control over production and distribution in this country, which is more than possible.

## 2. The Essential Economic Identity Between
## Socialism and Universal Price Controls

The most important principle to grasp about socialism is that *its economic consequences are essentially the same as those which result from universal price controls*. If socialism is introduced in response to the chaos created by universal price controls, its effect is to perpetuate that chaos; if it is introduced without the prior existence of universal price controls, its effect is to inaugurate that very chaos. This, of course, is ironic insofar as the government uses the chaos created by price controls as the grounds for its socialization of the economic system. Nevertheless, socialism and universal price controls are fundamentally the same in their economic nature and therefore produce the same effects. It is for precisely this reason that Soviet Russia has so consistently provided such excellent examples of the consequences that follow from universal price controls.

The essential economic identity between socialism and universal price controls consists in the fact that *both of them destroy private ownership of the means of production and its offshoots the profit motive and the price system.*

Price controls destroy private ownership of the means of production in the very fact of destroying the right to bid and ask prices. In a division of labor economy, in which buying and selling are indispensable to production and all other economic activity, the right to bid and ask prices is a fundamental, indispensable right of ownership. Without it, all other rights of ownership are meaningless. For example, the right to own a factory is meaningless if the owner is prohibited from charging or paying the prices required to keep his factory in existence. Essentially, price controls are fully as destructive of the rights of ownership as socialism itself.

Furthermore, *what makes price controls produce the chaos they do is precisely the fact that they interfere with the property rights of businessmen.* Specifically, they prohibit businessmen from using their capitals in the ways that would be most profitable to themselves. If they did not interfere with the right of businessmen to use their capitals in the most profitable way, then they could produce none of their chaotic effects. Try to imagine the government *not* interfering with the businessman's property rights and profit motive, and yet the consequences of price controls developing. Think back to Chapters III, IV, and V, and recall the following elements of chaos that we saw resulting from price controls: shortages and the destruction of vital industries; the impotence of consumers accompanied by hatred between buyer and seller; the impetus to higher costs; chaos in the personal distribution of goods to consumers; chaos in the geographical distribution of goods among various local markets; chaos in the distribution of a factor of production among its various products; chaos in the distribution of capital and labor among the various industries.

Consider. All of these elements of chaos result from just one thing: *interference with the businessman's property rights and profit motive*. For example, would businessmen voluntarily sell their goods too cheaply and thus cause shortages? Obviously not. Their property rights must be violated and they must be forced to do so. Would businessmen abandon the production of vital goods if they were free to charge profitable prices for them? Obviously not. Would they drive away customers offering them profitable business? Again, no. Would they run up the costs of production if those costs came out of profits (as they would have to in the absence of price controls and shortages)? Clearly not. Would businessmen saturate some markets at low prices, while starving others offering them high prices? Would they use a factor of production to produce some products to excess at low prices, while producing not enough of other products offering them high prices? Would they overinvest in some industries at low profits or losses, while underinvesting in other industries offering high profits? Again, the answer is clearly no to all of these questions. What makes businessmen behave in these ways is that their property rights are violated and they are thus prevented from doing what is profitable to themselves.

The wider principle that emerges is that the entire price system and all of its laws and harmonies depend on one essential fact: *the observance of private property rights and thus the freedom of businessmen to act for their own profit*. It is private property rights and the profit motive that are the foundation and the motive power that underlie and drive the entire price system. It is they which underlie and actuate all of the benevolent economic laws we observed in our study of the free market, such as the uniformity-of-profit principle, the various principles of price and wage uniformity, the cost of production principle, the principle that prices are set high enough to limit demand to the supply, and the principle that factors of production are channelled to their most important employments. All of these laws and all of their benevolent consequences are the result of just one thing: private property rights and the profit motive.

*Now socialism destroys all property rights. And with them it destroys the operation of the profit motive and the entire price system.*

Socialism produces the same chaotic effects as price controls, *because it destroys the same thing as price controls*, namely, the one and only source of economic order and harmony in the world: private property rights and the profit motive.

The essential fact to grasp about socialism, which explains why it is essentially identical to price controls, is that *it is simply an act of destruction*. Like price controls, it destroys private ownership and the profit motive, and that is essentially *all* it does. It has nothing to put in their place. Socialism, in other words, is not actually an alternative economic system to private ownership of the means of production. It is merely a *negation* of the system based on private ownership.

3. The Myth of Socialist Planning
—the Anarchy of Socialist Production

Of course, socialism is not usually perceived simply as a negation. The first economist fully to grasp the destructive nature of socialism was von Mises, and he has not had many followers.[1] Much more often, socialism is perceived as a source of economic order and harmony. In fact, the most popular synonym for socialism is "economic planning." The belief in social-ism's ability to plan is why a government turns to socialism when confronted with the chaos created by price controls. Indeed, the belief in socialism's ability to plan may be one of the reasons for instituting price controls in the first place—namely, as a deliberate step leading directly to socialism. Cer-tainly, the belief in socialism's ability to plan is a major factor in the pop-ularity of socialism. Without it, it would be difficult for socialism to find supporters.

Nevertheless, a socialist government is helpless to bring order out of the chaos created by price controls. And if price controls do not exist when it assumes power, then it proceeds to create the same chaos as price controls by the very fact of socializing the economic system. For the great joke of socialism, of "planning," as it is called, is that it *cannot plan*; it *destroys* planning and substitutes chaos.

In order to understand why socialism cannot plan, we must look again at capitalism. This will enable us to form an idea of what is required for eco-nomic planning and, therefore, why socialism is incapable of it.

Observe. *Under capitalism each individual engages in economic planning.*

I must stress this fact and I am going to give a very extensive list of examples of it, because it is very important and because socialist propaganda has created exactly the opposite impression in the minds of most people. It has created the impression that what individuals do under capitalism is run about like chickens without heads in an "anarchy of production," and that rational action—planned action—is a prerogative of government. The truth is that each individual under capitalism is engaged in economic planning almost continuously. Unfortunately, most of us are in the position of M. Jourdan—the character in the Molière play—who spoke prose without ever knowing it. We are all engaged in economic planning under capitalism, practically every day, but hardly any of us realize it—least of all, today's intellectuals. Let us see in just what ways we practice economic planning.

An individual is engaged in economic planning when he plans how much of his wealth and income to save and invest and how much of it to consume; when he plans where to invest it and in what ways to consume it. He is engaged in economic planning, for example, when he plans to put his money in a bank or in the stock market, and in which specific shares in the stock market; when he plans to buy more clothes or a new stereo; even when he plans to drive to work or take the train, instead.

Every businessman under capitalism is engaged in economic planning when he plans to expand or contract the production of any item; when he plans to introduce a new product or discontinue an old product; when he plans to change his methods of production or retain his existing methods; when he plans to build a new factory or not to replace an existing one; when he plans to change the location of his business or let it remain where it is; when he plans to buy new machinery or not; to add to his inventories or not; to hire additional workers or let some of his present workers go.

Every wage earner under capitalism is engaged in economic planning when he plans to seek new employment or to retain his present employment; when he plans to improve his skills or rest content with the ones he has; when he plans to do his job in one particular area of the country, or in one particular industry, rather than in another.

In short, every one of us under capitalism is engaged in economic planning every time he plans any aspect of his personal finances or business affairs. We are engaged in economic planning every time we *think* about a course of action that would benefit us in our capacity as a buyer or seller.

It is simply amazing that all of this planning could be overlooked, and that the socialists have been able to proceed as though capitalism lacked planning. Capitalism *has* planning—the planning of each and every person who participates in the economic system.

Let us observe another, equally important fact: Namely, that the planning of capitalism—which, as I say, takes place on the part of everyone—*is based on prices*.

Prices have a twofold function in the planning of capitalism. First, *they enable the individual planner of capitalism to perform economic calculations.* That is, they enable him to compute the money cost and/or money revenue of various modes of conduct. If the planner is a businessman, he weighs a money cost against a money revenue. If he is a consumer, he weighs a money cost against a personal satisfaction. If he is a wage earner, he weighs a money revenue against his personal efforts. *These economic calculations provide a standard of action for the planner under capitalism.* They tell businessmen to produce the products and use the methods of production that are anticipated to be the most profitable. They tell consumers to consume in the ways that, other things equal, occasion the lowest cost. And they tell wage earners to work at the jobs that, other things equal, pay the highest wages. Thus, prices are an indispensable guide both to the planning of production and to the living of one's personal life under capitalism.

The second, corollary function of prices is that *they coordinate the plans of each individual under capitalism with the plans of all other individuals.* That is, prices serve to make each individual adjust his own plans to the relevant plans of all other individuals in the economic system. In this way, *capitalism and the price system bring about a harmoniously integrated plan-*

*ning of the entire economic system.* Our whole discussion of the free market's price system demonstrated this process of coordination and mutual adjustment. It is only necessary to say the following, by way of summary of that discussion: Namely, that concern with money revenue makes one adjust to the plans of the prospective buyers of one's goods or services and to the plans of all competing—and even potentially competing—sellers of those goods or services. And that concern with money costs makes one adjust to the plans of all other buyers seeking either the things one buys or the factors of production from which they are made, and to the plans of the sellers in their capacity as individuals having definite personal values and preferences. The desire to earn a money revenue leads one to produce things that the buyers want and that are not being produced excessively by other sellers. The desire to limit costs leads one to economize on things in degree that other buyers value them and in degree that they can be provided only at some special inconvenience to the sellers engaged in producing them.

*Now socialism, in destroying the price system, destroys the possibility of economic calculation and the coordination of the activities of separate, independent planners. It therefore makes rational economic planning impossible and creates chaos.*

As an illustration of the consequences, consider the problems confronting a socialist government in trying to plan the production of a simple item, such as shoes. Shoes can be produced in varying quantities, in various styles or combinations of styles, by various methods, such as by machine or by hand, and in different combinations of machine and hand production; they can be produced from different materials or combinations of materials, such as leather, rubber, and canvas, and in different geographical locations, again, in both instances, in varying proportions. Under capitalism, all of these choices are determined on the basis of economic calculations. Thus, shoe production as a whole tends to be carried to the point where further production would make the shoe industry relatively unprofitable in comparison with other industries; the styles are those which the consumers are willing to make profitable; the methods of production, the materials used, the geographic locations are all the lowest cost except insofar as they provide special advantages for which the consumers are willing to bear the extra cost.

Under socialism, the lack of economic calculation makes it impossible to make any of these choices on a rational basis. The extent of attempted shoe production is determined arbitrarily—most likely on the basis of some official's judgment about how many pairs of shoes are "necessary" per thousand inhabitants, or some such criterion. Style is determined arbitrarily—according to what suits the tastes of those in charge. The methods, materials, and locations planned must be selected arbitrarily. And then—for reasons that will soon become clearer—the actual carrying out of production, as opposed to what is called for in the plans, may very well have to be undertaken on the accidental basis of the means of production that happen to be available.

Now it must be stressed that the decisions about all of these choices—quantity, styles, methods, and so on—are important not only from the standpoint of the consumers of shoes, *but, no less, from the standpoint of the production of all other goods.* It must be borne in mind that shoe production, or the production of any good whatever, requires factors of production which are thereby made unavailable for other purposes. Shoe production requires labor that could be employed elsewhere. It requires leather or other material that either might be employed elsewhere or which is produced by labor that could certainly be employed elsewhere. In the same way, the tools or machines required, or the labor and the materials used to make them, have alternative employments. Moreover, each of the different choices respecting shoe production makes a *different* combination of factors of production unavailable for alternative employments. For example, shoes produced by hand reduce the number of handicraft workers available for other purposes. Those produced by machine reduce the number of machine makers and the amount of fuel available for other purposes. Shoes produced in Minsk leave less labor available for other purposes in Minsk than if they were produced in Pinsk, and so on.

It is, therefore, clearly not enough, as most socialists appear to believe, for a socialist government—having inherited or stolen the technology of shoe production—to simply decide how many shoes to produce, determine on a style, quality, method, and locations for production, and then give the orders to produce them. In planning the production of shoes, or any other individual item, a socialist government is logically obliged to consider its effect on the production of *all other items in the economic system.* It is logically obliged to try to plan the production of shoes, or any other good, in a way that least impairs the production of other goods. In drafting its plans for shoe production, a socialist government is obliged to consider the extent of shoe production in relation to the production of all other goods using the same factors of production. It is obliged to consider such questions as whether shoe production might be expanded with factors of production drawn from the production of some other good, and whether the production of that other good might be maintained by drawing factors of production from a third good, and so on.

For example, it must consider whether it would be advisable to use more labor in Minsk for shoes and less for making clothing, say, and perhaps to expand clothing production in Pinsk, at the expense of some third good. It must consider *all* of the industries using *any* of the factors of production used in the shoe industry. It must consider what depends on the output of those industries and what alternative factors of production are available to those industries. Indeed, it must go even further. It must consider all of the industries using the alternative factors of production. It must consider what depends on *their* products, and what further alternative factors of production may be available to *them.* And so on. And at each step, it must consider the possibility of expanding the overall supply of the factor of production in question, and, if so, by what means, where, and at the expense of what.

To make these problems real, let us continue with the example of shoes. In order to plan shoe production rationally, it would be necessary for a socialist government to consider all of the alternative employments of each of the factors of production used to produce shoes. Let us start just with leather. A socialist government would have to consider the alternative employments of leather, such as upholstering furniture and providing belting for machinery. It would have to consider the consequences of having more or less furniture and machinery versus more or less shoes. It would have to consider alternatives to the use of leather in upholstering furniture and making belting for machinery—for example, various fabrics, and plastic and steel. It would have to consider the alternative uses for the various fabrics and for the plastic and steel. It would have to consider what depended on those alternative uses, and what substitutes were available for them. It would have to consider whether the total supply of leather, its substitutes, or the substitutes for its substitutes, should be expanded, and, if so, by what means, where, and at the expense of what. Then, of course, the socialist government would be obliged to repeat the same procedure for all of the other factors of production employed to produce shoes, or which potentially could be employed to produce shoes.

All of this raises the insuperable difficulty of socialist planning: *Namely, under socialism, it is necessary to plan the production of the entire economic system as an indivisible whole.* That would be the only rational procedure.

*But the planning of the economic system as an indivisible whole is simply impossible.*

It would require a superhuman intellect to be able to grasp the physical connections among all the various industries and to be able to trace the consequences of alterations in any one industry on all the others. What would be required for the rational planning of a socialist economy would be the existence of an omniscient deity willing to descend from heaven and assume the management of the socialist economy.

This deity would have to be able to hold in mind at one time a precise inventory of the quantities and qualities of all the different factors of production in the entire economic system, together with their exact geographical locations and a full knowledge of the various technological possibilities open to them. That is to say, it would have to be able to hold in mind at one time all of the millions of separate farms, factories, mines, warehouses, and so forth, down to the last repair shop, together with a knowledge of the quantity and quality of all the machines, tools, materials, and half-finished goods that they contained, and exactly what they were potentially capable of accomplishing and when.

It would then have to be able to project forward in time all of the different new combinations of factors of production that might be produced out of the existing factors, together with where and precisely when they would come into existence and the technological possibilities that would then be open to them. It would have to be able to make this projection for an extended period of time—say, a generation or more—in order to avoid the possibly wasteful production of machines and buildings lasting that long.

And then, out of all the virtually infinite number of different possible permutations and combinations of what might be produced, it would have to pick one that on some undefined and undefinable basis it considered "best," and then order it to be undertaken. That would be its economic plan. *That* is what would be required to even begin to duplicate what capitalism accomplishes through the price system.

For observe. Under capitalism, different individuals in combination—that is, when their knowledge is added together—*do know* the precise quantities, qualities, locations, and technological possibilities open to all the various factors of production in the economic system. And everybody's production is based on the sum of all of this knowledge, because the knowledge is reflected in the prices of all the various factors of production and products. For example, the price of wheat at any given time reflects the knowledge of each owner of wheat concerning the amount, quality, and location of the wheat he owns; it also reflects the knowledge of each user of wheat about the technological possibilities open to wheat. All of this knowledge enters into the supply and demand and hence the price of wheat. It is the same with every other good: its price reflects the sum of existing knowledge about the amount of it available, the technological possibilities open to it in production, and every other relevant consideration. And the future supply, locations, and production possibilities of factors of production are taken into account in the anticipation of their future prices.

The deity needed for the planning of socialism would require intellectual powers even surpassing those I have described. For under socialism any unanticipated event, such as a train wreck, an early snowstorm, a warehouse fire, an unexpectedly bad harvest—even unanticipated favorable events, such as the opposite of all of these—is a calamity, for it requires *the replanning of the entire economic system.* For example, if a tank train carrying a shipment of oil is destroyed, how is the socialist economy to decide where to take out the loss? It would have to look at all of the different uses for oil, all the possible remote consequences of its withdrawal from this or that area of production, and it would have to look at all of the alternative employments of factors of production that might be used to replace the lost oil, and all the permutations and combinations entailed in that, and then decide. By the same token, if, as a result of good fortune, a socialist economy had fewer wrecks of tank trains than anticipated, it would have to replan the entire economic system to find the right use for the extra supply of oil.

Capitalism, on the other hand, as we have seen in previous chapters, responds easily and smoothly to unforeseen changes in economic conditions.

Such changes simply bring about a change in the structure of prices and thus generate the most efficient response on the part of all concerned. Thus, the wreck of a tank train—to continue with that example—acts to raise the price of oil a little. The rise in price diminishes the consumption of oil in its marginal employments and simultaneously encourages its production —and, of course, at the least possible expense to other productive activities. The reason capitalism responds so smoothly and efficiently is that every individual in the economic system is involved in planning the response. Each individual acts on the basis of his knowledge of his own personal or business context, and the actions of all individuals are harmoniously integrated through the price system.

*The essential problem of socialism is that it requires economic planning to take place without benefit of a division of intellectual labor.* It requires that one man (the Supreme Director), or each of several men (the Supreme Board of Directors), hold in his head and utilize the knowledge that can be held and utilized only by millions of separate individuals freely cooperating with one another on the basis of private ownership of the means of production and its offshoots the profit motive and the price system. The essential economic flaw of socialism is that in destroying these basic institutions of capitalism, it destroys the foundations of the intellectual division of labor that is indispensable to rational economic planning.

As I say, therefore, the planning of the economic system as an indivisible whole—by single individuals—let alone its continuous replanning in response to every unforeseen change, is simply impossible. The ruler of socialism, after all, is simply not an omniscient deity.

As a result, although it is called "central planning," socialism can never have anything even approaching a rationally integrated plan for the entire economic system. In reality, the actual planning of socialist countries is undertaken by separate government ministries, each responsible for different industries or regions. Even the individual factories undertake part of the planning process. The plans of these separate ministries and individual factories are only superficially integrated into an economy-wide plan. In this sense, the actual planning of socialism must be called "decentralized planning." There is no alternative to decentralized planning, because it is simply impossible for any one individual to try to plan everything. Decentralized planning exists as soon as two or more people assume separate responsibilities in the planning process.

However, the decentralized planning of socialism necessarily causes chaos. Because without a price system—without the foundation and mainspring of the price system, i.e., private ownership of the means of production and the profit motive—the individual planners must operate at cross purposes. First of all, there is nothing to stop their various discoordinated plans from presupposing the availability of the same factors of production. In such conditions, the execution of any plan necessarily absorbs factors of production whose absence then makes the execution of other plans impossible. For example, if the shoe industry is planned by one ministry, the clothing industry by a second ministry, the steel industry by a third ministry, and so on, there is nothing to prevent all of these industries from drafting mutually contradictory plans. There is nothing to prevent them from basing their plans on the availability of the same labor, or the same material, fuel, transport facilities, or whatever. In such a case, to whatever extent one industry succeeds in obtaining the factors of production necessary to execute its plan, it simultaneously wrecks the plans of other industries.

Observe what is involved here. Because planning under socialism is necessarily both decentralized and lacks coordination, the production of each of the various goods can be expanded more or less randomly at the expense of destroying the production of other, more important goods. *This is exactly the same chaos that prevails under universal price controls and universal shortages.*

Furthermore, to whatever extent individual industries or factories are given discretion in the plans, the products that are produced can very well be unsuited to the needs of other industries that depend on them, and in that way wreck the plans of these other industries. For example, the plan for agriculture can be wrecked by the poor quality of tractors that break down too often or aren't suited for the terrain. Observe. Under socialism, suppliers do not have any incentive of profit and loss in meeting the requirements of their customers. Nor are they subject to any form of competition. Each branch of industry under socialism is a protected legal monopoly that is totally disinterested in the requirements of its customers. This, too, is exactly the same situation we observed in the case of price controls and shortages. And it applies, as I say, not only at the consumer level, but at the producer level as well.

Under socialism, each industry, as well as each consumer, is at the mercy of disinterested monopoly suppliers. To understand what this is like, think back first to our discussion of the problems at service stations and in the relations between tenants and landlords resulting from price controls on gasoline and from rent controls.[2] Now observe that similar or even worse problems exist around us in the present-day United States in practically every case in which the government is the supplier. For example, think of the services provided by municipal bus lines and subway systems, the public schools, the motor vehicle bureau, and the Post Office. All of these operations are notorious in the utter indifference and contempt they display toward customers and in the low quality and lack of dependability of their services. These characteristics are the result of the fact that these operations are government owned and therefore operate without the incentives of profit and loss; in addition, they are generally immune from the threat of competition. Because of the lack of profit and loss incentives, it doesn't matter to them whether they gain customers or lose customers—whether they perform fast and efficient service or slow and inadequate service.

Now imagine the steel industry being owned by the government and run in the same way, and the customers of the steel industry having to contend with its performance. The industries needing steel would not be able to make their plans with very great confidence. Moreover, since they too would be owned by the government, they would not particularly *care* about not receiving the quality and service or even the kind of products they were supposed to. The effects on *their* customers, in turn, and on the plans of their customers would be compounded.

For example, an industry waiting for a new factory, say, called for by its plan, would have to contend with the indifference and bad service of a construction industry suffering from the indifference and bad service of the steel industry. And so it would go, with the plans of each industry wrecked by the lack of incentives and poor performance of every other industry further back in the chain of supply. It is for these very reasons that suppliers in the Soviet Union are so unreliable that each factory there strives as far as possible to be self-sufficient and thus independent of suppliers.[3]

To think of socialism as a "planned economy" is absurd. It is, in fact, an "anarchy of production"—a true anarchy of production.

The Russian Quota System

The fact that socialism is an anarchy of production could not be better illustrated than by the famous Russian "quota system." Socialist planning in Russia assigns to each farm and factory a specified physical production goal, called its "quota"—for example, so many bushels of wheat or so many pounds of nails. And each farm or factory is encouraged *to exceed its quota*.

Now this situation is identical to the one we discussed under a system of universal price controls and universal shortages, for it means that there is a ready and waiting employment for more factors of production in every branch of production, with the result that any branch is capable of expanding at the expense of any other, more important branch. This, of course, is a system of pure chaos. The Russian quota system, moreover, illustrates the anarchy of socialist production in another major respect as well. The central planning authority does not even attempt to issue really precise production quotas because of the enormous additional detail that would be required. For example, at times it has not even attempted to specify the number of each particular size nail or screw and so forth that is to be produced. It has simply ordered the production of so many pounds or mere units of nails or screws or whatever, overall. As a result, depending on whether the orders were in terms of weight or mere number of units, the factories concerned were led to try to concentrate on items that were giant size and enormously heavy, or pin size and very large in number. For these were the ways most easily to meet and exceed the quotas. The disastrous results for subsequent production can be imagined.

The quota system and its stress on meeting and exceeding quotas is an inevitable consequence of the fact that socialism cannot rationally plan. It results from the fact that a socialist government wants to expand production, but is unable to trace the connections among the different industries. It is unable to determine—and is not even aware that it is necessary to determine—the effects of producing more of any one item on the ability to produce other items. A socialist government sees the particular product it wants to produce in each case, but, because it lacks a price system, it has no concept of the cost of producing that product or, therefore, of what other products it must forgo in the process. As a result, it simply gives orders to produce as much as possible of everything.

Socialism is simply unable to determine costs and is not concerned with costs. It should be realized how much more profound this lack of concern with costs is in a socialist economy than in the case of isolated socialized enterprises operating in an economy that is based on private ownership of the means of production. Today, for example, the Post Office is not overly concerned with costs, because there is no one in the Post Office who stands to make a profit by reducing costs or suffer a loss by allowing them to run up. In the context of a socialist economy, the problems of the Post Office, or any other enterprise, would be far more profound. In that case, it could not even know what its costs were, because of the absence of a price system. As a result, the Post Office, and every other enterprise under socialism, would be operated totally in the dark, with an unknown impact on the rest of the economic system.

### Shortages of Labor and Consumers' Goods Under Socialism

Because this will be an important matter for consideration in the next chapter, it should be realized that socialism's inability to determine costs and consequent lack of concern with costs produces exactly the same kind of *labor shortage* as exists under universal price controls. A labor shortage exists under socialism both because of a socialist government's desire to produce more of everything and because of its inefficiency in how it produces anything in particular. The latter circumstance increases the amount of labor required to produce each good. In addition, of course, shortages of consumers' goods contribute to the labor shortage.

A few words must be said specifically about the reasons for the existence of shortages of consumers' goods under socialism, especially since it is often claimed by socialist economists that such shortages could be avoided by a socialist society. Shortages of consumers' goods exist under socialism even without inflation. They exist as a result of the following factors. First, the chaos in the production and geographical distribution of the various goods: at any time, goods can cease being produced, or cease being sent to particular localities. This can occur because particular plans are fulfilled that snatch away the necessary factors of production or perhaps the very consumers' goods themselves from other plans. Second, when this happens, the managers of the local stores and warehouses of the socialist society have no incentive and no authority to raise prices. Nor do they have the incentive or authority to try to anticipate such events and build up stockpiles—that would be speculation. In the same way, they have no incentive or authority to bring in supplies from other areas (or send supplies to other areas)—that would be another form of activity possible only under capitalism, namely, arbitrage. In addition, all of the moral and political pressures of a socialist society work against prices being raised.

A basic moral postulate of socialism is that goods should be free to whomever needs them, or, if not free, then at least as inexpensive as possible. The political pressures of socialism are likewise overwhelmingly against price increases (a fact which was confirmed in the summer of 1976, when the Communist government of Poland was forced to rescind announced price increases in the face of widespread rioting). The reasons for such political pressures are exactly the same as those which make rent control so popular in New York City, namely, whoever succeeds in buying at the low price sees his benefit and applauds the government officials responsible; on the other hand, those who are victimized by the shortage the too low price creates rarely see any connection between the too low price and their inability to obtain the goods they want; they view the low price as being in their interest, too, and hope to be able to buy at that price.

All of these circumstances create shortages of consumers' goods under socialism, which, of course, are worsened by the desire to hoard that necessarily accompanies them. On top of all this, the socialist government can issue additional money to the consumers and probably does so, which, of course, further intensifies the shortages by expanding aggregate demand in the face of a given level of prices.

### 4. Further Economic Flaws of Socialism: Monopoly, Stagnation, Exploitation, Progressive Impoverishment

The most fundamental fact about socialism is that *government ownership of the means of production constitutes an attempt to make intelligence and initiative in production a monopoly of the state.*

Production depends on the possession of means of production. If the means of production are monopolized by the state, because it arbitrarily claims to own them all, then no one is free to produce on his own initiative and to regard his own intelligence and judgment as the ultimate authority for his action. In a socialist economy, no one can produce without the permission, indeed, without the orders, of the state.

This attempted monopoly of intelligence and initiative is the cause of socialism's anarchy of production. Socialism simply *prohibits* all of the independent planning of millions of free, self-interested individuals that is required to run an economic system in a rational and ordered way.

There are additional, corollary consequences of socialism's monopoly character that must be stressed, namely, *the necessary technological backwardness of socialism and the utter powerlessness of the plain citizen under socialism.*

To understand these points, compare the conditions of socialism with those of capitalism. Under capitalism, whoever sees a profitable opportunity for action is free to act on his own initiative. He is powerfully motivated to do so by the prospect of the profit he can make. At the same time, he is restrained from rash action by the risk of losing his own money. In addition, his action constitutes a challenge to the established ways of doing things. For if what he is doing is in fact an improvement over present products or methods of production, then those producing the present products or practicing the present methods must copy his or be driven out of business.

Competition exists, too, in the fact that if an innovator lacks capital of his own, he can turn to any one of hundreds or even thousands of independent sources of financing. Thus, under capitalism, he has hundreds or even thousands of chances to obtain backing for his idea, while all he needs is success in just one of those chances. And, of course, his potential backers have powerful incentives, for they will share in the profits—or losses. Thus, it is not necessary under capitalism for an innovator to convince everyone, a majority, or even a significant size minority of people of the value of his idea. All he has to do is convince any one person or handful of persons who possess the capital necessary to give his idea a chance.

Because of its freedom of initiative, its incentives to use that initiative, and its freedom of competition, the products and methods of production of capitalism tend to be literally the very best that anyone in the entire society can think of, and to improve further as soon as anyone can think of any still better idea. We saw all this, of course, back in Chapter I.

Under socialism, on the other hand, individual initiative is paralyzed by the fear of punishment. Prison replaces profit for the man who would seek to implement an idea on his own initiative, for it is against the law under socialism to act outside the government's "plan." If an individual does manage to think of some improvement under socialism, he must submit it to the government, whose officials, of course, have no economic incentives to adopt it and who, therefore, will be inclined to reject it, in order to spare themselves the difficulties and uncertainties that are always entailed in implementing an innovation—such as, the need to find new suppliers of raw materials, obtain new workers, or discharge or relocate present workers. The officials will not want to run the risk of the innovation failing, while if it succeeds, the effect on them is likely to be merely an increase in the production quotas they are assigned. These are the conditions that prevail in the Soviet Union.[4] Under such circumstances, very few new ideas are thought of, fewer still are implemented, and virtually none at all are of benefit to the plain citizen.

The complete and utter powerlessness of the plain citizen under socialism can hardly be exaggerated. Under socialism, the plain citizen is no longer the customer, "who is always right," but the serf, who must take his rations and like it. For no official of a socialist government stands to make a profit by supplying him better or a loss by supplying him worse. These officials both lack the incentive of profit and loss and need not fear any competition from the initiative of outsiders. Thus, the plain citizen is economically powerless against them.

It is not even necessary to speak of the absence of any improvements for the plain citizen. Even if it had the ability, socialism has *no reason* to supply the plain citizen even with such goods as already exist and to which he has grown accustomed in the preceding era of capitalism. Indeed, it has no reason to supply him with *anything more than is necessary to prevent an uprising*. Consider a simple example. Assume there is a neighborhood somewhere that needs a grocery store. Under capitalism, this need represents a profitable opportunity for someone. Whoever sees it and has no better opportunity available simply opens a grocery and proceeds to make money, at the same time satisfying the need.

Under socialism, on the other hand, the residents of the neighborhood can only obtain a grocery by petitioning the economic planning board for one. Even if the residents actually went so far, which is itself highly doubtful, the officials of the board would have no compelling reason to comply with their request. They would certainly be far less likely to do so than officials presently accede to requests for traffic lights at dangerous intersections, which is often only after repeated deaths have occurred. It is for these very reasons, incidentally, that even Moscow, the leading city of socialism, is grossly lacking in retail and service establishments; residents living in outlying suburbs must often travel all the way to the center of the city to obtain even such things as food supplies.[5]

To take a second example: if ten million citizens of a socialist state are without shoes and must go barefoot, this does not and cannot mean any more to the officials of the socialist state than it means to the officials of New York City that everyday tens of thousands of New Yorkers are subjected to inhuman, cattle-like conditions in the city's municipalized subway system. No government official ever has been or ever will be motivated seriously to work to do anything about such conditions, for his own welfare does not depend on improving them. The only people who really do work to provide the general public with a decent standard of living, who—literally—stay up nights thinking of ways to provide them with such things as shoes and transportation, are *capitalists*, who are motivated by the prospect of making a fortune. The simple fact is that under socialism the consumers must accept whatever the government decides to give them, however meager and inadequate that may be. For the rest, they are helpless, and whatever pleas they might make, fall on deaf, indifferent, and often hostile ears.

The paralysis of initiative and incentives under socialism knows no limit—it extends to death itself. For example, if one asks how it is that Russia can periodically be threatened by famine despite the fact that it possesses the world's richest farm land, in the Ukraine, and was a major wheat exporter even under the Czars, the answer is that the individual Russians are prevented—by physical force—from taking the actions necessary to save their lives. Russian peasants, however ignorant they may be, are not so ignorant that they do not know that to eat they must grow food, nor do they lack the knowledge to grow sufficient food. They could grow not only enough to feed themselves, but the urban population of Russia as well, and far more. The urban population of Russia could produce things of value to the peasants, and they could mutually exchange and both live far removed from the threat of starvation.

The reason they do not is quite simple: The Russian government has arbitrarily declared the whole of Russia to be its property, and refuses to allow the peasants to farm for their own profit or the urban population to produce for its own profit. It threatens, quite literally, to kill anyone who tries to do so. Thus, a Russian peasant may look at virgin forest land that he could clear and make his farm, and which would feed himself and ten others. He may look, but he will not lift a finger, because he would be killed for trying. People starve to death under socialism because the actions they would have to take to prevent starvation would bring them a more immediate death from the government. It is that simple.

It follows from the powerlessness of the plain citizens that *the government of a socialist country is not and has no reason to be interested in anyone's values but those of its rulers*. This principle applies both to technological developments and to the whole of production. The only kind of technological developments that a socialist government is interested in are those which are of value to its rulers: above all, improvements in weapons production and in the kinds of things that add to the rulers' prestige, such as "sputniks"—or pyramids. Of course, even these, or their base, it must steal from capitalist countries, because it is impossible significantly to develop military technology, or any other aspects of technology of special interest to the state, while repressing civilian technology. For example, the tank and the military airplane could not have been developed in the absence of the automobile. Radar and rocketry could not have been developed in the absence of radio. But the automobile and radio would never have been introduced under socialism.

The only kind of production a socialist government is interested in is the production of weapons, spectacles, and monuments, which enhance the power and prestige of the rulers—and of just enough consumers' goods to prevent a revolt or mass starvation, either of which would weaken its power. Ironically, in *Das Kapital*, Karl Marx refers to capitalists as "blood-sucking," "vampire-like" "exploiters." It is clear, however, that it is not capitalists, but the rulers of socialism who are the genuine "blood-sucking," "vampire-like" "exploiters" of labor. Minimum physical subsistence is the most they will ever voluntarily give to the masses, for they have absolutely no reason to give more. Over sixty years of communism in Russia confirm this principle. But in the long run they cannot even provide this much. For, as should be apparent, as a result of its "anarchy of production," socialism "cannot even maintain its slaves in their slavery": the workers of socialism "sink deeper and deeper into poverty"—to borrow some other of Marx's choice clichés and apply them truthfully for once.

If anyone doubts that the standard of living under socialism tends to sink below the level of minimum physical subsistence, let him consider where the Russians would be right now without American wheat—given to them, at the expense of the American taxpayer, for nothing or on credit they will never repay. Let him consider how many Russians would die from the famines that would then result. Indeed, three times in the last fifteen years—in 1964, 1972, and 1975—the Russians have averted famine only because of the existence of an outside, capitalist world. They have no doubt averted countless other disasters only because a capitalist world has existed to provide them with all sorts of supplies to make good the errors of their chaotic economy.

Without the aid of capitalist countries, socialism must revert to feudalism, for it could not feed an extensive urban population. Such urban population as it might begin with would be destroyed by famines or flee to the countryside to avoid such destruction. These results must ultimately occur even if socialism were to begin with the present economy of the United States, the inheritance of two centuries of capitalism. For the chaos of socialism would so reduce production as to make it impossible to replace the existing stock of capital goods. Then, as a result of fewer capital goods, production would drop again, and the supply of capital goods would thus decline still further. Socialism would find itself caught in the vicious circle I described in the last chapter of less production causing fewer capital goods causing less production.[6] The day would come when, no matter how high the level at which it began, it could not feed the population. Socialism is an utterly destructive and self-destructive economic system.

### 5. Socialism's Last Gasp: The Attempt to Establish a Socialist Price System and Why It Is Impossible

Von Mises' demonstration of the chaotic consequences of socialism's lack of a price system has not gone entirely unnoticed. While practically all socialists continue to denounce the "wages system" and to extol what they call "production for use" above the hated "production for profit," a handful of academic socialists who are conversant with economics have recognized the devastating power of von Mises' criticisms.

According to these socialists, it was a minor oversight of all other socialists to have failed to understand the operations of the price system and to have sought to destroy it, and thus to destroy all of civilization along with it, for over a century. Fortunately, however, before socialism could destroy civilization, the material productive forces came to the rescue and made von Mises see the problem, and his criticisms have now led this handful of academic socialists to recognize what must be done to avert disaster. I do not exaggerate. Oskar Lange, formerly of the University of California and the University of Chicago and later deputy premier of Communist Poland, writes:

"Socialists have certainly good reason to be grateful to Professor Mises, the great *advocatus diaboli* of their cause. For it was his powerful challenge that forced the socialists to recognize the importance of an adequate system of economic accounting to guide the allocation of resources in a socialist economy. Even more, it was chiefly due to Professor Mises' challenge that many socialists became aware of the very existence of such a problem. . . . a statue of Professor Mises ought to occupy an honorable place in the great hall of the Ministry of Socialization or of the Central Planning Board of the socialist state. . . . a socialist teacher might invite his students in a class on dialectical materialism to go and look at the statue, in order to exemplify the Hegelian *List der Vernunft* [cunning of 'reason'] which made even the stanchest of bourgeois economists unwittingly serve the proletarian cause."[7]

The alleged solution to the economic problems of socialism offered by Lange and the others (whom we must view as a kind of self-styled vanguard of the vanguard of the proletariat, trying to teach the vanguard not to act as a barbarian horde) is known as "liberal socialism" or, sometimes, "market socialism." It consists in the construction of a mythical economic system that is analogous to the centaur of Greek Mythology, the beast that was supposed to be half man, half horse. That system is *capitalism's price system appended to the body of socialism.* Socialism is to have free-market prices for all goods and services. It is to have wages, interest, and profits. The hated "wages system," that Marx spent his life attacking, is to be retained. Production is to be "production for profit," not, as all socialists have always said previously, "production for use." In this way, socialism is allegedly to be able to have all the advantages of capitalism, plus more; for it will simultaneously pocket all of the profits that under capitalism would go to the capitalists. Profits will serve as a "parameter," that is, as a guide to what to do—though, of course, no one will actually profit from doing what he is supposed to do.

This doctrine, incidentally, was presented for consideration in Russia under Khrushchev. It was known as "Libermanism," after a Russian professor of that name. The proposed role of profits was described with great fanfare at the time, in practically the very words I have used. "Libermanism" has not been heard from since, and with good reason, as we shall see.

Now the way socialism is to achieve a price system is by dividing the socialist economy up into separate sections or firms. Each will be assigned a balance at the government's central bank. The government will set prices for all goods and services. At least on paper, these firms will then buy from and sell to each other; they will also sell to consumers and pay wages. They will pay interest on capital to the government's central bank and even to other enterprises, and they will record profits and losses.

There is really nothing astonishing in any of this. It is similar to socialism on the German or Nazi pattern, in that seemingly separate, independent enterprises will exist. Lange, Liberman, and the others simply want to convert Russian-style socialism into something more closely resembling German-style socialism.

They go further. They claim that many or most of the controls of German-style socialism can be abolished. They claim that a price system can be developed within the context of their German-style socialism, that would make it unnecessary for the government to engage in specific allocations of physical factors of production. They claim, in effect, that all the government need do is allocate capital in money terms to different enterprises or individuals, tell them to invest and produce in the lowest-cost, most profitable way, and then everything will take place as under capitalism except that the government will rake in the profits. There allegedly need be no problem of shortages as a result of the government's prices being set too low, or unsaleable surpluses as a result of its prices being set too high; for as soon as such shortages or surpluses appear, it is claimed, the government can raise or lower the prices concerned and thus achieve a balance between supply and demand.

Now the absurdity of what Lange, Liberman, and the others propose can be grasped most simply by starting with the existence of capitalism and then imagining two alternative things to occur: 1) the government imposes price and wage controls, 2) the government obtains the power to expropriate any firm's or individual's capital and turn it over to any other firm or individual at its discretion. After we look at the consequences of each of these measures separately, we can consider their operation in conjunction; and that will describe what to expect from any attempt at a "price system" under socialism.

According to Lange, Liberman, *et al*, a socialist government could have a price system and make it work by varying prices in response to changing conditions of supply, demand, and cost. In the case of price controls imposed on an existing capitalist system, the individual capitalists have a powerful personal incentive to try to push the government to change its controls every time there is a change in supply, demand, or cost. It is absurd to believe, however, that the government could be made to change its controls in the same way that the capitalists would have changed their prices in a free market.

To make this as concrete as possible, what Lange, Liberman, and the others are implying—though apparently without being aware of it—is that the government could control the price of oil and gasoline and apartment rents and so forth, and would then vary its controls every day in just the same way as a free market would have varied its prices. Now if this were really so, we must ask why the Federal Energy Administration did not listen to the oil companies and raise the price of oil and gasoline during the oil shortage, or why the New York City rent-control authorities have never listened to the landlords and raised rents in the face of the shortage of controlled housing? We must ask why price controls are imposed in the first place, for what purpose could they serve if they were really to duplicate the prices charged in a free market?

The fact is that government price-control officials do not and cannot control prices in the way a free market would have set them. For the basis of the free market's prices is the *self-interests* of the different individuals concerned, acting in an environment of freedom of competition. A gas station owner, an oil company, a landlord, and so on, sets his price on the basis of what is most profitable *for him*, given the same endeavor of all others in setting their prices and in choosing whether or not to pay his. *Self-interest and the freedom of competition are the driving force of price determination under capitalism. Government control of prices thwarts this driving force.*

While price controls thwart this driving force, the socialization of the economic system destroys it utterly, and more besides.

There is one, indispensable control that socialism must have, even under the most relaxed imaginable variant of the German-style socialism envisioned by Lange, Liberman, *et al*; and that is *the right to withdraw capital at any time from any enterprise and make it available to any other enterprise*. This minimum control on the allocation of capital is inescapably implied in the very nature of government ownership: if the government is to be the owner, the enterprises and those in charge of them can have no right to regard the capital at their disposal as theirs for one moment longer than the government wishes it.

To grasp the significance of this fact, let us forget about price controls for the moment. Let us return to an existing capitalist system, and assume that all the government does is obtain the power to expropriate the capital of any firm or individual and turn it over to any other firm or individual at its discretion. This is the equivalent to what it must be able to do, as a minimum, under the most "liberal" variant of so-called market socialism. Thus, for example, one year, it uses this power to halve or totally eliminate the capital of the General Motors Corporation and build up the capital of other enterprises. The next year, it gives the real estate of Manhattan Island to a different group of owners. In the following year, it dispossesses the farmers of New Jersey and turns their farms over to others. The government can do this in the same way that a private business today can close down some branches and open others, or fire existing managers and replace them with new ones—for the property is the government's, not that of the private firms or individuals any longer.

Now this measure would totally destroy all the incentives of ownership.

*Nevertheless, it is to people in such a position that "market socialism" in its logically consistent form wants to entrust the supreme management of the socialist economic system.* "Market socialism" wants the socialist government to place capital in the hands of firms and individuals who will have absolutely no incentives of ownership, and then to give them discretion as to its investment. It wants the government to delegate its responsibility for investment to them, by giving them capital and then telling them to go and make believe they are capitalists. As I have said, it expects that then everything will work as under capitalism except that the state will be able to claim all of the profits.

If this system were actually implemented, those to whom the socialist state entrusted the use of its capital at any time would be in the position of owners of capital at the pleasure of the state. Their powers of discretion in investment would be genuine powers of ownership, but they would last no longer than the state desired. They would be in the position of people facing the constant threat of expropriation. They would, in effect, be property owners, but they would be less secure in their possession of property than were the owners of fields along the coast of Europe in the era of the Viking raids. It is obvious that the self-interest of people in such a position is very different from that of capitalists under capitalism. Not being secure owners of property, they are not in a position to think of enhancing its value on a long-range basis. Their horizon extends no further than the immediate moment. If they are given significant discretion in its use, their self-interest lies with personally consuming as much of the capital entrusted to them as possible, or converting it to some concealable form, such as gold or jewels. If the socialist state effectively thwarts this motive, it succeeds merely in securing the services of people who are disinterested in the most literal sense of the term.

To grasp the nature of this disinterest, simply think again of our example of the General Motors Corporation, the owners of Manhattan real estate, the New Jersey farmers, and so on. Under "market socialism," all of them have the threat of impending expropriation hanging over their heads. Their self-interest is to consume or conceal as much of their property as possible. We may assume that to prevent this, the government issues orders severely punishing such acts, and that it thereby actually succeeds in stopping them. Now what? Now, the "market socialists" believe, these property owners will be willing to simply go to work for the state with the same zeal with which they would have worked for themselves, and will continue in loyal service until the day the state expropriates them and turns their property over to a new set of owners. Then this new set will do the same thing.

It should be clear that what all of the abstruse talk of the "market socialists" about the "parametric" function of profits in a socialist society boils down to is this: It is profitable to a man to clear and cultivate a field, to develop a business, to construct a factory, which is why under capitalism he does it. Under socialism he will allegedly still do it, not because it is profitable *to him*, but because it is "parametrically" profitable—that is, profitable *to his expropriators*. If traditional socialism requires that an omniscient deity assume command of the socialist economy to make it work, "market socialism" requires the descent of Jesus of Nazareth, Francis of Assisi, and all the other saints of altruism, who will, in the meantime, assume the garb of hard-nosed, calculating businessmen. "Market socialism" is the same old line of "from each according to his ability, to each according to his need," but dressed up in the ludicrous guise of the businessman's quest for profit.

I have not mentioned the opportunities for corruption that a system of "market socialism" would create, nor, having now mentioned them, will I dwell on them. It is clear, however, that under such a system vast personal fortunes could rotate, as it were, among succeeding sets of government favorites who were awarded the right to invest the capital of the economic system.

It is really a nonessential under "market socialism" whether the government explicitly controls prices or not. It could delegate this responsibility to the individual enterprises if it wished. If it did, it might achieve an economic system at the level of, say, Turkey under the arbitrary, despotic rule of the sultans, when no one could be secure in the possession of any property—when no one dared to improve his house or fields, let alone build a factory, for fear of having them seized by the government.

If the government does control prices, as Lange and the others actually suggest, it is absurd to believe that the enterprises to whom it entrusts capital will be zealously besieging the price-control office with requests to raise or lower them so as to balance demand and supply; or, of course, that the price-control office would have any more reason to listen to their requests than when price controls are imposed on an existing capitalist system.

It is obvious that socialism cannot rationally entrust its management to people who either have no incentive at all or an incentive to grab what they can while the opportunity exists. And, in fact, none of the so-called market socialists is actually consistent enough to go very far in his proposals. Without ever explicitly mentioning it, and certainly without ever stressing the fact, they all take for granted that the discretion of the enterprises will be severely limited. They all take for granted that the state will give precise orders to each enterprise concerning what industry or industries it is to operate in, what products it is to produce, how many factories it is to have, and where, and what kind and how many machines it is to have. The discretion they are actually willing to allow is in the relatively minor and very narrow area of how best to use the existing quantity and quality of plant and equipment assigned, for the purposes assigned.

But this brings "market socialism" back to all of the problems of socialist "planning" that it claims to have solved. For in this case, the state must still decide the relative size of the various industries, the quantity and composition of their output, their basic methods of production, and their physical location. And, as we have seen, it has no rational way of deciding these things, for it must try to do so without the aid of a price system.

The limited discretion the "market socialists" want to allow would only introduce further disruption into the already anarchic conditions of socialist production. For it would allow enterprises on their own initiative to snatch away materials, supplies, and labor from other enterprises in ways that could not be controlled by the government planners, and which would thus disrupt even such limited, partial planning as they are presently able to accomplish in behalf of projects of special priority. Imagine, for example, the Russian government trying to build a tank factory, only to find that it cannot do so because some of its own enterprises have snapped up all the supplies of some vital material or part. It is for this very reason, I am sure, that "market socialism"—even of the very timid variety actually recommended by Lange and the others—has never been tried in the socialist countries, is unlikely ever to be tried, and, if tried, would soon be abandoned.

The only solution for the problems of socialism is, as von Mises saw almost sixty years ago, the restoration of capitalism.

# The Tyranny of Socialism
# VII

1. The Tyranny of Socialism

The chaos of socialism is equalled only by the tyranny of socialism. In abolishing economic freedom, socialism absolishes political freedom. In abolishing property rights, it abolishes civil rights. In a word, socialism means the establishment of a totalitarian dictatorship.

It must be stressed again that when I refer to socialism, I am referring to *all* variants of socialism—the socialism of the allegedly respectable socialists, such as the Social Democrats, as well as the socialism of the Nazis and Communists. I stress this fact because a widespread misconception prevails that somehow the "good" socialists could achieve socialism by peaceful means and thereafter preserve political freedoms and civil liberties. That is not so, and it has never been so. And no one should make the mistake of thinking that countries like Great Britain, Israel, and Sweden are exceptions. As we have seen, these countries are not in fact socialist countries, but mixed economies.[1]

In every instance in which socialism has actually been enacted, as, for example, in Nazi Germany, Soviet Russia, Communist China, Communist Cuba, and all the other communist-bloc countries, its totalitarianism has been manifest. It is only necessary to show why the violent, bloody means that have been employed to achieve socialism, and the perpetual reign of terror that follows thereafter, are no accident, but are caused by the very nature of socialism; why, in other words, socialism is a thoroughly evil end, necessitating evil means for its achievement, and necessarily producing the most evil consequences.

## 2. The Necessity of Evil Means to Achieve Socialism

Let us begin by considering the means employed to achieve socialism. We observe two phenomena that are not unrelated. First, wherever socialism has actually been enacted, as in the communist-bloc countries and Nazi Germany, violent and bloody means have been used to achieve it and/or maintain it. And, second, where socialist parties have come to power but abstained from wholesale violence and bloodshed, as in Great Britain, Israel, and Sweden, they have *not* enacted socialism, but retained a mixed economy, which they did not radically or fundamentally alter. Let us consider the reasons for these facts.

*Even if a socialist government were democratically elected, its first act in office in implementing socialism would have to be an act of enormous violence, namely, the forcible expropriation of the means of production.* The democratic election of a socialist government would not change the fact that the seizure of property against the will of its owners is an act of force. A forcible expropriation of property based on a democratic vote is about as peaceful as a lynching based on a democratic vote. It is a cardinal violation of individual rights. The only way that socialism could truly come into existence by peaceful means would be if property owners *voluntarily donated their property to the socialist state.* But consider. If socialism had to wait for property owners to voluntarily donate their property to the state, it would almost certainly have to wait forever. If socialism is *ever* to exist, therefore, it can only come about by means of force—force applied on a massive scale, against all private property.

Further, in the case of the socialization of the entire economic system, as opposed to that of an isolated industry, no form of compensation to the property owners is possible. In the case of an isolated nationalization, the government can largely compensate the loss of the former owners by taxing the rest of the property owners to some extent. If the government seizes all property, however, and simply abolishes private ownership, then there is just no possibility of compensation. The government simply steals everyone's property lock, stock, and barrel. In these circumstances, property owners will almost certainly resist and try to defend their rights by force if necessary, as they properly should.

This explains why it takes the Communists to achieve socialism, and why the Social Democrats always fail to achieve socialism. The Communists, in effect, know that they are out to steal all of men's property from them and that if they expect to succeed, they had better come armed and prepared to kill the property owners, who will attempt to defend their rights. The Social Democrats, on the other hand, are held back by fear from taking the steps that would be necessary to achieve socialism.

In sum, the essential facts are these. Socialism must commence with an enormous act of theft. Those who seriously want to steal must be prepared to kill those whom they plan to rob. In effect, the Social Democrats are mere con men and pickpockets, who engage in empty talk about pulling the "big job"—socialism—someday, and who flee before the first sign of resistance by their intended victims. The Communists, on the other hand, are serious about pulling the "big job." They are armed robbers prepared to commit murder. This is why the Communists are able to implement socialism, while the Social Democrats are unable to implement socialism. Of the two, only the Communists are willing to employ the bloody means that are necessary to implement socialism.

### 3. The Necessity of Terror Under Socialism

If socialism is not to be achieved by open force, the only other way it can be achieved is behind people's backs—i.e., by fraud—which is the method of price and wage controls. This was the route chosen by the Nazis.

But however socialism may be achieved, whether by open force or by fraud, its maintenance requires a reign of terror. It requires an environment in which people cannot trust even their friends, an environment in which they are afraid to express any ideas of their own, or even to ask questions. It requires precisely the kind of environment that existed in Nazi Germany and that exists in every communist country today.

In order to begin to understand this point, let us consider merely the requirements of enforcing price and wage controls in an economy that is falling under the rule of *de facto* socialism. Let us imagine our own economy suffering from universal price controls and universal shortages and observe what would be required just to enforce the price-control regulations and prevent the development of a black market so large as to make the price controls largely meaningless.

Imagine, therefore, that we have a fully price-controlled economy, and that enough time has gone by to create shortages of practically everything. Imagine that we have gasoline shortages, meat shortages, power shortages, shoe shortages—shortages of all goods. In these conditions, every seller would have a powerful self-interest in charging higher prices than the law allowed, and every buyer would have a powerful self-interest in offering to pay such higher prices as a means of outbidding others, in order to obtain a larger supply for himself. How could the government stop the buyers and sellers from pursuing their mutual self-interests and transacting business above its ceiling prices?

Obviously, there would have to be penalties imposed for selling above the ceiling prices. But what kind of penalties? If a seller stood to make the equivalent of an extra ten or twenty thousand dollars a year, say, by defying the price-control regulations, an occasional small fine would certainly not be a sufficient deterrent. And probably even the smallest neighborhood shops would stand to take in far more than that amount of extra income by defying the regulations. If the government were serious about its price controls, therefore, it would be necessary for it to impose severe penalties—penalties comparable to those for a major felony.

But the mere existence of such penalties would not be enough. The government would also have to be able actually to catch the violators and obtain convictions. It would have to make it actually dangerous to conduct black-market transactions. It would have to make people fear that in conducting such a transaction they might somehow be discovered by the police, and actually end up in jail. In order to create such fear, the government would have to develop an army of spies and secret informers. For example, the government would have to make a storekeeper and his customer fearful that if they engaged in a black-market transaction, some other customer in the store would report them. Because of the privacy and secrecy in which many black-market transactions could be conducted, the government would have to make anyone contemplating a black-market transaction fearful that the other party might turn out to be a police agent trying to trap him. The government would have to make people fearful of their long-time associates, even of their friends and relatives, lest even they turn out to be informers.

And, finally, in order to obtain convictions, the government would have to place the decision about innocence or guilt in the case of black-market transactions in the hands of an administrative tribunal. It could not rely on jury trials, because it would be unlikely that many juries could be found willing to bring in guilty verdicts in cases in which a man might have to go to jail for several years for the crime of selling a few pounds of meat or a pair of shoes above the ceiling price.

In sum, therefore, the requirements merely of enforcing price-control regulations would be the adoption of essential features of a totalitarian state, namely, the establishment of the category of "economic crimes," in which the peaceful pursuit of material self-interest is treated as a criminal offense, and the establishment of a totalitarian police apparatus replete with spies and informers and the power of arbitrary arrest and imprisonment. Clearly, the enforcement of price controls requires a government similar to that of Hitler's Germany or Stalin's Russia. If the government is unwilling to go to such lengths, then, to that extent, its price controls prove unenforceable and simply break down. The black market then assumes major proportions.

Now observe that in a socialized economy, a black market also exists. Only in this case, its existence entails the commission of further crimes. Under *de facto* socialism, the production and sale of goods in the black market entails the defiance of the government's regulations concerning production and distribution, as well as the defiance of its price controls. For example, the goods themselves that are sold in the black market are intended by the government to be distributed in accordance with its plan, and not in the black market. The factors of production used to produce those goods are likewise intended by the government to be used in accordance with its plan, and not for the purpose of supplying the black market. Under a system of *de jure* socialism, such as exists in Soviet Russia, all black-market activity necessarily entails the misappropriation of state property. From the point of view of the legal code of a socialist state, most black-market activity must be regarded simply as the theft of state property. For example, the factory workers or managers in Soviet Russia who turn out products that they sell in the black market are considered as stealing the raw materials supplied by the state.

Observe further. In a socialist state, the government's economic plan is part of the supreme law of the land. We have already seen in the last chapter how chaotic the so-called planning process of socialism is. Its further disruption by workers and managers siphoning off materials and supplies to produce for the black market, is something which a socialist state is logically entitled to regard as an act of *sabotage*. And that is how the legal code of a socialist state does regard it. Consistent with this fact, black-market activity in a socialist country often carries the death penalty. In Nazi Germany, people were beheaded for it. In Soviet Russia, they are shot.

Even apart from possible indulgence in black-market activity, every socialist official who has responsibility for production necessarily leads a dangerous life. On the one hand, any use of factors of production in a way different than that specified by the state's economic plan lays such an official open to a charge of sabotage. On the other hand, it is generally impossible for the state's economic plan to be very precise, as we have seen; and so some discretion must be used. Since a socialist economic system functions in a state of continuous chaos and chronic crisis, it is very easy for any given official to be singled out and blamed for some disaster caused by socialism's anarchy of production. It becomes an essential talent under socialism for an official to be able to know how to cover himself and always to have scapegoats of his own at hand. From the top to the bottom, an incredible game of buck passing, favor trading, and mutual blackmail takes place. Ever-shifting alliances and factions are formed for mutual protection. And, periodically, victims are sacrificed: usually, subordinate officials here and there; sometimes, entire factions in giant purges.

The fundamental fact driving socialism to a reign of terror is the incredible dilemma in which the socialist state places itself in relation to the masses of its citizens.[2] On the one hand, the socialist state assumes full responsibility for the individual's economic well-being. It openly avows this responsibility—this is the whole source of socialism's popular appeal. On the other hand, in all of the ways we have shown, the socialist state makes *an unbelievable botch of the job*. It makes the individual's life a nightmare. Every day of his life, the citizen of a socialist state must spend time in endless waiting lines. For him, the problems we experienced in the gasoline shortage are normal; only he does not experience them in relation to gasoline—for he does not own a car and has no hope of ever owning one—but in relation to simple items of clothing, to vegetables, even to bread. Even worse, as we will see, he is frequently forced to work at a job not of his choice and which he therefore must certainly hate. And he lives in a condition of unbelievable overcrowding, with hardly ever a chance for privacy. To put it mildly, such a man must seethe with resentment and hostility.

Now against whom would it be more logical for the citizens of a socialist state to direct their resentment and hostility than against that very socialist state itself? The same socialist state which has proclaimed its responsibility for their life, has promised them a life of bliss, and which *in fact* is responsible for giving them a life of hell. Indeed, the leaders of a socialist state live in a further dilemma, in that they daily encourage the people to believe that socialism is a perfect system whose bad results can only be the work of evil men. If that were true, who *in reason* could those evil men be but *the rulers themselves*, who have not only made life a hell, but have perverted an allegedly perfect system to do it?

It follows that the rulers of a socialist state must live in terror of the people. By the logic of their actions and their teachings, the boiling, seething resentment of the people should well up and swallow them in an orgy of bloody vengeance. The rulers sense this, even if they do not admit it openly; and thus their major concern is always to keep the lid on the citizenry.

Consequently, it is true but very inadequate merely to say such things as that socialism lacks freedom of the press and freedom of speech. Of course, it lacks these freedoms. If the government owns all the newspapers and publishing houses, if it decides for what purposes newsprint and paper are to be made available, then obviously nothing can be printed which the government does not want printed. If it owns all the meeting halls, no public speech or lecture can be delivered which the government does not want delivered. But socialism goes far beyond the mere lack of freedom of press and speech. It totally *annihilates* these freedoms. It turns the press and every public forum into a vehicle of hysterical propaganda in its own behalf, and it engages in the relentless persecution of everyone who dares to deviate by so much as an inch from its official party line.

The reason for these facts is the socialist rulers' terror of the people. To protect themselves, they must order the propaganda ministry and the secret police to work 'round the clock. The one, to constantly divert the people's attention from the responsibility of socialism, and of the rulers of socialism, for the people's misery. The other, to spirit away and silence anyone who might even remotely suggest the responsibility of socialism or its rulers—to spirit away anyone who begins to show signs of thinking for himself. It is because of the rulers' terror, and their desperate need to find scapegoats for the failures of socialism, that the press of a socialist country is always full of stories about foreign plots and sabotage, and about corruption and mismanagement on the part of subordinate officials, and why, periodically, it is necessary to unmask large-scale domestic plots and to sacrifice major officials and entire factions in giant purges.

It is because of their terror, and their desperate need to crush every breath even of potential opposition, that the rulers of socialism do not dare to allow even purely cultural activities that are not under the control of the state. For if people so much as assemble for an art show that is not controlled by the state—as they tried to do in Moscow not so long ago—the rulers must fear the dissemination of dangerous ideas. Any unauthorized ideas are dangerous ideas, because they can lead people to begin thinking for themselves and thus to begin thinking about the nature of socialism and its rulers. The rulers must fear the spontaneous assembly of a handful of people in a room, and use the secret police and its apparatus of spies, informers, and terror either to stop such meetings or to make sure that their content is entirely innocuous from the point of view of the state.

Socialism cannot be ruled for very long except by terror. As soon as the terror is relaxed, resentment and hostility logically begin to well up against the rulers. The stage is thus set for a revolution or civil war. In fact, in the absence of terror, or, more correctly, a sufficient degree of terror, socialism would be characterized by an endless series of revolutions and civil wars, as each new group of rulers proved as incapable of making socialism function successfully as its predecessors before it.

The inescapable inference to be drawn from this discussion is that the terror actually experienced in the socialist countries has not been simply the work of evil men, such as Stalin, but springs from the nature of the socialist system, *and is still going on at this very moment.* Stalin could come to the fore because his unusual willingness and cunning in the use of terror were the specific characteristics most required by a ruler of socialism. He rose to the top by a process of socialist natural selection: the selection of the worst.[3] His heirs are still resorting to the same techniques. As examples, consider the invasion of Czechoslovakia and the use of drugs to destroy the sanity of dissidents in Russia. And, of course, there is no way of knowing what is not reported to the outside world, which is probably a good deal worse than what is or even can be reported. For most of Russia is inaccessible to foreign correspondents, and contacts with Russian citizens are severely limited by the Russian government.[4]

The only reason for these restrictions is that the Russian government still has a great deal to hide. If Stalin's heirs do not find it necessary to be fully as brutal as Stalin himself, it is only because they are able to coast on the environment of fear and the habit of unquestioning obedience that he created. Periodically, fresh demonstrations of terror on the scale applied by Stalin will be required to prevent socialism from collapsing into continuous civil war and revolution.

In the meanwhile, the Russian people do experience all the hostility and resentment I have described, but they are so fearful and so contemptible that they channel it against each other rather than against socialism and its rulers. Hedrick Smith writes: ". . . Soviet society in general is peopled by mini-dictators inflicting inconvenience and misery on the rest of their fellow citizens, often, it seems, as a way of getting back at the system for the hardship and frustration they themselves have suffered."[5] He quotes a Russian scientist: " 'Put a Russian in charge of a little plot of ground or a doorway somewhere, and he will use his meager authority over that spot to make life hard on others.' " Smith notes that he has heard Russians describe this phenomenon as "a mass settling of scores on a personal level."[6]

*This* is the psychological and moral climate of a socialist society—a society blinded by terror and reduced virtually to the punishment of all by all. It is terror and universal hatred that socialism and its rulers require lest they be blasted off the earth.

### 4. The Necessity of Forced Labor Under Socialism

Socialism necessitates a system of forced labor—slavery. Forced labor is implied in the very ideal of socialist planning. If the state is to plan the production of all commodities, it must also plan the skills that the workers will possess who are to produce those commodities, and where those workers are to live and work. It is incompatible with socialist planning for private individuals to have the freedom to acquire the skills *they* want and to live where *they* want. Such freedom would alone make socialist planning impossible.

Of course, socialism cannot plan in any case. Nevertheless, forced labor remains an essential feature of socialism. As shown in the previous chapter, the economic conditions of socialism are the same as those which prevail under universal price controls and universal shortages. Accordingly, socialism is characterized by a labor shortage, in which there is a ready and waiting employment for more labor in the production of virtually every good. The labor shortage under socialism results from the fact that a socialist government wants to expand production, but is unable to trace the connections among the different industries; it is unable to determine the effects of producing more of any one item on the ability to produce other items.

As a result, it establishes a quota system, as in Soviet Russia, in which it tries to encourage the maximum possible production of *each* item. This creates a need for additional labor and all other factors of production in every industry and factory. The labor shortage is compounded by all of the inefficiencies of socialism, which cause a larger amount of labor to be required to produce each unit of a good. Finally, the shortages of consumers' goods under socialism act to reduce the supply of labor by destroying the incentive to work and earn money, leading people to stop working.[7]

In the face of such conditions, if the government is unwilling to abandon socialism (or price controls, however the case may be), its only alternative is *to freeze people into their jobs, order them into those jobs and those geographical areas where it considers their work vital, and extract work from them by the threat of physical force.* The government must freeze people into their jobs to stop them from quitting in response to the shortage of consumers' goods. It must order them into specific jobs in specific areas for the same reasons it finds it necessary when a shortage exists to allocate crude oil or any other factor of production to the production of specific products in specific places, namely, to avoid the chaos of products it considers vital not being produced because other products it considers less important are produced instead. It must extract work by the threat of force because, with the money that jobs offer no longer a value to the workers, it lacks adequate positive incentives to offer them.

This, of course, is a system of slavery.

## Forced Labor in Soviet Russia

The extent to which forced labor exists right now in Soviet Russia must be considered, because this is a matter which is almost entirely ignored by the press.

Forced labor exists in present-day Russia in the following ways. First, all people living on collective farms—at least 40 percent of the Russian population, according to the Russian government's own statistics—are prohibited from moving away from those farms without the permission of the collective-farm managements. In addition, at harvest time, all available urban workers are forced into the countryside to help bring in the harvest. (Observe, incidentally, that the collective farming system is so inefficient that 40 percent of the population is insufficient to bring in the harvest. In the United States, by way of comparison, about 4 percent of the population is more than sufficient for agriculture.) Second, every graduate of a university or technical school in Russia is compulsorily assigned to a job for a period of two to three years following graduation. Third, every remaining worker in Russia is compelled to have a labor book that details all of his previous employment, including comments by his former employers, reasons for changing jobs, and so on. This book must be presented to each new employer. Employment cannot be obtained without it. The employer then keeps the book so long as the worker is employed at that particular job. Theoretically, since Khrushchev, the employer is supposed to return the labor book at the worker's request. Nevertheless, this system certainly discourages the worker's leaving any given job against the employer's wishes, and is, in fact, a forcible deterrent to changing jobs. In addition, it is illegal in Soviet Russia to be unemployed.[8]

Since most of Soviet Russia is closed off to foreigners, it is impossible to have any direct knowledge of what goes on in most of the country; but one must assume that it is worse than in the parts that are open to foreigners. Based on my knowledge of the nature of socialism, I see no reason not to believe that there are still enormous numbers of people shipped off to do forced labor under deadly conditions, just as under Stalin. Recent estimates place the number of inmates currently in Russian concentration camps at between one and two million people.[9] It could be substantially higher.

If the severity of forced labor in Soviet Russia today is not as great as it was under Stalin, the explanation is largely a more flourishing black market. The black market is now estimated to account for about 20 percent of Russia's economy.[10] In addition, it is legal for the members of collective farms to farm small, one-acre plots on their own account and to sell the produce in the cities for whatever prices it can bring. These small plots account for less than 3 percent of the cultivated land in Russia and produce about 30 percent of its agricultural output.[11] This agricultural output and the black market make it worthwhile for people to work and earn money; within limits they provide people with something to spend the money on.

Notice, however, how the mitigation of forced labor and, indeed, the very survival of the socialist system, depend on the extent to which socialist principles are violated. Strictly, according to socialist principles, there should be no black market and no quasi-private farming plots. But it is only by permitting them that the system can survive. For the rest, the fact that forced labor is not as severe as it was under Stalin is the result of a willingness on the part of Russia's present rulers to tolerate enormous rates of labor absenteeism and a general breakdown of what the regime calls "labor discipline."[12] (To illustrate how pervasive these problems are, Hedrick Smith describes a popular comedy routine in Russia, in which three workers sneak away from their jobs to get haircuts. They receive miserable service because their barbers sneak off too. The barbers, in turn, cannot obtain the things they want, because the dentist, repairman, and grocer they were seeking are the very customers left sitting in their chairs.[13])

### The Imposition of Forced Labor in the United States

It must be stressed that a system of forced labor could be imposed even in the United States. This could happen either as a result of the open socialization of the economic system, or, as is much more likely, as part of a program of *de facto* socialization carried out in response to the chaos created by price controls. None of our traditions, none of our past record of freedom, would be enough to stop it.

It should be realized that such slavery was actually instituted during World War II in countries with very similar traditions as the United States.

It was imposed in Great Britain, Australia, and even Canada. During World War II, workers in those countries could not quit or change their jobs without government permission, and they could be ordered to work wherever the government required them. Similar legislation was proposed to the Congress of the United States by President Roosevelt in his State of the Union Message of January 1944.[14] Fortunately, the legislation did not pass. But had the United States been at war longer and the effects of the labor shortage become more severe, as a result of the continued operation of inflation and price controls, it is very likely that such legislation would have been enacted even here. For the only alternative, given the continuation of price controls, would have been chaos in the allocation of labor and the massive stoppage of work.

Thus, if we adopt socialism in this country, no matter what its form, we must expect the same consequences as exist in Soviet Russia.

### 5. Socialism as a System of Aristocratic Privilege and a Court Society

Once the government assumes the power to determine the individual's job, it obtains the power to decide whether he must spend his life working in a coal mine in a remote village somewhere, or in the comparative comfort of one of its offices in the capital. It obtains the power to decide whether he will pass his life as an obscure nobody living in poverty, or enjoy a flourishing career, celebrated in his field, and living in comparative opulence.[15] This, of course, goes along with the government's power over the distribution of consumers' goods—a power which every socialist government naturally possesses. In accordance with its powers of distribution, a socialist government decides what kind of house or apartment the individual is to occupy, what kind of clothing he is to wear, what kind of food he is to eat, whether or not he is to own an automobile, and so on.

In Soviet Russia today, for example, the government assigns different grades of housing based on rank in the government or Communist Party. On the same basis, it decides who can and who cannot buy an automobile. It even maintains special stores that are closed to the general public and which exclusively serve high government and party officials and their favorites in the arts and sciences. These stores carry many kinds of Western imports, from clothing to tape recorders, and the limited supplies of whatever worthwhile goods as are produced in Russia itself. While such things as meat may be unavailable throughout most of Russia for months on end, the privileged customers of these stores are supplied with caviar.[16]

The existence of a system of naked aristocratic privilege is not a contradiction of the principles of socialism, but their natural outgrowth. It follows directly from socialism's fundamental moral and political premise, which is that the individual does not exist as an end in himself, but as a means to the ends of "Society." Since Society is not an independent entity with a will and voice of its own, the alleged ends of Society are necessarily ends determined by the rulers of the socialist state. This means that under socialism the individual is a means to the ends of the rulers. It is difficult to imagine a system that could be more aristocratic in nature.

The existence of a system of aristocratic privilege does not contradict the slogan "from each according to his ability, to each according to his need."[17] The rulers of socialism can and do assert that they and their favorites have "special needs." Moreover, that slogan was intended by Marx to be achieved only under "socialism in its higher phase"—that is, after generations of socialism had changed human nature. If one thinks seriously about the meaning of the phrase "a change in human nature," one must realize that it is a contradiction and therefore impossible. A change in human *nature* is as absurd an idea as a change in the nature of water or lead. Men will be able to practice the principle "from each according to his ability, to each according to his need," when water is able to flow uphill and lead to float. Meanwhile, while it is waiting for human nature to "change," a socialist state is free to adopt any system of distribution it pleases.

What positively generates the system of aristocratic privilege under socialism is the fact that the only values that actually count in a socialist society are the values of its rulers. It should be recalled from the previous chapter that the absence of competition and profit-and-loss incentives in supplying the consumers makes the plain citizens economically impotent under socialism. Production thus takes place exclusively in accordance with the values of the rulers. What the rulers value is what contributes to their military strength, their prestige, and their amusement. The goods required by the masses for survival enter into the rulers' valuations only to the extent that the rulers need subjects and do not wish to lose too many of them.

The nature of the rulers' values determines the nature of the incentives and inequalities of a socialist society. It is not true that a socialist society exists entirely without incentives. That would be true only if it tried to practice consistently the absurd ideal "from each according to his ability, to each according to his need." In actual fact, a socialist society does have some incentives. But the incentives are geared entirely to the achievement of the values of the rulers. There are no incentives to the achievement of the values of the plain citizens.

The kind of incentives and inequalities that prevail under socialism are similar to those which prevail in an army. In an army there are incentives for privates to make corporal and for everyone to advance to a higher grade. But all the incentives in an army are geared to achieving the objectives of the supreme commander. The objectives of the supreme commander are the ultimate ends, definitely not the improvement of the life of the privates. Indeed, neither in an army nor under socialism is the improvement of *anyone's* actual life the goal. The goal is always some impersonal achieve-ment, whether victory in the battle with the neighboring country or victory in the battle of the new dam or truck factory, which is just how the socialists describe their construction projects.[18] The closest socialism ever comes to making the improvement of life its goal is its alleged concern with the improvement of the life of unborn future generations. But no sooner does the generation of the grandchildren arrive, than socialism's concern switches to the grandchildren of the grandchildren.[19]

Socialism is essentially a militaristic-aristocratic type society. It rests on a base of starving serfs, comprising the great majority of the population, who live at or below the level of minimum physical subsistence and whose only function in life is to toil for the values of the rulers. Workers with special skills of value to the rulers may be somewhat better off, if that is what is necessary to make them deliver their skills and if it is practicable to offer them such incentives. But they too are essentially just serfs—they too work under force, and what they receive is subsistence or sub-subsistence plus a small bonus for their skill. Above the serfs come various grades of officials and favorites, who help the rulers to exploit the serfs or who provide the rulers with weapons of war, the means of gaining greater prestige, or simply amusement. In this category are all the production managers, all the lower and middle party and police officials, the propagandists, the intellec-tuals, the scientists, the artists, the athletes. These are the tools, the hench-men, the flunkies, and the simple court favorites of the socialist society. Finally, at the very top, come the supreme rulers themselves—the men who have outmaneuvered and outgunned all of their rivals. These are the Neanderthals whose power lust and gluttony socialism elevates to the ulti-mate end of human existence.

A few further words need to be said in reference to the middle strata of a socialist society, especially its intellectuals. As a result of a socialist state's twin powers over the individual's work and consumption, everyone's life comes to depend unconditionally on the good graces of every government official with power or influence. In such circumstances, not only are people stopped by terror from criticizing anything the government or any govern-ment official does, but a competition breaks out in the positive *praise and adulation* of the government and its officials. As illustration of the lengths to which such self-abasing flattery can be carried, it should be remembered that educated Germans proclaimed that Hitler spoke with God, the "Führer of the Universe"; and that educated Russians praised Stalin as "the leader genius," the sight of whom made them want "to howl from happiness and exaltation."[20]

The same sort of thing still goes on today in Soviet Russia, though, for the time being, it appears to be somewhat more subdued. In Soviet Russia, no one can rise in his field without the backing of influential friends in the

Party. Major advancement, including the highly coveted privilege of traveling abroad and thus being able to buy foreign goods simply unavailable in Russia, requires serving as an informer for the KGB—the secret police. In Soviet Russia, men betray friends and relatives for the meanest material gains: to be able to buy such things as a Western refrigerator, Western furniture, even a Western toilet.[21]

Ironically, the American sympathizers of Soviet Russia, who work for the establishment of a similar regime here, frequently write books and plays denouncing corporate executives under capitalism for allegedly having sold their souls for material advantage. The socialist society that these authors and playwrights yearn for is a society in which the only way that intellectuals can advance is by means of displaying the most abject servility to Neanderthals, who, in the absence of a capitalist world outside, could offer them no more than a few extra scraps of food wrung from some poor serf. It is pitiable, but that is evidently the path that today's intellectuals find most secure and the reward they find commensurate with their abilities, since a socialist society is what they are striving to bring about.

### 5. From Forced Labor to Mass Murder Under Socialism

There is a further consequence of forced labor under socialism that must be considered, namely, its potential for developing into mass murder. To understand how this can happen, we must contrast forced labor under socialism with forced labor under different conditions.

Slavery existed in ancient Greece and Rome and in the southern United States before the Civil War, and was, of course, a moral abomination. Nevertheless, abominable as slavery was, there was an important factor in these cases which restrained the slave owners and the overseers in their treatment of the slaves. That was the fact that *the slaves were private property*. A private slave owner was restrained in his treatment of his slaves by his own material self-interest. If he injured or killed his slave, he destroyed his own property. Of course, out of ignorance or irrationality, this sometimes happened; but it was the exception rather than the rule. Private slave owners were motivated to treat their slaves with at least the same consideration they gave to their livestock, and to see to it that their overseers acted with the same consideration.

But under socialism, the slaves are "public property"—the property of the state. Those who have charge of the slaves, therefore, have no personal economic interest in their lives or well-being. Since they are not owners of the slaves, they will not derive any personal material benefit if the slaves are alive to work in the future, nor suffer any personal material loss if the slaves are not alive to work in the future. In such conditions, slave labor results in mass murder. The officials in charge of the slaves are given orders to complete certain projects as of a certain time. Quite possibly, they are threatened with being reduced to the status of slaves themselves, if they fail. In these circumstances, the slaves are treated as valueless natural resources. Brutal punishments are inflicted on them for trifling reasons, and they are worked to the point of exhaustion and death. The slaves of socialism are slaves, but they are no one's property and therefore no one's loss.

In this way, slave labor under socialism results in mass murder. In just this way, tens of millions of people have been murdered.

Of course, the economics of slavery under socialism is not a sufficient explanation of mass murder. Those who participate in the system must be utterly depraved. But observe how socialism creates the conditions in which depravity flourishes—the conditions in which depravity can express itself, is freed of the restraints of better motives, and is positively nurtured and encouraged. For it is socialism that delivers men into slavery. It is socialism that removes the restraint of self-interest from those in charge of the slaves. And it is socialism that creates an environment of hatred and sadism. In such conditions, the most depraved and vicious element of the population finds a place for its depravity and viciousness and steps forward to run the labor camps and the whole socialist society.

# Appendix

President Carter's Speech on "Voluntary Guidelines"

In a televised address to the nation on October 24, 1978, President Carter announced his latest program to combat inflation—the program of "voluntary" wage and price "guidelines."

According to *The Wall Street Journal*, the guidelines impose a limit of 7% on wage increases and a limit on price increases of one-half of one percent below a firm's average annual rate of price increase in 1976-77. What the price guidelines mean is that if a company's prices rose 10% in 1976-77, it is allowed to increase them a further 9½% in the coming year. If they rose only 2% in 1976-77, the company will be allowed to increase them in the coming year by only 1½%.

The most decisive objection to the "guidelines" is not that they will not "work," but that they will be economically destructive if they do work. They will be destructive precisely if they are obeyed.

To state the matter as simply and as forcefully as possible: *If we obey the President's guidelines, we will damage the economic system.*

The obvious reason for this is that the guidelines arbitrarily perpetuate relatively low rates of profit in many industries after the economic justification for those low rates of profit has passed. Indeed, they tend to reduce low rates of profit even further. If an industry was not able to increase its prices significantly in 1976-77, because of a temporary oversupply of its products, it is not to be allowed to increase its prices significantly in 1979, either; even though the oversupply problem may well have been solved, and the industry is experiencing growing difficulty in meeting demand. Indeed, the low profits of 1976-77 must be cut still further, because while the industry's price increase is again strictly limited, it must pay 7% higher wages.

The President's guidelines, therefore, are a sure formula for damaging all those companies and industries unfortunate enough to have been earning low profits in the 1976-77 base period. As a result, these companies and industries will not be able to obtain additional capital to expand, and probably will begin to lose capital. Some of the companies may actually be driven out of business.

It is not only these companies and industries that will be harmed, however, but the entire economic system. For many of these firms and industries supply vital materials, parts, tools, or machines, and so on, to other firms and industries. If, for example, the guidelines should damage companies producing common nails, the producers of lumber and plywood must suffer, along with the whole construction industry. If producers of ball bearings or lubricants are damaged, all the firms requiring these products must be damaged; similarly, if the producers of steel, cement, or sulphuric acid are damaged; and so on.

President Carter expressed the conviction that while his program would allow wages to increase by 7%, the average, economy-wide increase in prices would soon only be 5¾%. The difference, he said, would be made possible by an improvement in the productivity of labor. This would reduce the amount of labor needed to produce a unit of goods, and so keep labor costs to a 5¾% increase while wages rose 7%. It is clear, however, that the President's program must act to *reduce* the productivity of labor, not increase it, and, therefore, that if the goal of his program is to hold price increases below wage increases, it will tend sharply to reduce profits throughout the economic system. The reduction in profits, of course, will be accompanied by reductions in business saving and investment and thus by further declines in the productivity of labor.

The President spoke of a reduction in government regulation of industry as a means of improving the productivity of labor. Certainly, a reduction in regulation could substantially help in this regard. But it is absurd to hear about it from a President who by virtue of his "guidelines" is in process of extending government regulation to total control over the economic system—and in the very same speech!

The President's promises to reduce the federal deficit and federal employment cannot be taken with any greater seriousness. If the President were even remotely serious about these matters, he would, at the very least, have proposed a moratorium on new government programs, which he did not do. As far as federal employment is concerned, it is probable that the only lasting effect of his program will be the employment of additional thousands of bureaucrats to implement it.

It should be clear that no amount of giving the President's program "a chance" is going to make it successful. The program is fundamentally misconceived; it is destructive by its very nature, as I have shown.

Every program of "guidelines" must be destructive. For there is simply no way rationally to apply a general formula about prices. This is because what the economic system needs is *prices and wages that are constantly changing in relationship to each other*, and, of course, changing at different rates and in different directions. Whether the government simply freezes all prices, or orders them to rise at a uniform rate, or, as President Carter is doing, to rise in accordance with some prescribed deceleration formula, its action is incompatible with this basic requirement of the economic system; thus it must be destructive.

In advancing his program, the President virtually admitted that he did not quite know what he was doing. No one, he said, really understands inflation or how to deal with it. His own program, he admitted, was imperfect; it represented, in effect, merely the best one could do in the circumstances, and, given a chance, might somehow work.

The President was wrong in his belief that no one really understands inflation or how to deal with it. All of the essentials about inflation have been understood for well over two centuries. Adam Smith understood the issue. David Ricardo understood it. John Stuart Mill understood it. Carl Menger and Eugen von Böhm-Bawerk understood it. Ludwig von Mises understood it. Today, Milton Friedman understands it. F. A. Hayek understands it. Henry Hazlitt understands it. Anyone can understand it who takes the trouble to study the works of these economists.

The President apparently spoke from total ignorance about the subject of inflation. Not once in his entire speech did he mention the essential element, the expansion of the quantity of money by none other than the government itself—i.e., by the administration of Mr. Carter and of his last several predecessors.

The U.S. government inflates the money supply in order to finance additional expenditures without having to raise taxes, or to be able to reduce taxes without having to reduce its expenditures—i.e., in order to be able to operate with budget deficits.

By following a policy of inflation—financed deficits, the government is able to foster the delusion that it has the power to provide people with free benefits of some kind. By creating the money it spends rather than collecting it in taxes, the government is able to appear to the citizens as a wonderful institution possessing independent means in no way derived from them; it appears as a sort of kindly grandfather—as Santa Claus.

The politicians of Mr. Carter's party have been especially adept at catering to this delusion. They regularly succeed in depicting their rivals as nothing more than hard—hearted curmudgeons bent on withholding one free benefit after another from a deserving citizenry.

The truth, of course, is that every "benefit" received from the government is paid for by the people. When the government finances the "benefits" by inflating the money supply, the people pay in the form of prices that rise more rapidly than their incomes.

Instead of acknowledging the government's responsibility for inflation, the President tried to shift the blame onto two scapegoats: big business and its alleged "monopoly power," and the alleged irrationality of the general public. In this way he sought not only to maintain the delusion that the government can provide free benefits, but to foster the corollary delusion that in raising their prices, private individuals are guilty of inflicting gratuitous evil; and thus that the government must assume still wider powers and control prices ("voluntarily," of course).

A few words are necessary to lay to rest these bugaboos of "monopoly power" and the alleged irrationality of the general public as causes of rising prices. First, even if big business possessed monopoly power (which it does not), it could not be responsible for steadily rising prices. It is in the interest of a monopolist to charge all that the traffic can bear, but not more than the traffic can bear. If every year a monopolist finds it profitable to raise his price, something must be happening that enables his customers to afford to pay more and more. That "something" is the *government's increase in the money supply,* which, in being spent and respent, raises people's money incomes and the money value of their assets, and thus allows them to pay more for everything they buy.

As for the irrationality of the general public, Mr. Carter tried to explain inflation in terms of a simplistic spiral in which prices and wages allegedly chase each other ever upwards, fueled by self-fulfilling expectations that the process will continue. He likened the process to the self-defeating efforts of a "crowd at a football stadium," where "no one can see any better than when everyone is sitting down—but no one is willing to be the first to sit down."

The deficiency in this explanation is that it does not tell us how prices and wages are able to go on rising without causing falling sales volume and mounting unemployment. Certainly, we should expect that people would not be able to afford to buy as many goods at higher prices, nor employers to employ as many workers at higher wages or in the face of declining sales of their goods. Further, we should expect that price increases would moderate as sales volume fell off, and that demands for higher wages would also taper off in the face of growing unemployment. Thus, we should expect any sort of wage-price spiral to come to an end if simply left alone.

The reason the wage-price spiral does not come to an end is because of the policies of politicians like Mr. Carter. Mr. Carter declared that there were two things he would not do to end inflation: impose "mandatory" price and wage controls, or allow a recession to develop.

What he meant by not allowing a recession to develop was that he would *not* stand back and allow the wage-price spiral to burn itself out, in the way I have just indicated. He did not explain how he would avoid this, but the actual explanation is that he will force the Federal Reserve System to go on creating money ever more rapidly, to enable people to pay rising prices and wages. In this way, President Carter and his predecessors have continuously fueled the wage-price spiral (and, incidentally, steadily increased the size of the temporary recession needed to stop it).

Along the same lines, the President also pledged—incredibly—that he would fight inflation by holding down interest rates. Once more, he did not explain how he would do this, but the actual explanation is, again, by forcing the Federal Reserve System to create additional billions of dollars out of thin air, to be dumped into the loan market. This policy, too, has been a favorite of the last several administrations. (I must note, incidentally, that its long-run effect is not to reduce interest rates, but to raise them.)

Further along the same lines, the President promised that if prices rose by more than 7%, workers who did not receive wage increases in excess of 7% would be compensated by tax rebates. While the President did not explain how the government would obtain the necessary funds to pay the rebates, the answer, of course, comes back yet again to the Federal Reserve System and its creation of money.

Given the nature of the policies pursued by Mr. Carter and his predecessors, it is no wonder that people have begun to develop an "inflation psychology." Their growing expectation that prices and wages will go on rising is perfectly logical in view of the policies of our government. What is surprising is only that this expectation is not much more widespread and intense than it is.

The presidency of Mr. Carter highlights the tragedy of the present American monetary system.

Our present monetary unit—totally divorced from gold or silver—is virtually costless to produce: billions of dollars can be created at a cost of pennies in terms of the paper and ink or ledger entries required. The only thing that enables our money to maintain a value substantially above the paper it is printed on is that its creation is a monopoly privilege of the government. (If everyone were allowed to create paper money, its quantity would be so rapidly increased by the efforts of individuals to gain from the process that its value would be destroyed almost immediately.)

Mr. Carter presides over the government's monopoly of paper money. His administration, like its last several predecessors, derives an enormous advantage from it in that—at virtually no cost—it obtains billions of dollars with which to finance programs designed to reelect itself. There is money to meet every "emergency"—to combat or prevent a recession (that is always brewing because of previous expansions of money); to bail out companies, banks, cities, even states; to subsidize here, underwrite there; to finance this or rebuild that; to lend; to "fund"; to "rescue," "restore," "revitalize"; there is nothing for which "Washington"—i.e., the printing press—cannot be called upon for funds.

Mr. Carter and his associates have the power to destroy the value of paper money by overissuing it, or by creating the impression that they will overissue it. This power entails the power to destroy the value of every contract payable in dollars.

The tragedy of the American monetary system is that everyone's financial well-being depends upon the purchasing power of the dollar; the purchasing power of the dollar depends upon the quantity of dollars created; and the quantity of dollars created depends upon the knowledge of economics of politicians like Mr. Carter, who believes that "guidelines" and an easy money policy are the solution to inflation.

The Real Solution to Inflation

The solution to inflation is not "guidelines," but an end to the government's arbitrary increase in the quantity of money. This is a point on which every competent economist is now agreed.

Unfortunately, widespread disagreement prevails concerning the *means* of achieving this vital goal.

On the one side are Milton Friedman and the "monetarists," who advocate a predetermined "monetary rule" which the government is to follow in increasing the money supply—such as by two, three, or five percent per year. (Professor Friedman himself has changed his mind on the precise rate.)

On the other side are the supporters of the gold standard, who advocate tying the quantity of money to the quantity of gold. Here again, however, differences exist, for there are various types of gold standards. There is the gold coin standard, in which gold coins constitute at least part of the actual circulating money supply. There is the gold bullion standard, in which the entire money supply consists of paper currency and demand deposits which are convertible into gold bullion on demand. There is the 100% gold reserve standard and the fractional gold reserve standard: under the former, the monetary unit is not only defined as a definite quantity of gold of a definite purity, but no more paper currency and checking deposits can exist than equals the quantity of gold possessed by its issuers. There are also other variations.

While it is not possible to enter too far into the pros and cons of each specific position, I must state my conviction that the ideal monetary system would be the closest possible approximation consistent with the principle of laissez faire to a 100% gold reserve system, in which gold (and silver) coins constituted a significant proportion of the actual circulating money supply. Such a system, I believe, would be both inflationproof and deflation-depressionproof.

Under it, the increase in the quantity of money would be no more rapid than the increase in the supply of precious metals, which is usually quite modest. And even when relatively rapid, as in the days of the California gold rush, the increase is substantially less than the rate at which paper money is now being created by the world's most financially "conservative" governments. (It should be noted that while prices rose somewhat in the generation following the California gold rush, they had been falling in the previous generation and resumed their fall in the generation following 1873, as a result of the production of goods in general growing faster than the production of gold.)

Moreover, once a gold or silver money comes into existence, it remains in existence; it cannot be wiped out by financial failures, which was the major flaw of the fractional gold reserve system of the 19th century. (Under that system, business failures caused bank failures, thereby reducing the money supply, which was backed in large part by loans the banks had made, rather than by gold. The drop in the money supply then caused a drop in total spending and thus in business sales revenues; as a result, more business failures occurred, followed by more bank failures. Under the 100% gold reserve system, such a situation would be impossible.) Given the 100% reserve system's absence of monetary contractions, the gold standard means secularly stable or even falling prices without depressions.

By the same token, the "monetarists' " principle of allowing the government to expand the money supply at a predetermined rate must be rejected, I believe, on at least five distinct grounds.

First, and most fundamentally, it is incompatible with the principle of individual freedom, in that it rests entirely on the creation of money being a monopoly privilege of the government (otherwise, the value of any irredeemable paper money must quickly be destroyed, as I have explained). A gold money, on the other hand, does not require the existence of any monopoly privilege in its creation. The value of gold is protected by its high cost of production; thus, the manufacture of gold money can be thrown open to all, as the principle of freedom of competition demands.

Second, as a result of the existence of different sovereign governments, each with its own monetary unit, its own rate of increase in that unit, and changing conditions in the various countries, the monetarist scheme implies fractionalization of the world monetary system and fluctuating exchange rates. The gold standard, on the other hand, means a unified world monetary system, as each government acknowledges gold as money.

Third, the monetarist "rule" is itself essentially arbitrary, in that different governments, at different times and under different circumstances, are to be guided by different "rules." If the system were enacted, each government, one may be sure, would constantly be seeking to prove why its circumstances required that it adopt a more liberal "rule." The tendency to return to unrestrained inflation would be greatly reinforced by the fact that a basic premise of the monetarists—their reason for rejecting the gold standard in the first place—is their belief that the supply of gold increases too slowly and that government intervention is required to make the supply of money increase more rapidly. Thus, the monetarists cannot easily oppose those who argue for a still higher rate of increase in the money supply; they themselves are inflationists, though of a relatively mild variety.

Fourth—and this closely relates to my first point—if the monetarist proposals were to be adopted, it would eventually be necessary either to adopt the gold standard or to adopt repressive measures against gold. That this is the choice can be understood if we project the long-run consequences of any monetarist rule that accords with the inflationist philosophy of monetarism and increases the quantity of money significantly more rapidly than gold.

If, for example, the supply of gold increases on the average at two percent per year, while the monetarist rule calls for increasing the money supply at five percent per year, the day will eventually come when the price of gold will begin to rise on an average of three percent per year. From that point on, because of the negligible costs of storing gold, and the negligible spread between the retail and wholesale price of gold, it will pay people to acquire gold holdings as a form of savings.

As gold ownership becomes more widespread, the base is laid for gold reemerging as a medium of exchange. For example, if an owner of gold wants to buy a piano and the seller wants to save the price in gold, the parties can exchange gold for the piano. When it becomes known that a significant number of people are willing to accept gold for goods, because they want to save in gold, more people become willing to accept it, because they know they can exchange it with the first group. Thereafter the process intensifies; eventually, gold becomes universally acceptable in exchange, i.e., it becomes money.

The point here is that because of its great suitability for saving, a gold money has been the repeated choice of the free market in the past and is likely to be so in the future. (The process of a growing number of individuals saving in the form of gold holdings is, in fact, underway right now, and, if not stopped by governmental repression, may well lead at some point to a spontaneous remonetization of gold as inflation of the paper money continues.)

It is difficult to understand, therefore, how supporters of liberty as stanch as many monetarists are can advocate a monetary system that both ignores and is incompatible with the free choice of the market and which must ultimately rest on forcibly repressing the competition of gold. For in the long run, there is no other way but force to stop the reemergence of gold as money if the money it competes against increases at a significantly greater rate than it does, and therefore steadily and perceptibly loses value against it.

Fifth, and finally, monetarism must be rejected in favor of gold, because, despite impressions to the contrary, the practical difficulties of inaugurating any sort of reasonable monetarist rule are actually much greater than making a clean sweep and going over to gold.

The great practical—political—problem of stopping inflation is how to do it without causing a catastrophic contraction in spending on the order of the early 1930s, or worse. The difficulty is that decades of inflation have seriously undermined the demand for paper and checkbook money, i.e., the desire to hold it in reserve. As a result, more and more individuals and business firms have come to operate with smaller and smaller cash reserves relative to the size of their financial dealings. An end to inflation would be followed by a major increase in the demand for money—as people sought to rebuild their cash holdings. A sudden end to inflation—even just a substantial reduction in the rate at which money is created—would mean a tremendous contraction in the volume of financial dealings. Suddenly going over even to a monetarist rule of a five percent annual increase in the quantity of money would certainly produce such consequences today.

Thus, at best, monetarism could only be implemented after a lengthy transition period, in which the government sought very gradually to reduce the rate of increase in the money supply. It is virtually certain, however, that long before such a transition period could be completed, the monetarists would be overwhelmed by demands from strong political interests for a more rapid increase in the quantity of money, which they would be powerless to resist. For the success of their transition period would require that for many years aggregate spending in the economic system increase by less than the increase in the quantity of money—in order that cash holdings could be rebuilt relative to the size of financial dealings. By the logic of their opposition to gold, however, the monetarists could not be satisfied if for many years a six or a five percent annual increase in the money supply produced only a three or a two percent annual increase in aggregate spending. Thus, they would have to yield to demands for more rapid increases in the money supply to stimulate spending. (And then they would find that spending would once again begin to increase more rapidly than the quantity of money.)

The gold standard, on the other hand, holds out the possibility of ending inflation quickly and permanently, without a major depression. For if the transition to gold were made at a sufficiently high price of gold, the gold stock could be made equal to a large enough number of dollars to offset the effects on spending of a greater desire to hold money in reserve. The transition to a gold money, in other words, could be accompanied by a simultaneous enlargement in the nominal—dollar—value of the money supply that would offset the drop in the rate at which money was spent. (In order for this not to represent merely one more burst of inflation, it would be necessary for the gold to be physically turned back to the people and the banks; this would ensure that money would be more tightly held and thus not be spent with the same or even greater rapidity than it is today.)

The solution to inflation is neither "guidelines" nor "monetarism."

It is *the end of government intervention in money.*

It is the government's acknowledgment that gold money is the choice of the free market.

It is the restoration of the gold standard.

# NOTES

## Introduction

1. On this subject, see Robert G. Kaiser, *Russia* (New York: Atheneum, 1976) and Hedrick Smith, *The Russians* (New York: Quadrangle Books, 1976).
2. Actually, it could be shown that falling supply can practically never be the cause of a sustained significant rate of increase in prices and that at no time can it be the cause of the full *complex* of symptoms that people complain of in discussing inflation, such as the enormously greater number of prices rising compared with the number of prices falling and the effects on the relations between debtors and creditors. In addition, it can be shown that falling supply is itself usually a consequence of rapid inflation.
3. Cf. Ludwig von Mises, *Human Action*, Third Edition (Chicago: Henry Regnery Co., 1966), pp. 426-428; *The Theory of Money and Credit*, New Edition (reprint; Irvington-On-Hudson, New York: The Foundation for Economic Education, 1971), pp. 227-230.
4. Statistics of the money supply are published every Friday in *The New York Times* and *The Wall Street Journal*. Historical statistics are available from the Board of Governors of the Federal Reserve System. The Federal Reserve Bank of St. Louis regularly publishes data showing the trend of growth in the money supply on a short-term and long-term basis.

## Chapter I

1. For elaboration and related discussion of these points, see below, pp. 32f., pp. 47–54, pp.58ff.
2. I limit the discussion to the resources available on earth. Actually, advances in space technology are making it clear that this restriction is far too narrow.
3. The quotation appears in W. T. Jones, *The Medieval Mind*, Volume II of *A History of Western Philosophy*, Second Edition (New York: Harcourt, Brace, and World, 1969), p. 6.
4. Cf. *Commodity Yearbook 1976* (New York: Commodity Research Bureau, Inc., 1976), pp. 264f.
5. For an important exception to the principle that sellers are led to sell too rapidly, see below, p.70.
6. This accords with the views of the great classical economist David Ricardo. Cf. his *Principles of Political Economy and Taxation*, Third Edition (London: 1821), Chapter XXX especially. (Several reprints of this book are available.)
7. This analysis of the relation between cost of production and supply and demand is the work of the great economist Eugen von Böhm-Bawerk, one of the founders of the "Austrian" School of Economics. Very similar ideas are also propounded by John Stuart Mill, the last major representative of the "British" Classical School. Cf. Eugen von Böhm-

Bawerk, *Capital and Interest*, 3 volumes (South Holland, Illinois: Libertarian Press, 1959), Vol. II, especially pp. 168-176, but also pp. 248-256, and Vol. III, pp. 97-115; John Stuart Mill, *Principles of Political Economy*, Ashley Edition (reprint; Fairfield, New Jersey: Augustus M. Kelley, 1976), Book III, Chapters II-IV.

## Chapter II

1. While the economic system is in process of adjusting to a change in the quantity of money, the demand for the various goods and services is affected unevenly. Cf. von Mises, *Human Action, op. cit.*, pp. 412ff.; *The Theory of Money and Credit, op. cit.*, pp. 137-141. Von Mises argues that there are also permanent effects on the relative demands for the various goods and services, and thus on their relative prices.
2. This insight is one of the great contributions of Böhm-Bawerk. See above, Chapter I, n. 7.

## Chapter III

1. For a further, related discussion of the effects of price controls on natural gas, see below, below, pp. 130ff.
2. Cf. above, pp. 26f.
3. On these points, cf. John Stuart Mill, *Principles of Political Economy, op. cit.*, Book IV, Chapter II, Section 5.
4. Cf. above, pp.28-31.
5. *The New York Times*, April 28, 1976, p. 1, p. D9.
6. *The New York Times*, January 29, 1977, p. 22.
7. Cf. Ludwig von Mises, *Bureaucracy* (reprint; New Rochelle, New York: Arlington House, 1969), *passim*.
8. Cf. Ludwig von Mises, *Socialism* (reprint; London: Jonathan Cape, 1974), pp. 40ff.
9. Cf. above, p.79
10. *The New York Times*, April 11, 1974, p. 49, p. 55.
11. The following discussion is an application of principles set forth by Ayn Rand in criticizing the use of the word "censorship" in reference to the actions of private individuals. Cf. Ayn Rand, "Man's Rights," in Ayn Rand, *The Virtue of Selfishness* (New York: New American Library, 1964), especially pp. 131-134.
12. It could be argued that freedom is also violated by the initiation of force on the part of private individuals, i.e., by common criminals, such as murderers, robbers, and rapists. However, criminals are always a small minority and do not constitute a significant threat if the government fulfills its proper function of apprehending them and removing them from society. The essential problem of freedom pertains to the relationship between the citizen and the government.
13. For a refutation of the related tissue of fallacies that constitute the doctrines of "oligopoly," "monopolistic competition," and "pure and perfect competition," and of the charge that a free economy lacks "price competition," see George Reisman, "Platonic Competition," *The Objectivist*, Vol. 7, No's. 8 & 9, August and September, 1968.

## Chapter IV

1. These results are reinforced by the fact that the more economical models, being more popular and therefore selling faster, tend to carry lower profit margins in a free market than do the higher priced models. For example, $1 million of capital invested in a fast-moving inventory of low-priced models may generate $2 million of sales revenue in a year, while the same size capital invested in a slow-moving inventory of high-priced models may generate only $1 million of sales revenue in a year. In order to earn the same rate of profit on capital, say 10 percent, when invested in either inventory, it is only necessary to have a 5 percent profit margin on the low-priced models, while a 10 percent profit margin is required on the high-priced models. If price controls are imposed and costs rise by any given percentage, the reduction in profit margins will be more severe in the case of the low-priced models. For example, a 5 percent rise in costs will just about totally eliminate profits on the low-priced models, while it will roughly halve them on the high-priced models. This too tends to cause the discontinuance of low-priced models ahead of high-priced models.

2. I am indebted to von Mises for this point and for the example used to illustrate it. Cf. von Mises, *Human Action, op. cit.*, pp. 762ff.; *Socialism, op. cit.*, pp. 532ff.; *Planning For Freedom*, Third Edition (South Holland, Ill.: Libertarian Press, 1974), pp. 73ff.
3. Cf. above, pp. 120f
4. Cf. above, pp. 89-93, pp. 77-83.
5. Cf. above, p.9, pp. 15-20, pp. 105ff.

## Chapter V

1. Cf. above, Chapter IV, note 2.
2. Cf. Hedrick Smith, *op. cit.*, pp. 62-65; Robert Kaiser, *op. cit.*, pp. 46ff.
3. Smith, *op. cit.*, p. 65.
4. Cf. above, pp. 10f., pp. 58ff.
5. Cf. above, pp.111ff.
6. Cf. Smith, *op. cit.*, pp. 60f.
7. Cf. Kaiser, *op. cit.*, pp. 315-356.
8. Cf. Kaiser, *op. cit.*, p. 16, p. 324; Smith, *op. cit.*, p. 267.
9. Cf. Ludwig von Mises, *Human Action, op. cit.*, pp. 717ff., pp. 758f., p. 764; *Socialism, op. cit.*, pp. 533f.; *Planning For Freedom, op. cit.*, pp. 4f., pp. 22-27, p. 30, pp. 72-78.; *Omnipotent Government* (reprint; New Rochelle, New York: Arlington House, 1969), pp. 55-58.

## Chapter VI

1. Cf. von Mises, *Socialism, op. cit.*, pp. 111-142, pp. 211-220, pp. 516-521; *Human Action, op. cit.*, pp. 689-715. Von Mises' leading supporter on this issue is F. A. Hayek, to whom I am also greatly indebted in the following discussion. See his *The Road to Serfdom* (Chicago: The University of Chicago Press, 1944), pp. 48ff; and *Individualism and Economic Order* (Chicago: University of Chicago Press, 1948), pp. 33-56, pp. 77-91, pp. 119-208.
2. Cf. above, pp. 99-103.
3. Cf. Kaiser, *op. cit.*, p. 338.
4. Cf. *ibid.*, pp. 330-335.
5. Cf. Smith, *op. cit.*, p. 59; Kaiser, *op. cit.*, p. 338.
6. Cf. above, pp. 139-143
7. Oskar Lange, *On the Economic Theory of Socialism*, Benjamin E. Lippincott, editor (Minneapolis: The University of Minnesota Press, 1938), pp. 57f.

## Chapter VII

1. Cf. above, pp. 147f.
2. Cf. Frederic Bastiat, "The State," in Frederic Bastiat, *Selected Essays On Political Economy* (New York: D. Van Nostrand, 1964; reprint, Irvington-On-Hudson, New York: The Foundation For Economic Education, 1968), pp. 140-151. Also cf. Hayek, *The Road to Serfdom. op. cit.*, p. 107.
3. Cf. Hayek, *The Road to Serfdom, op. cit.*, pp. 134-152.
4. Cf. Kaiser, *op. cit.*, p. 87, pp. 141f.; Smith, *op. cit.*, pp. ix f., pp. 3-6, pp. 11-22.
5. Smith, *op. cit.*, p. 265.
6. *Idem.* Smith and Kaiser, incidentally, are both aware of the fundamental insecurity of the Soviet regime. Cf. Smith, *op. cit.* pp. 253f.; Kaiser, *op. cit.*, pp. 10ff., pp. 21ff., pp. 172ff., pp. 451ff., p. 459, p. 473.
7. Cf. above, pp. 143f., pp. 161f.
8. Concerning these various points, cf. G. Warren Nutter, *The Strange World of Ivan Ivanov* (New York: World Publishing Co., 1969), pp. 87ff.; Kaiser, *op. cit.*, pp. 336f.; Smith, *op. cit.*, p. 267, p. 285.
9. Cf. Smith, *op. cit.*, p. 341, p. 456.
10. Cf. Kaiser, *op. cit.*, pp. 111ff., pp. 341ff.; Smith, *op. cit.*, pp. 82-85, pp. 92f.
11. Cf. Nutter, *op. cit.*, pp. 99f.; Smith, *op. cit.*, pp. 200f.; Kaiser, *op. cit.*, pp. 46f.
12. Cf. Smith, *op. cit.*, pp. 222-225; Kaiser, *op. cit.*, pp. 339f.
13. Cf. Smith, *op. cit.*, p. 223.
14. Cf. *The New York Times*, January 12, 1944, p. 12.

15. Cf. von Mises, *Socialism, op. cit.*, pp. 185-191.
16. Cf. Kaiser, *op. cit.*, pp. 175-181, p. 192, p. 328; Smith, *op. cit.*, pp. 7f., pp. 25-52, pp. 355-360, pp. 464-467.
17. For a critique of this slogan and its underlying moral philosophy, see Ayn Rand, *Atlas Shrugged* (New York: Random House, 1957), especially pp. 660-672 and pp. 1009-1069; also *The Virtue of Selfishness, op. cit.*, pp. 1-34.
18. Cf. Smith, *op. cit.*, pp. 219ff., pp. 230f., p. 334, pp. 338-343. For a novel that makes real the feeling of life under socialism, see Ayn Rand, *We The Living* (New York: Random House, 1959).
19. Cf. Ayn Rand, *Capitalism: The Unknown Ideal* (New York: New American Library, 1966), p. 21.
20. Cf. von Mises, *Omnipotent Government, op. cit.*, p. v; *Bureaucracy, op. cit.*, p. 106.
21. Cf. Alexander Solzhenitzyn, *et al, From Under The Rubble* (Boston: Little, Brown and Company, 1974), pp. 246f.; Kaiser, *op. cit.*, pp. 360-380; Smith, *op. cit.*, pp. 25-52, pp. 109f., pp. 464-467.

# INDEX

www.ingramcontent.com/pod-product-compliance
Lightning Source LLC
Chambersburg PA
CBHW060549200326
41521CB00007B/538